Adobe® GoLive®

Classroom in a Book®

Adobe

www.adobe.com/adobepress

Contents

Getting Started

About Classroom in a Book 1

Prerequisites 2

Installing Adobe GoLive 2

Copying the Classroom in a Book files 2

Additional resources 3

Adobe certification 4

Lesson 1

Creating Design Diagrams

About this lesson 8

About design diagrams 8

Getting started 9

Looking at the first design diagram 13

Creating a new design diagram 14

Adding sections 18

Adding color 21

Adding pages 22

Adding objects 28

Adding a SWF animation 35

Aligning and distributing objects 37

Adding annotations 39

Adding items to every page 41

Labeling the diagram levels 45

Printing and exporting a design diagram 47

Anchoring a design diagram 48

Submitting a design diagram 50

Review questions 52

Review answers 52

Lesson 2 **Developing Web Sites with Adobe GoLive CS**

About this lesson 56

The GoLive workflow 57

Getting started 63

Creating a new site 65

Adding files and folders 67

Designing a first Web page 69

Previewing a Web page 80

Creating a second Web page 83

Creating a third Web page 92

Creating links 94

Comparing the files on your desktop with the site files ... 96

Managing sites 97

Review questions 99

Review answers 99

Lesson 3 **Getting to Know the Work Area**

About this lesson 104

Getting started 105

Opening and viewing a site 106

Using the document window 117

Using the toolbar 124

Creating a custom workspace 126

Using the Objects palette 132

Using the Inspector 135

Using context menus 136

Setting GoLive preferences 137

Previewing in GoLive 138

Previewing in a Web browser 140

Review questions 141

Review answers 141

Lesson 4

Designing Web Pages

About this lesson 146

Getting started 147

Creating a new Web site 148

Adding files to the Web site 151

Creating a component to be used as a navigation bar ... 154

Designing the home page 165

Creating a custom color palette and adding
color to text 174

Adding a component to an existing Web page 182

Updating the custom color palette 183

Designing a Web page using layers 184

Editing a component 191

Previewing in GoLive 193

Review questions 194

Review answers 194

Lesson 5

Working with Text and Tables

About this lesson 200

Getting started 201

About converting layout grids to tables 202

Creating a new Web page 203

Adding text 206

Adding a table 216

Applying fonts 227

Capturing a table style 231

Editing text 232

Converting a layout grid to a table 236

Previewing in GoLive 237

Exploring on your own 237

Review questions 240

Review answers 240

Lesson 6   **Creating Navigational Links**

About this lesson 244

About links 244

Getting started 245

Opening a site 246

Creating a navigational link from a graphic 247

Testing a link 250

Creating anchors 251

Testing anchors 254

Creating hypertext links 255

Creating an action 266

Using image maps 269

Setting preferences for link warnings 277

Finding and fixing broken links 278

Previewing links 280

Review questions 281

Review answers 281

Lesson 7   **Using Smart Objects**

About this lesson 286

About Smart Objects 288

Using Smart Photoshop objects 289

Using Smart Illustrator objects 299

Using Smart LiveMotion objects 300

Editing a variable in a Smart Photoshop image 302

Review questions 304

Review answers 304

Lesson 8   **Working with Frames**

About this lesson 310

About frame sets 310

Getting started 312

Creating a frame set 314

Making changes to the frame set 316

Setting up the content frames 319

Adding content to frames 321

Creating targeted links 324

Creating a return link to the home page 324

Linking the frame set to your home page 326

Adding an action to always load the frame set 327

Previewing in a Web browser 329

Review questions 330

Review answers 330

Lesson 9 **Creating Rollovers**

About this lesson 334

Getting started 334

Opening the home page 336

Adding a layer to hold a rollover button 340

About naming rollovers 343

Creating a rollover button 344

Adding an image to a layer 347

Creating a drop-down menu 348

Previewing in a Web browser 356

Review questions 357

Review answers 357

Lesson 10 **Using Actions and JavaScript**

About this lesson 362

Getting started 363

Creating head actions 364

Using actions to manipulate layers 369

Creating actions on call 374

Assigning JavaScript scripts to page elements 384

Review questions 388

Review answers 388

Lesson 11 **Creating Forms**

About this lesson 392

Getting started 392

About forms 394

Creating the Personal Information section of the form .. 396

Storing frequently used objects 410

Adding an image that spans two columns 413

Adding radio buttons 414

Modifying a list box 417

Adding a clickable image 419

Adding a Reset button 421

Changing the main table's border and cell spacing 421

Creating a tabbing chain 422

Review questions 425

Review answers 425

Lesson 12

Using Cascading Style Sheets

About this lesson 430

Getting started 430

About style sheets 431

Exploring style sheets 432

Working with styles 442

Creating a style sheet 448

Saving and linking a style sheet 451

Linking and unlinking a style sheet to multiple pages ... 453

Creating a class style 454

Importing an external style sheet 456

Duplicating a style 457

Changing the background color 458

Previewing the results in current browsers 460

Review questions 462

Review answers 462

Lesson 13

Managing Web Sites

About this lesson 468

About Adobe GoLive Web site management 468

Getting started 469

Importing an existing site into GoLive 470

Exploring the site in the site window 472

Reviewing the expanded site window 475

Correcting errors 478

Managing folders 484

Adding new pages to your site 487

Solving the site hierarchy 489

Changing the Navigation view 491

Creating new pages in the Navigation view 499

Changing all links and file references 503

Cleaning up a site 504

Exploring on your own 506

Review questions 507

Review answers 507

Index 509

Working with Version Cue 515

Adobe Certification Programs

Getting Started

Welcome to Adobe® GoLive® CS—the complete solution for Web site design, development, and management for novices and professionals alike. GoLive provides easy-to-use site design tools, site-building tools, editors, and powerful site-management features that help you develop professional-quality Web sites quickly and easily. Integrate your Web design and development work seamlessly with other Adobe applications, including Adobe Photoshop®, Adobe Illustrator®, Adobe InDesign®, and Adobe LiveMotion®. Create rollovers and animations easily, and add Macromedia® Flash™ (SWF) files and QuickTime movies to your Web pages.

About Classroom in a Book

Adobe GoLive CS Classroom in a Book® is part of the official training series for Adobe graphics, Web, and publishing tools developed with the support of experts at Adobe Systems. The lessons are designed to let you learn at your own pace. If you're new to Adobe GoLive, you'll learn the fundamental concepts and features that you'll need to master the program. If you've been using GoLive for a while, you'll find Classroom in a Book teaches many advanced features, including tips and techniques for using this exciting Web design tool.

The lessons in this edition include information on the GoLive workflow, customizing the work area, converting layout grids to tables, creating stationery, spell checking, using variables with Smart Objects, adding date and time stamps, creating HTML styles, and working with Smart rollovers. Additionally all lessons have been revised to incorporate updated information on GoLive CS commands and tools. Lesson 1, "Creating Design Diagrams," shows you how to use the powerful presentation and Web site creation tool to lay out the structure or architecture of a site before you create pages. You can develop multiple prototype design diagrams as you build and revise a site. You can present design diagrams in print or online in Adobe PDF or SVG format for review. When you are ready to work with real pages, you can convert the design diagram's pages to editable HTML pages in a site.

Although each lesson provides step-by-step instructions for creating a specific project, there's room for exploration and experimentation. You can follow the book from start to finish, or do only the lessons that correspond to your interests and needs.

Prerequisites

Before using the *Adobe GoLive CS Classroom in a Book*, you should have a working knowledge of your computer and its operating system. Make sure that you know how to use the mouse and standard menus and commands, and also how to open, save, and close files. If you need to review these techniques, see the online documentation included with your Windows or Mac OS documentation.

Installing Adobe GoLive

Before you begin using the *Adobe GoLive CS Classroom in a Book*, make sure that your system is set up correctly and that you've installed the required software and hardware. You must purchase the Adobe GoLive software separately. For system requirements and complete instructions on installing the software, see the How to install file on the application CD.

Copying the Classroom in a Book files

The Classroom in a Book CD includes folders containing all the electronic files for the lessons. Each lesson has its own folder, and you must copy the folders to your hard drive to do the lessons. To save room on your drive, you can install only the necessary folder for each lesson as you need it and remove it when you're done.

To install the Classroom in a Book files:

1 Insert the *Adobe GoLive CS Classroom in a Book* CD into your CD-ROM drive.

2 Create a folder named GL_CIB on your hard drive.

3 Copy the lessons that you want to the hard drive:

• To copy all of the lessons, drag the Lessons folder from the CD into the GL_CIB folder.

• To copy a single lesson, drag the individual lesson folder from the CD into the GL_CIB folder.

If you are installing the files in Windows, you need to unlock them before using them. You don't need to unlock the files if you are installing them in Mac OS.

4 In Windows, unlock the files that you copied:

• If you copied all of the lessons, double-click the unlock.bat file in the GL_CIB/Lessons folder.

• If you copied a single lesson, drag the unlock.bat file from the Lessons folder on the CD into the GL_CIB folder. Then double-click the unlock.bat file in the GL_CIB folder.

Note: *As you work through each lesson, you'll overwrite the Start files. To restore the original files, recopy the corresponding Lesson folder from the Classroom in a Book CD to the GL_CIB folder on your hard drive.*

Additional resources

The *Adobe GoLive CS Classroom in a Book* is not meant to replace the online help that comes with the program. Only the commands and options used in the lessons are explained in this book. For comprehensive information about program features, refer to these resources:

• Online Help, an online version of the User Guide. You can view the online Help by choosing Help > GoLive Help.

• The Adobe Web site (www.adobe.com). You can view the Adobe Web site by choosing Help > Adobe Online, if you have a connection to the World Wide Web.

Adobe certification

The Adobe Training and Certification Programs are designed to help Adobe customers improve and promote their product proficiency skills. The Adobe Certified Expert (ACE) program is designed to recognize the high-level skills of expert users. Adobe Certified Training Providers (ACTP) use only Adobe Certified Experts to teach Adobe software classes. Available in either ACTP classrooms or on-site, the ACE program is the best way to master Adobe products. For Adobe Certified Training Programs information, visit the Partnering with Adobe Web site at http://partners.adobe.com

1 Creating Design Diagrams

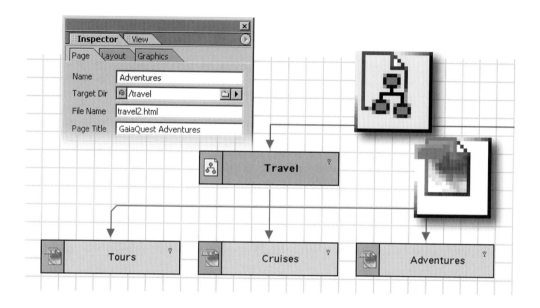

With the design diagram tool, you can layout your Web site before you create any content. You can create multiple diagrams as you refine your site structure. You can create paper or electronic versions of the design diagram for review, and when you're ready to work with Web pages, you can convert your design diagram to live, editable Web pages.

About this lesson

In this lesson you'll learn how to do the following:

- Create a design diagram.
- Add pages and elements that create a link hierarchy in the Web site architecture.
- Move, distribute, and align elements in a design diagram.
- Add annotations, boxes, graphics, and level labels to a design diagram.
- Create logos and elements on the master page.
- Print and export to PDF for presentation and design review.
- Check the staging of a design diagram.
- Submit a design diagram to convert the pages to editable HTML pages.

This lesson takes approximately 1 hour to complete.

If needed, copy the Lessons/Lesson01/ folder onto your hard drive. As you work on this lesson, you'll overwrite the start files. If you need to restore the start files, copy them from the *Adobe GoLive CS Classroom in a Book* CD.

Note: Windows users need to unlock the lesson files before using them. For more information, see "Copying the Classroom in a Book files" on page 2.

About design diagrams

The Adobe GoLive design diagram feature is a powerful presentation and Web site creation tool that lets you lay out the structure or architecture of a site before you create pages and helps you manage the site creation process. You can use multiple prototype diagrams as you build and revise a site, creating and testing designs for review. You can present design diagrams in print or online in Adobe PDF or SVG format. When you are ready to work with real pages, you "submit" a diagram—that is, you convert its pages to actual pages in the site.

Getting started

In this lesson you'll create a Web site architecture design diagram for GaiaQuest, an online travel company. An advantage of design diagrams is that you can easily revise them to determine how many sections there should be in a site and how the content is grouped. The design diagram you'll create in this lesson is a revision of an existing diagram. Template and stationery pages have already been created for the site. You'll create a Main page and two subsections, one for Travel and one for Customer Service. You'll create subpages for each section, grouping some elements within the subsections. When the design is complete, you'll anchor the index.html page, check the staging for file name errors, and submit or convert the design diagram, making the pages "live" in the Files tab of the project site file.

The design diagrams you'll work on in this lesson are prototypes developed for this lesson. The URL, www.gaiaquest.net and www.cometstudios.net, and their company names, GaiaQuest and Comet Studios, are used with generous permission of Dianne McKenzie and John Halley of Comet Studios and GaiaQuest.

First you'll view the completed design diagram that you'll create in GoLive.

1 Start Adobe GoLive.

By default an introductory screen appears prompting you to create a new page, create a new site, or open an existing file.

Note: You can set preferences for the introductory screen to not appear when you start GoLive. If the introductory screen doesn't appear, choose File > Open and go to step 3.

2 Click Open to open an existing file.

3 Open the *Design Diagram.site* file in Lessons/Lesson01/01End/Design Diagram folder/.

4 Click the Diagrams tab in the site window, and double-click GaiaQuest_design_02 to open the design diagram.

Due to variables in system configurations, you may see an erroneous warning message regarding printing. you may safely disregard this message.

5 Scroll vertically and horizontally through the document, and explore the design diagram. You may want to maximize the window.

The site starts with a Home Page that connects to a Main page on Level 1. Notice that from the Main page, the site branches into two sections, one on Travel and the other on Customer Service. To make it easy to follow the site hierarchy, the two sections have different color coding. Notice that some pages are grouped, under Order and Press Releases, for example. Grouping items can help define areas of your site, such as an e-store or catalog area, for example. Groups don't affect the underlying HTML—they're purely to help organize your design diagram.

6 Scroll to the top of the page and notice the anchor icon (⚓) on the Home Page. Every design diagram must be anchored to an existing page in the site for its pages to be visible in a navigation view after the diagram is submitted. You'll learn how to do this later in the lesson. If you submit a design diagram without anchoring it, its pages become scratch pages.

Notice the pages in the design diagram have a symbol (⚓) in the upper right corner indicating that the design is anchored and currently submitted. You'll learn more about this later in the lesson.

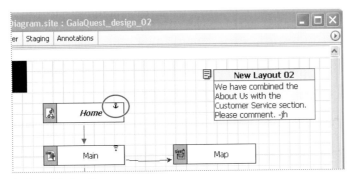

Anchored design diagram

The site design diagram also has annotations.

7 Double-click the yellow annotation icon at the top of the page to close it. Double-click the annotation icon again to open it.

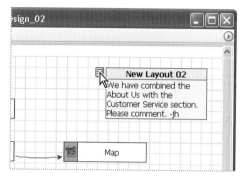

Double-clicking an annotation icon opens it

8 If you maximized the design diagram, minimize so that you can see both the design diagram and the site window.

9 In the site window, select the Files tab, and notice that two folders, the travel folder and the services folder, have been created to hold pages for the two main sections in the Web site, travel and customer service.

10 In the design diagram, select the page named Adventures. You may have to scroll to see it.

11 Choose Window > Inspector to open the Inspector, or click the tab if the Inspector is collapsed. In the Page tab of the Page Inspector, notice that the page has been created from a template, template_01.html.

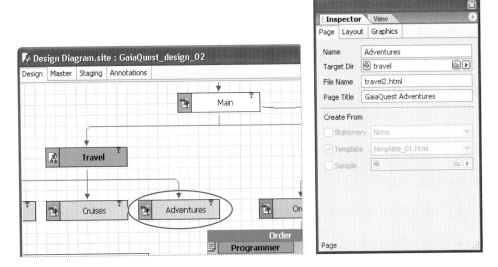

Click the Main page in the design diagram. In the Page tab of the Inspector, notice that the page is created from stationery_01.html.

The stationery_01.html file is used in the creation of the Main page (main.html) in this site. Because you are refining an existing design diagram in this lesson, the decisions on when to use generic pages and pages based on templates and stationery have already been made.

12 When you have finished viewing the design diagram, close the site window without saving any changes. The design diagram closes automatically when you close the site window.

A PDF file of the design diagram has been included for your convenience. The file, gq_diagram_02.pdf, is located in Lessons/Lesson01/01End/. You can keep this file open or print the page to serve as a visual reference as you work through the lesson to help you lay out your site more easily.

Looking at the first design diagram

First you'll explore an example of an in-progress design diagram. Examine this first draft design to familiarize yourself with its architecture.

1 In GoLive, choose File > Open, and double click the *Design Diagram.site* file in Lesson01/01Start/Design Diagram folder/ to open the site window.

2 In the site window, select the Diagrams tab, and double-click the design diagram GaiaQuest_design_01 to open it. You may wish to maximize the design diagram window.

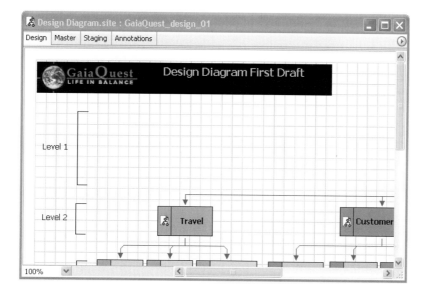

There are four tabs in the design diagram window.

The Design tab is where you layout the architecture of the Web site.

3 Click the Master tab to open the master view where you add objects that will appear on every page (in a multipage diagram), such as the design company's logo for branding purposes.

4 Click the Staging tab to see how your design diagram relates to the live site. This view also displays error and warning icons if you use the Check Staging command to validate your site.

5 Click the Annotation tab to see a summary of all the comments on your design diagram.

6 When you have finished reviewing the design diagram, choose File > Close and close the GaiaQuest_design_01 design diagram.

Creating a new design diagram

Now you'll create an alternative version of the Web site proposed for GaiaQuest.

You'll develop a design diagram by adding objects that represent pages, sections (hierarchies of pages), and other items. After adding objects, you'll create new links, group and rearrange objects, and anchor the diagram to an existing page in the site.

1 Choose Diagram > New Design Diagram to create a new design diagram.

2 In the Diagrams tab of the site window, select the newly created design diagram, which has the default name "untitled_diagram," and change the default name to "GaiaQuest_design_02." Press Enter or Return.

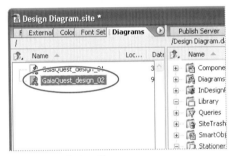

Renaming a design diagram

3 Double click the file GaiaQuest_design_02 in the Diagrams tab of the site window to open the design diagram.

The title bar in the design diagram window reflects the title of the design diagram.

Now you'll add your first page to the Design tab.

4 Choose Window > Objects to open the Objects palette, or click the Objects tab if the palette is collapsed.

5 In the Diagram set (⛁) of the Objects palette, drag a Page icon to the design diagram. Drop the page icon approximately two inches from the top of the page and in the center.

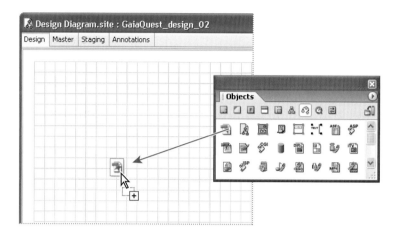

Design diagrams are always anchored to a page in the Web site, often the home page. You'll anchor the diagram later in the lesson. For the moment, be sure to leave enough space (approximately two inches) above the page icon to add the anchor page, annotations, and a logo.

💡 *If you place a page or object incorrectly, you can drag it to a new location in the design diagram. Alternatively you can delete a selected page or object by pressing the Delete key on your keyboard, and then add the page or object again in the correct position.*

6 Select the untitled.html icon, and in the Page tab of the Page Inspector, enter **Main** for the Name of the page. Change the File Name to **main.html**.

7 In the Create From section, select the Stationery option and select stationery_01.html from the Stationery pop-up menu. Any stationeries that you have added to the Stationeries folder in the Extras tab of the site window will be listed in this pop-up menu.

Notice the Page Title becomes GaiaQuest, which is inherited from the stationery file.

We used the stationery developed for the site to make the development of Web pages easier after the design diagram is submitted.

Now you'll change the display of pages and icons in the design diagram.

8 Choose Window > View to open the View palette, or click the tab if the palette is collapsed.

9 Click the Display tab of the View palette.

10 Select Icon Frames for the Show Items As option, and select Design Name for the Item Label option. The Design Name is the value you entered in the Name text box in the Inspector.

11 Choose Wide from the Frame Size pop-up menu.

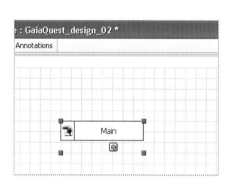

12 Click the Grid tab of the View Palette, and select the Collision Avoidance option to have other objects move out of the way when you move or insert an object in the diagram.

13 Select the Canvas As Single Page option to allow the design diagram canvas to be viewed on a single page. Depending on the size and complexity of your page, you might want to view the design diagram on multiple pages.

You can change other aspects of the appearance and behavior of the design diagram grid in the Grid tab of the View palette. For the moment, you'll use the default values.

14 Choose File > Save to save your design diagram.

15 Click the site window to make it active, and choose File > Save to save the site project file as well.

Note: When you work on your own projects, you should save both the file you are working on, such as the design diagram, and the site window regularly.

Adding sections

You can add single pages to a design diagram as separate objects, or you can add pages in a family relationship—parent, child, previous sibling, or next sibling, for example—to an existing page or section. You can also add sets of child pages to a page or section. When you add new child pages, you can make the child pages and their parent a section. Note, however, that a child page can have only one parent.

A section is a hierarchy of pages, usually a sub-tree, which is part of a larger hierarchy. The section and its children are descendents of some other object or parent. A section is treated as a unit to simplify file management—the children of the section inherit section properties. Pages in a section will often have the same base filename. Sections can contain other sections (subsections) as well as pages.

In this proposed Web site design, the Main page links to two pages, one leading into the travel section and the other leading into the customer service section. Now you'll add these two sections to your design diagram.

1 Click the design diagram title bar to make the window active.

 2 Drag a Section icon from the Diagram Set ( ) in the Objects palette to your design diagram. As you drag, a black bar appears above, to the side of, or below the existing Main page, indicating a family relationship to the new page. Drag the Section icon below the Main page. Drop the icon to add a child relationship when the black bar is visible below the Main page.

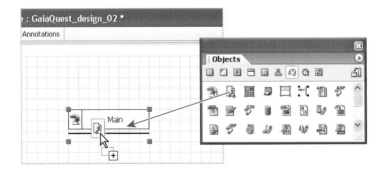

3 Drag a second Section icon from the Diagram set of the Objects palette to form second child relationship to the Main page.

4 Select the right Section placeholder, and press the right arrow button on your keyboard about 24 times to move the placeholder far enough over to the right to make room for the child pages that you will add. Notice that the design grid expands as you move the placeholder over. (By default the squares on the grid are 16x16 pixels.)

5 Select the Main page, and press the right arrow key 16 times to move the Main page to the right so it is between the two sibling pages.

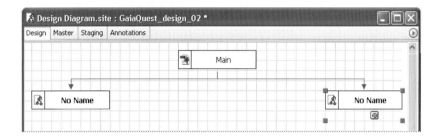

6 Select the left Section placeholder, and click the Page tab in the Section Inspector. Enter **Travel** for Name and enter **travel** for Target Dir (Directory).

The name you give to the target directory is the name that GoLive assigns to the folder that it creates to hold any child pages in the Files tab of the site window when you submit the design diagram.

7 In the Create From section, select Template, and choose template_01.html from the pop-up menu. Notice that the Page Title is automatically inherited from the template.

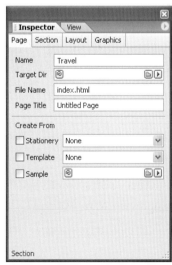

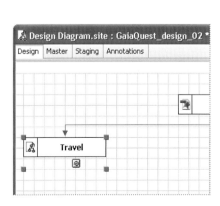

As with the use of stationery for the Main page, you've used a template to facilitate Web page development after the design diagram is submitted.

The parent page for a section or subsection is called its section page. The filename for a newly created section page is index.html by default, unless you change the home page filename in the site preferences. Section pages are displayed with boldface labels and have the section icon ().

Now you'll name the right placeholder.

8 Select the right Section placeholder. You may need to scroll to the right in the design diagram to see the placeholder. In the Page tab of the Section Inspector, enter **Customer Service** for Name. Enter **services** for the Target Dir (Directory). In the Create From section, select the Template option, and choose template_02.html from the pop-up menu. Again, the Page Title is automatically inherited from the template.

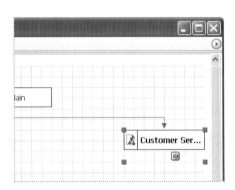

9 Choose File > Save.

Now you'll set the colors for the travel section and then create the child pages that will inherit the colors and the template properties.

Adding color

Now you'll add color to the design diagram to better distinguish between the different sections of the diagram. To simplify the lesson, all the custom colors you'll use for this design have already been added to your Colors tab in the site window. For information on adding custom colors to the Color tab in the site window, see "Updating the custom color palette" on page 183.

1 Select the Travel page in the design diagram window.

2 In Graphics tab of the Section Inspector, click the Fill Color field to open the Color palette. You may have to click the tab of the Color palette to open it if it is collapsed.

3 Select the Swatches tab. Click the triangle in the upper right side of the palette and select site colors. Select the color labeled travel #9999FF.

4 In the Section Inspector, make sure the Fill Color slider is centered.

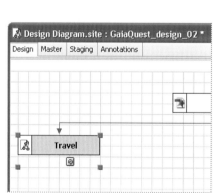

5 Click the Header Fill Color color field.

6 In the Swatches tab, select the color labeled travel #9999FF again.

7 In the Inspector, drag the Fill Color slider to the right to increase the intensity of the color. We dragged the slider all the way to the right.

Next you'll add color to the customer service section.

8 Repeat steps 1-7 for the Customer Service page, using the color labeled customer service #669999.

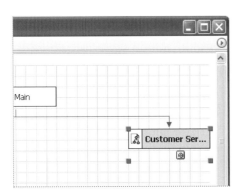

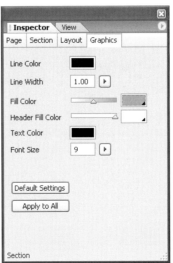

9 Choose File > Save to save your work.

Adding pages

In the next two sections you'll add pages using two different methods. First you'll add new pages to the Travel section using the New Pages dialog box. With this method, new pages inherit minimal properties from the parent page. Properties inherited by the child pages are the properties displayed in the Page tab of the Inspector for the parent page. You can override inherited properties at any time by changing the values in the Page tab of the Inspector for the child page. This method of adding pages is often used when the site architecture is not fully developed or there is little or no commonality among the child pages.

Then you'll add new pages to the Customer Service section using the Section tab of the Section Inspector. With this method, the child pages inherit all the properties in the Section tab of the Inspector for the parent page. When you select the child pages, the target directory and template do not show up in the Page tab of the Inspector, as it is assumed that the child inherits the parent properties. You can override the inherited properties at any time by changing the properties in the Page tab of the Inspector for the child page. Adding pages using the Section tab is preferred when the site architecture structure is more developed.

Adding new pages with the New Pages dialog box

In this section you'll add three child pages for the travel section.

1 In the design diagram, select the Travel page, and right-click (Windows) or Control-click (Mac OS) to show the context menu. Choose New Pages from the context menu.

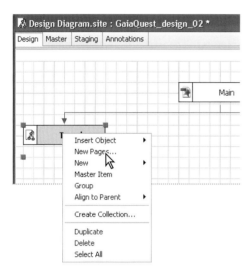

2 In the New Pages dialog box, enter **3** as the Number of pages to create. Enter **travel** for the Filenames, and enter **travel** for the Folder.

The travel folder (target folder) in your site window holds all the child pages in this section and their descendents when you submit the diagram. This target folder should be a subfolder of the root folder, either an existing subfolder or one that will be created when you submit the diagram.

3 In the Create Pages From section, select the Template option and choose template_01.html.

4 Click Create to create three child pages that inherit some of the qualities from the Travel section page, including color.

Now you'll adjust the color of the Travel page to differentiate it from the child pages.

5 Select the Travel page, and in the Graphics tab of the Section Inspector, drag the Fill Color slider to the right. The darker color will visually distinguish the Travel page as the first page in the section.

Next you'll set properties for each of the child pages. You'll identify the first child page that you just added as a page containing tour information.

6 Select the left-most child page of the Travel page.

7 In the Page tab of the Page Inspector, enter **Tours** for Name, and change Page Title to **GaiaQuest Tours**. Notice that the file name and the target directory are inherited from the parent.

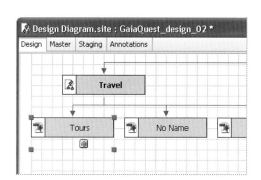

Now you'll identify the second and third pages as pages for cruise and adventure information, respectively.

8 Repeat steps 6 and 7 for the remaining two child pages. For the middle page, enter **Cruises** for Name and enter **GaiaQuest Cruises** for Page Title. For the right-most page, enter **Adventures** for Name and enter **GaiaQuest Adventures** for the Page Title.

9 Choose File > Save.

Adding new pages with the Section Inspector

Now you'll use the Section tab of the Section Inspector to add a second level of pages for the customer service section. With this method of creating new pages, the child pages inherit all the properties of the parent page. You also have the option to change the individual page properties for each child page in their respective Page tabs.

1 Select the Customer Service page.

2 Click the Section tab of the Section Inspector.

The Section tab in the Section Inspector is where you can change the settings for the child pages if you wish. In this lesson, you'll use the inherited properties.

3 Type **services** for the New Filename, and type **services** for the Folder.

4 In the Create Pages From section, select the Template option, and choose template_02.html from the pop-up menu.

5 Enter 3 in the Count field to create three new pages, and click Create New Pages. Notice that the design diagram expands to accommodate the new pages.

Next you'll refine the color of the Customer Service section as you did for the Travel section.

6 Select the Customer Service page.

7 In the Graphics tab of the Section Inspector, drag the Fill Color slider to the right to intensify the color and identify the page as the parent of the Customer Service section.

Now you'll identify the first child page of the customer service section as a page containing ordering information.

8 Select the left-most child page of the Customer Service section.

9 In the Page tab of the Page Inspector, enter **Ordering** for Name.

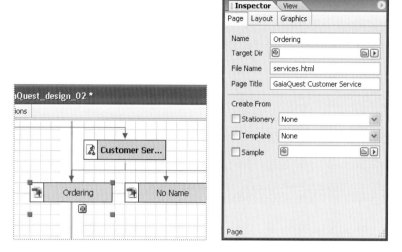

These child pages have inherited the properties of the parent page, even though the Page tab of the Page Inspector doesn't reflect this inheritance. For example, in the design diagram, double-click the page you just named Ordering to open the page. Notice that it has inherited the template template_02.html even though this is not reflected in the Inspector. (Close the page when you have finished viewing it.) When you submit this diagram later in the lesson, you'll see that GoLive has automatically named these pages services.html, services1.html, and services3.html and placed them in the services folder of the Files tab of the site window. (You can check this by opening the Design Diagram.site file in the 15End folder.)

10 Repeat steps 8 and 9 to name the other two child pages of the Customer Service page, naming the middle page **FAQs** and the right page **About Us**.

You may need to rearrange the pages icons so they don't overlap.

You'll probably need to resize the page icons to read their names.

11 Choose File > Save to save your work.

Adding objects

You are not limited to adding pages to the design diagram. You can add other objects, such as SWF files, PDFs, video, forms, wireless objects, database objects, and more. The Diagram set of the Objects palette has icons for all these objects. Note, however, that the icons you drag from the Objects palette only represent the various elements in the Web site. For example, if you drag a database icon into your design diagram, you are adding a representation of a database; you are not adding a real database.

Now you'll add an ASP element. An ASP page (Active Server Page) handles orders submitted from the Order page and is used to develop customer profiles. ASP code opens connections to databases, extracts or updates information, and performs other functions in a dynamic content site.

Adding an ASP element

1 Select the Ordering page on the design diagram.

2 From the Diagram set ( ) of the Objects palette, drag an ASP element to the area below the Ordering page. As you drag, a black bar appears above, to the side of, or below the existing page, indicating a family relationship to the new page. Drag the ASP element icon below the "Ordering" page to add a child relationship. Drop the icon when the black bar is visible below the Ordering page.

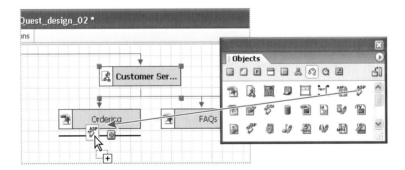

GoLive provides native support for several common scripting languages. For example, the Dynamic Content module in GoLive supports Microsoft® Active Server Pages (ASP), Sun® JavaServer Pages (JSP), and PHP: Hypertext Preprocessor (PHP) server scripting technologies.

3 In the Object tab of the Object Inspector, type **Profile** for the Name of the ASP element, and enter **profile.asp** for the File Name.

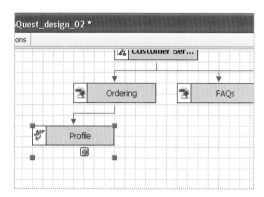

Notice that the services file name was inherited. The Target Directory (Folder) value is inherited from the parent page even though it doesn't show here, just as the template option was inherited above.

4 Click the Graphics tab in the Object Inspector to change the color of the Profile page. Click the Fill Color color field to open the Color palette.

5 In the Swatches tab of the Color palette, choose the color labeled customer profile #FFCC00.

6 Use the same procedure to apply the same color to the Header Fill Color, dragging the slider all the way to the right.

7 Use the arrow keys on your keyboard to move the ASP page so that it is positioned under the ordering page.

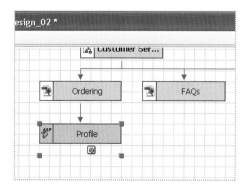

Adding a Secure object

Now you'll add a Secure object to the design diagram that represents the back-end programming that makes the page secure. Realize that you are simply adding a representation of the function, not the actual security function.

1 Select Profile page in the design diagram.

2 From the Diagram set (♣) of the Objects palette, drag a Secure object below the Profile page to create a child page.

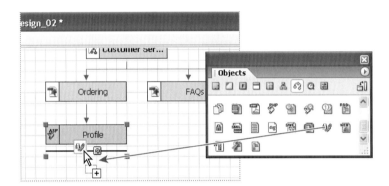

3 In the Object tab of the Object Inspector, type **Secure Order** for Name and enter **secure.html** for File Name. Select the Create From option and the Stationery option, and choose stationery_01.html from the pop-up menu.

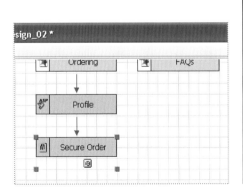

4 In the Graphics tab of the Object Inspector, change the color of the Secure page. Click the Fill Color color field to open the Color palette.

5 In the Swatches tab, choose the color labeled ordering #669933. Apply the same color for the Header Fill.

6 If necessary, move the secure page to the right so that it is positioned under the ASP Profile page.

7 Choose File > Save to save your work.

Organizing items into groups

Grouping items is a useful layout tool. It can help define areas of your site, such as an e-store or catalog area, for example. A group is simply a container that encloses a number of diagram items (pages or other items), allowing you to treat the items as a unit. You can move, copy, or delete a group. Groups don't affect the underlying HTML—they're purely to help organize your design diagram visually.

1 Click to select the Profile page and Ctrl-click (Windows) or Shift-click (Mac OS) to add the Secure Order page in the design diagram to the selection.

2 Right-click (Windows) or Control-click (Mac OS) to show the context menu, and choose Group from the context menu.

3 Drag one of the Group's handles to resize the Group container as necessary. Drag the group by its title bar to adjust its position on the page. You can also use the Align palette to align the Group container with the parent Ordering page, as described in "Aligning and distributing objects" on page 37.

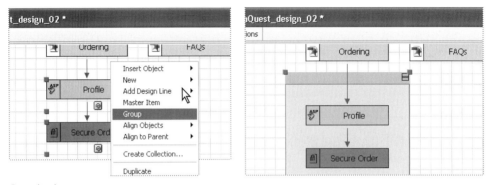

Grouping items

4 With the Group object selected, enter **Order** for Name in the Group tab of the Group Inspector. Press Enter or Return.

5 In the Graphics tab of the Group Inspector, click the Fill Color field. In the Swatches tab of the Color palette, choose the color labeled ordering #669933. Set the Header Fill Color color to the same color, but drag the slider all the way to the right.

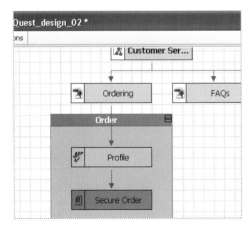

6 Choose File > Save to save your work.

Adding a database and PDF objects

The plan for the GaiaQuest Web site includes a database of press releases linked to the About Us page. To represent this part of the plan, you'll add a Database object and two Press Release PDFs to the design diagram.

Because the steps for adding a database object and two PDF files are very much the same as for adding any other objects, the following steps are brief. If you need help with the process, review the steps in "Adding an ASP element" on page 28.

 1 Drag a Database object from the Diagram set ( ) of the Objects palette into the design diagram and create a child relationship with the About Us page.

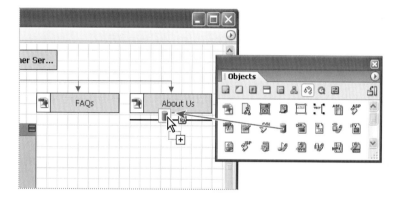

2 In the Object tab of the Object Inspector, type **Press Releases** for Name, and enter **press.db** for File Name.

3 In the Graphics tab of the Object Inspector, set the Fill Color to white (#FFFFFF) and leave the Header Fill Color set to the color labeled customer service #669999.

4 Drag a PDF object from the Diagram set of the Objects palette to below the Press Release Database object to create a child relationship.

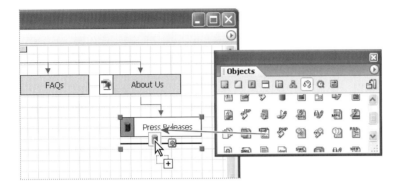

5 In the Object tab of the Object Inspector, type **Jan 02** for Name and enter **jan_02.pdf** for File Name. In the Graphics tab, leave the Fill Color and Header Fill Color unchanged, but move the Header Fill Color slider to the middle.

Add the second PDF object as a sibling of the PDF object you just added. Adding the second PDF object as a sibling here is equivalent to adding a second child to the parent database object.

6 Add a PDF object as a sibling to the right of the jan_02 PDF. Enter **Feb 02** for Name and **feb_02.pdf** for File Name. In the Graphics tab, leave the Fill Color and Header Fill Color unchanged, but move the Header Fill Color slider to the middle.

Now you'll group the two PDF files.

7 Click to select one of the two PDF objects, and Ctrl-click (Windows) or Shift-click (Mac OS) to add the second to the selection. Right-click (Windows) or Control-click (Mac OS) to show the context menu, and choose Group. In the Group tab of the Group Inspector, type **Press Releases PDF** for Name.

8 In the Graphics tab of the Group Inspector, change Fill Color to the color labeled main #99CC00 (green) and the Header Fill Color to the color labeled about us #9933FF (purple).

You'll align the objects later in the lesson.

Adding a SWF animation

The design concept for the GaiaQuest Web page included an animation on the Main page. In this section you'll add a SWF object (representing this animation).

First you'll format the Main page in the design diagram.

1 If necessary, scroll up in the design diagram so that you can select the Main page.

2 In the Graphics tab of the Page Inspector, leave the Fill Color as white (#FFFFFF). Change the Header Fill Color to the color labeled main #99CC00 in the color palette. Drag the slider all the way to the right. If you need help setting the fill and header fill colors, review the steps in "Adding an ASP element" on page 28.

Now you'll add the animation.

3 Drag the SWF object from the Diagram set (品) of the Objects palette and place it to the right of the Main page. Don't create a family relationship with the Main page.

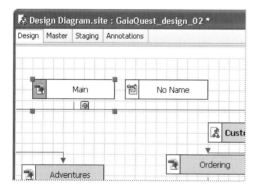

4 In the Object tab of the Object Inspector, enter **Map** for Name and **map.swf** for File Name.

5 In the Graphics tab of the Object Inspector, leave the Fill Color as white (#FFFFFF) and change the Header Fill Color to the color labeled map #FF66FF in the Color palette. Drag the slider to the right.

Next you'll add a pending link from the Main page to the map.swf object. Pending links are useful for mapping out the flow of a site. In the design diagram you can add pending links between pages, sections, and custom objects; change the type of link (parent, child, hyperlink, next and previous links); and change the deflection of the arrow and its appearance. Additional properties for the appearance of links can be set in the Link Type panel of the Design Diagram.site Settings dialog box (choose Site > Settings to open the dialog box). After the design is submitted, you can use the Pending Links palette to resolve links from HTML pages.

6 Select the Main page, and drag from its Point and Shoot button (located below the Main page) to the SWF object to create a link.

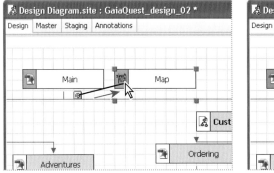 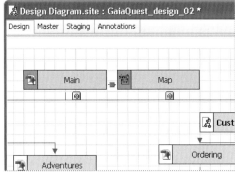

Creating a pending link

7 In the Link tab of the Link Inspector, check the style of link defined. For this lesson you'll use the default settings. You can experiment with other styles if you wish.

8 Choose File > Save to save your work.

Adding custom objects

You can create custom objects that represent items that you might add or link to a site and add these objects to the Diagram set of the Objects palette. The Diagrams set of the Objects palette contains a number of pre-defined custom objects representing items such as forms, elements, databases, applets, and scripts. You can edit or delete these objects as needed.

Custom objects are images in GIF format, located in the Modules/Diagram Objects folder in the GoLive application folder. When you add a custom object to a diagram, you can specify whether to create a file for the object when it is submitted, and the type of file to be created. You must create the file from a template, stationery, or sample file. For example, you can add a movie to a site by creating a custom object that uses the movie file as a sample file. When the diagram is submitted, a new movie file is created from the sample file. All non-HTML files created from custom objects become scratch items.

–From the Adobe GoLive CS online Help.

Aligning and distributing objects

Now that you've added a number of pages and objects to the design diagram, you'll use the Align palette to organize objects more precisely.

1 Click to select the one of the three child pages of the Travel section, Cruises, Tours, and Adventures, and Ctrl-click (Windows) or Shift-click (Mac OS) to add the other two to the selection.

2 Choose Window > Align to open the Align palette, or click the tab if the palette is collapsed.

3 In the Align Objects section of the Align palette, click the Align to Top button (🖫) to align the tops of all pages.

4 Select the Use Spacing option and enter 16 in the text box. (A square on the grid is 16 pixels by default.) Click the Distribute Spacing button to add one space between the objects.

You can align the siblings of the Customer Service section and any other objects in the design diagram in the same way.

5 Click to select one of the three child pages of the Customer Service section, and Ctrl-click (Windows) or Shift-click (Mac OS) to add the other two pages to the selection. Then align the pages using the Align palette.

6 Reposition any other objects in the design diagram based on your preferences or the example given in the 01End folder.

7 Close the Align palette when you are finished.

8 With the design diagram active, choose File > Save to save your work.

Adding annotations

The design diagram is a presentation tool, so you'll probably want to add annotations or comments to the layout for discussion with the members of your team. Annotations are text comments that can be displayed or closed. Both the subject and text of annotations are summarized in the Annotations tab of the design diagram window.

Note: *If you want comments created for presentation purposes to appear on each page of a diagram, you can add them as master items on the Master tab of the diagram window.*

You'll add a note explaining to reviewers of the site design that you have moved the About Us page to the Customer Service section.

1 Drag an Annotation icon from the Diagram set ( ) of the Object palette to an area close to the Main page.

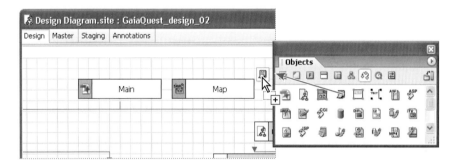

2 In the Annotations tab of the Annotation Inspector, enter **New Layout 02** for Subject and enter **We have combined the About Us with the Customer Service section. Please comment. -jh** in the Text box.

3 Select the Display Subject and Display Text options to make the subject and text of annotations visible in the design diagram.

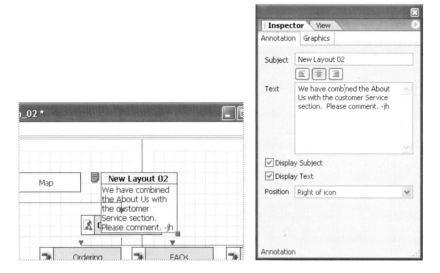

The Annotations tab of the Annotation Inspector offers options for formatting and displaying text. Select whether the subject and text are displayed to the right, left, above, or below the annotation icon from the pop-up menu. The Graphics tab allows you to personalize the font size and color for your comments.

4 Drop a second Annotation icon in the Order Group. In the Annotation tab of the Inspector, enter **Programmer** as the Subject, and enter **Get database set up for ordering. –dm** as the text. Select the Display Subject and Display Text options, and select Left of Icon from the Position pop-up menu. Annotations in groups will move with the group.

💡 *If you drag an Annotation icon to an object, such as a page, you'll see a gravity field or halo around the object. Drop the icon when you see this gravity field and the icon will always stay with that object.*

5 In the Swatches tab of the Color palette, change the Fill Color and the Header Fill Color to the color labeled about us #9933FF. Use the sliders to set the intensity of the color.

6 Both the text and subject of your icon are now visible in the design diagram. Before you save your work, deselect the Display Subject and Display Text options to hide the content of the annotation.

7 Choose File > Save.

Annotations can also be dropped on Link lines to describe the nature of the link. The annotation will stick to the line even if you move the line or change its deflection. You can try this by dropping an annotation on the link from the Main page to the SWF object, and then moving the SWF object. The annotation will move with the link. Restore the SWF object to its original position if you try this experiment.

Adding items to every page

If you have items that you want to add to every page of your design diagram, such as logos or copyright information, you can add them as master items. In this part of the lesson you'll add a client logo to the design diagram, and then you'll add a box to contain the design firm's logo and text.

1 In the design diagram window, select the Master tab.

2 Position the site window so you can see both the Files tab of the site window and the design diagram window.

3 From the Files tab of the site window, drag the client_logo.gif file from the media folder to the top left corner of the grid in the Master view. If you drop the image in the wrong place, you can simply drag it to a preferred location.

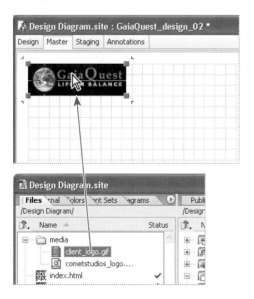

Now you'll add a box to contain text and the designer's logo. Boxes are graphical containers that can hold objects, including text, graphics, and other boxes. All contents within a box are contained in the box boundaries and move with the box. You can use boxes to provide captions or to contain text or graphics that represent items in a site.

4 Scroll to the bottom of the design diagram window so you can see the bottom left corner of the diagram.

 5 From the Diagram set (⚥) in the Objects palette, drag a Box icon to the bottom left corner of the Master view.

6 Select one of the box handles, and resize the box to the right allowing room for the logo and text.

7 With the box selected, in the Text area of the Box tab of the Inspector, enter the following text:

2nd Draft by Comet Studios
Confidential
www.GaiaQuest.net
© 2002

You can also type directly in the box if you click to create an insertion point.

8 If necessary, drag one of the corners of the box to resize it so that all the text is visible.

9 In the Box Inspector, click the button to align the text to the right (▤).

10 To add the design company logo, drag the cometstudios_logo.jpg file from the media folder in Files tab of the site window to the left side of the box. You may need to adjust the size of the box again to accommodate the logo and the text. Use the arrow keys to adjust the position of the logo.

11 Click the Design tab to return to the design diagram.

12 Click the arrow at the bottom of the design diagram window to open the magnification pop-up menu, and select Fit in Window to check your layout to date. When you are finished reviewing the page, use the magnification pop-up menu to return to your preferred magnification.

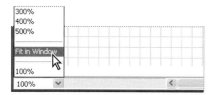

13 Drag a Box icon from the Diagram set of the Objects palette to the top of the page.

14 In the Text area of the Box tab of the Box Inspector, enter **Design Diagram Second Draft**. Select center text button (☰) to center the text.

15 In the Graphics tab of the Box Inspector, change the Fill Color to the color labeled banner #000000 and the Text color to the color labeled customer profile #FFCC00. Enter **12** for the Font Size.

Note: *If you want the left edge of the box you just added to line up with the right edge of the GaiaQuest logo so that the look is one seamless box, you'll need to temporarily deselect the Collision Avoidance option and the Horizontal Snap and Vertical Snap options in the Grid tab of the View palette. You can then use the arrow keys to align the two boxes. To move an object in one-pixel increments, press Ctrl+arrow key (Windows) or Option+arrow key (Mac OS). Remember to reselect the Collision Avoidance and the Snap options when you are finished. You can also select one of the box handles, and resize the box to the right allowing the text to place on a single line if you wish.*

16 Choose File > Save.

Labeling the diagram levels

Now that your design is almost finished, you'll add Level objects—brackets with optional text labels—that you can use to indicate the hierarchy of objects in your design diagram. You can place a bracket anywhere in the design diagram, and you can resize the bracket to include all the objects at a particular level.

1 Drag a Level icon from the Diagram set () of the Objects palette to the design diagram. Position the bracket by dragging it to the left of the Main Page, and resize the bracket by dragging any of its handles. You may find it easier to position the level labels if you change the view of the page using the magnification menu.

2 In the Level tab of the Level Inspector, enter **Level 1** in the text box. Click the Align in the Center of the Bracket button, and click the Right Align Text button.

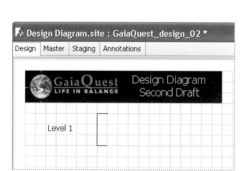

You'll add four more level brackets to the design diagram, positioning the brackets to correspond to each of the next four levels of the site hierarchy.

Note: Because you selected the Collision Avoidance option in the Grid tab of the View palette, the Level bracket adjusts objects on the page to make room where needed. As a result, you may need to realign objects on your page.

3 Add a Level 2 bracket for the row of Travel and Customer Service pages. Add a Level 3 bracket for the row of Tours, Cruise, Adventures, Ordering, FAQs, and About Us pages. Add a Level 4 bracket for the Profile and Press Release pages directly below. Add a Level 5 bracket for the Secure Order, Jan 02, and Feb 02 Press Releases. If you need guidance on the positioning of the level brackets, refer to the GaiaQuest_design_01 file in the Design tab of the site window.

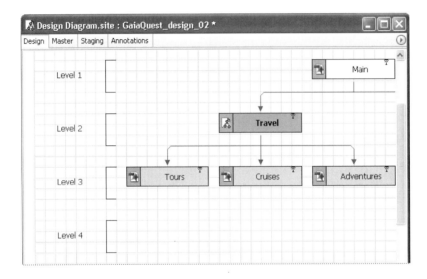

4 To align the Level brackets, click to select one and Ctrl-click (Windows) or Shift-click (Mac OS) to add the others to the selection.

5 Choose Window > Align to open the Align palette, and then click the Align Left button under Align to Parent to align the brackets to the left. Choose Window > Align to close the Align palette when you are finished.

You have one more note to add at Level 4. Because this is a note about missing material rather than a comment for review, you'll add it in a box so that it is visible all the time.

6 From the Diagram set of the Objects palette, drag a Box icon to the right of the Level 4 bracket.

7 Click in the box to create an insertion point, and enter the following text directly in the box:

Need to add templates for content from database for Tours, Cruises, and Adventures.....
-dm

8 Select the box and resize it by dragging one of the handles.

You can also enter text in the Text box of the Box Inspector.

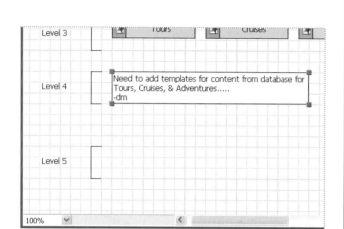

9 Choose File > Save.

Your design diagram is finished. Now you need to present it for review.

Printing and exporting a design diagram

You can print a design diagram in paper format, or you can export the diagram to Adobe PDF or SVG format for an online presentation. An exported diagram can contain live links and annotations.

Note: You can open both SVG files and PDF files in Illustrator and further brand the diagram with your company style as necessary. You can also edit the objects and individual lines as well as enhance the presentation. You can further enhance your exported files in Illustrator by replacing bitmaps (thumbnails, corporate logos, etc.) with higher-resolution versions (EPS, Illustrator files, etc.) of the same images; or choose different fonts and font sizes to replace the default fonts in the exported diagrams.

1 To export your design diagram as a PDF file, choose File > Export >Design Diagram. In the Export Options dialog box, select PDF from the Export Diagram As pop-up menu.

2 Select the Make Annotations Live option so that the annotations can be opened in the PDF file.

If you know the URL to which you'll upload your files, you can select the Make Diagram Objects Into Links option and enter the complete path where the site will be located. You'll not use this option in this lesson.

3 Click OK, and save the PDF file as "gq_diagram_02.pdf" in the Lessons/Lesson01/01Start/ folder on your hard drive.

4 Open the gq_diagram_02.pdf file. Notice that you can open annotations in the PDF file.

5 Close the PDF file, and save the design diagram.

Anchoring a design diagram

After your design diagram is complete and approved, you can submit it—that is, you can convert pages in the diagram to real pages in the site. Before you submit a design diagram, however, you must anchor it to a page in the site's navigation hierarchy.

For this design diagram, you'll anchor the index.html page to the Main page. The index.html pages will function as a splash page or introductory page that automatically takes a visitor to the Main page depending on the type of browser being used.

First you'll drag a live page from your site window to the design diagram window. This live page becomes the anchor page, representing a location in the existing site. Later you'll check and submit the design.

1 Drag the index.html page from the Files tab of the site window to the design diagram window and drop the page above the Main page without creating a hierarchy—that is, without associating it as a parent page of the Main page.

2 Drag the Main page over the bottom of the anchor page so that it becomes the child of the anchor page. A black bar appears below the "No Name" anchor page when the main page is a child of the anchor page.

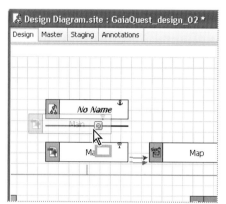 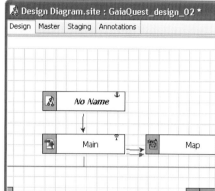

Anchoring a site

3 Select the new anchor page, and in the Page tab of the Section Inspector, name the page **Home Page**.

4 In the Graphics tab of the Inspector, leave the Fill Color as white (#FFFFFF). Change the Header Fill Color to the color labeled main #99CC00 in the Swatch tab of the Color palette, and drag the slider to the right.

Note: *If the design shifts when you add an anchor page, you can realign the pages for presentation.*

5 Choose File > Save.

Submitting a design diagram

When you have completed the design diagram and anchored the diagram with a page from the Files tab in the site window, you can submit your diagram, converting it into an active site and make it live. Submitting a design diagram converts the pages and sections to real, editable HTML pages that can be uploaded to the Web. The pages move from the Diagrams tab of the site window to the Files tab and from the Design Pages and Objects folders to the Live Pages and Live Objects folders in the Staging tab.

Before submitting (or converting) a design diagram, you should check the staging view and correct any errors. The staging view lets you see how your design diagram relates to the live site. It also displays error and warning icons when you check your site.

Note: Errors are often found in file and folder names (such as multiple files in the same directory having the same name or wrong folders specified in a directory). Checking your design alerts you to any changes you need to make before submitting the design.

1 To check the staging of the design, click the Staging tab of the design diagram window.

2 Choose Diagram > Staging > Check Staging.

A check mark in the Check column opposite a page or object means that no errors were detected. Other icons in the column indicate problems or potential problems. For example, the Stage in Scratch icon indicates that a page is not linked directly or indirectly to an anchor page. Unless you want such a page to be treated as a scratch page when the diagram is submitted, you need to anchor it by dragging an anchor page from the navigation view to a page in the design diagram or linking the page to an anchored page in the diagram to create a family link.

3 Choose Diagram > Staging > Submit All to submit the design diagram and convert its pages and sections to real, editable HTML pages. Or click the Submit All button (🖼) on the toolbar.

4 Click the Design tab in the design diagram window.

Notice that all pages (but not necessarily the objects, such as the database) have a symbol (⚓) in the right corner indicating that the design is anchored and currently submitted.

In the Files tab of the site window, notice the newly created pages, folders (travel and services), and their generic symbols. Also notice that none of the custom objects are represented except for the Secure object. For predefined custom objects—forms, elements, databases, applets, PDF files, and scripts—to be present in the site window, you must create the file from a template, stationery, or sample file for it to become a real file. The Secure object was created from stationery, which is why it is present in the Files tab of the site window. The PDF files are not yet linked to a stationery or template. The press release database has not been created and is not based on a real file.

5 Save and close both your design diagram and your site window.

After you make a design diagram live, you can recall it. You can then modify the design diagram and resubmit it any time. For example, you might submit a diagram in progress to examine it in context and then recall it for further design development. Or you might submit one of two alternative diagrams, and then recall the submitted diagram so that you can submit the other and choose between them. Submitted diagrams can be uploaded to the Web.

Review questions

1 What are some of the reasons for using design diagrams?

2 How do you create a design diagram?

3 How do you add pages and elements to a design diagram?

4 What is the purpose of the Master tab in the design diagram window?

5 Why should you check the staging of a design diagram?

6 When would you submit a design diagram?

Review answers

1 A design diagram lets you lay out the structure of a site before you create pages and helps you manage the site creation process. You can use multiple prototype diagrams as you build and revise a site, creating and testing designs for review. You can present design diagrams in print or online in Adobe PDF or SVG format. When you are ready to work with real pages, you submit a diagram, converting its pages to actual pages in the Web site.

2 In the site window, select the Diagrams tab. Then choose Diagram > New Design Diagram from the GoLive command bar to create a new design diagram.

3 There are several ways to add pages and elements to a design diagram. You can drag page and element icons from the Diagram set of the Object palette. After you add one page, you can also add pages and objects using the context menu. Right-click (Windows) or Control-click (Mac OS) on a page or object in the design diagram, and choose from the Insert Object menu or the New menu.

4 The Master view allows you to add items that will appear on every page of your design diagram if you have a multipage diagram. This is useful when you want to brand pages with a client logo or design team logo, for example, or when you want to add a legend.

5 Checking the staging of a design diagram lets you determine whether all of a site's pages are connected by links to an anchor page and whether there are folder or filename problems. Checking the staging gives you the opportunity to correct errors before submitting the design.

6 You submit a design diagram when you are ready to convert the design diagram's pages and sections to real, editable HTML pages. GoLive moves the pages from the Extras tab of the site window to the Files tab, indicating that they exist as files within the site. Files are created for custom objects that are linked to a template, stationery, or other file.

2 | Developing Web Sites with Adobe GoLive CS

This lesson gives you an overview of the Web site development process with Adobe GoLive and introduces you to key features of the application. During this lesson you'll create a simple Web site that includes a home page and two linked pages. The pages incorporate formatted text, GIF images, rollovers, and a Quick-Time movie. As you progress through the other lessons in this book, you'll look at these tasks in more detail.

About this lesson

In this lesson you'll do the following:

• Review the tasks involved in developing a Web site and Web pages using Adobe GoLive.

• Create a new Web site using the GoLive Site Wizard.

• Add folders and files to a site.

• Import existing Web pages into a site and create a new page.

• Add images and text to a Web page.

• Create rollovers so objects on a page change as you move the mouse over them.

• Create stationery.

• Work with a table.

• Add a QuickTime movie.

• Add navigational links to text and images.

• Preview Web pages in GoLive and in a Web browser.

• Examine the relationship of the files you see in the site window with the organization of files on your desktop.

This lesson takes approximately 90 minutes to complete. Although the lesson is long, it provides an important overview of the site building process and an introduction to the basic tools in GoLive that simplify and expedite this process. Most of the tasks introduced in this lesson will be covered in more detail in subsequent lessons, so relax and enjoy building your first Web site with GoLive. Don't worry about memorizing the details of each task; you'll revisit them in later lessons.

If needed, copy the Lessons/Lesson02/ folder onto your hard drive. As you work on this lesson, you'll overwrite the start files. If you need to restore the start files, copy them from the *Adobe GoLive CS Classroom in a Book* CD.

Note: Windows users need to unlock the lesson files before using them. For more information, see "Copying the Classroom in a Book files" on page 2.

The GoLive workflow

Creating a Web site that contains multiple pages is a complex task that is made much simpler by the creation and management tools in GoLive. Before you begin, you can make the task even easier by planning your Web site, thinking about your workflow, and understanding how GoLive can help you at each step of the way.

The following brief informational overview will help you understand how the different GoLive tools relate to the process of building Web pages and Web sites, and the subsequent hands-on tasks will give you experience in building a simple Web site and adding content to Web pages.

Before you begin

Before you begin building your Web site, it's best to have a basic design or hierarchy in mind. You can sketch out a plan using paper. You can use the GoLive site design diagram feature that allows you to design both simple and complex sites, and when you are ready to work with live pages, converts the pages to actual HTML pages in a site. If you already have a site in GoLive or imported into GoLive, you can manually add pages to the site, setting up the page hierarchy and links as you go, or you can add pages and move pages around using the Navigation view.

For information on creating a design diagram, see Lesson 1, "Creating Design Diagrams." For information on adding material to existing sites, see Lesson 4, "Designing Web Pages" and Lesson 13, "Managing Web Sites."

Working in the site window

Whether you are working on a single Web page or a complex, multipage Web site, you should always work in the GoLive site window. Although you can design and build Web pages outside of the site window (using the File > New Page command to create a page without creating a site), the site window is key to the building and management tools in GoLive. If you work outside the site window, for example, GoLive will not automatically check links and update them for you. Think of the site window as your desktop work area.

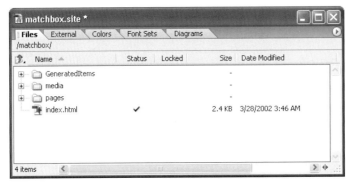

GoLive site window

You create a GoLive Web site using the New Site command. The GoLive Site Wizard automatically opens the GoLive site window, creates a home page for your site, and sets up folders to hold site resources and settings. Whether you create a blank site, import files from an existing Web site, or use one of the GoLive site templates, the Site Wizard will walk you through the process.

For more information on using the site window, see Lesson 3, "Getting to Know the Work Area."

Adding pages and page content

Once you have created a site with a home page (named index.html by default), you'll probably need to add more pages, images, and other media files. GoLive makes it easy—simply drag existing files into the site window or use the Import command. If you need a blank page, drag a Generic Page icon from the Site Items set of the Objects palette into the site window or create a new page using the New Page command.

When you're designing pages within a Web site, consider using reusable templates, stationeries, components, and snippets. These not only save you design and construction time, but they add consistency to your design.

• Templates are predesigned page layouts that you can use as the basis for new pages. When you update a template, you automatically update all pages based on that template.

• Stationery is similar to a template, except that pages based on stationery aren't linked to the source. In other words, if you update a stationery file, any pages you developed based on that stationery won't be updated.

• Components are HTML source files that you can add to a page as a single object. For example, a navigation bar that contains buttons, images, and text can be saved as a component and used on each page of a site to give a consistent look to pages. As with templates, whenever you update a component, all the pages that use the component are updated automatically.

• Snippets, like components, are source files that you can add to a page as single objects. Unlike components, library objects don't remain linked to their source files when they are added to a page. You collect Snippets either in the Snippets folder in the Extras tab in the site window or in the Snippets tab in the Library palette. Snippets are not limited to HTML—for example, you can drag image files from the site into the Snippets tab of the Library palette.

GoLive keeps track of a variety of other reusable site assets, including external URLs, e-mail addresses, and site colors. For more information on using reusable site objects, see Lesson 4, "Designing Web Pages."

Laying out Web pages

In GoLive, you can build simple or complex professional-quality Web pages without writing any source code. You can lay out pages using layout grids, tables, layers, or frame sets by simply dragging these objects from the Objects palette into a Web page. GoLive writes all the code for you.

• Layout grids let you create table-based designs without having to bother with the time-consuming process of manually adjusting table properties. Layout grids enable you to position table cells, images, and other content by simply dragging the items onto and around the grid. And when you're finished, you can easily convert a layout grid to a table that has less HTML code.

• Tables are useful for positioning items on a page in much the same way as layout grids, but tables are more challenging to use. Tables are also used whenever information needs to be organized in columns or rows.

• Layers, based on Dynamic Hypertext Markup Language (DHTML), allow you to specify absolute positioning, overlap text and images, and add animations. Because you can attach JavaScript actions to layers, they are often used to show and hide information based on mouse movements.

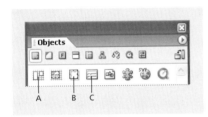

*A. Layout grid **B.** Layer **C.** Table icons
in the Basic set of the Objects palette*

You can also import Web pages created in other applications. For example, you can include a sliced Adobe Photoshop image (.psd) in your site window. When you drag the .psd file into your document window, GoLive converts the slices to Web-formatted images (.gif or .jpeg) and creates an HTML table to hold those images in place on the Web page.

For more information on laying out pages, see Lesson 4, "Designing Web Pages."

Designing pages in other applications

While you can create Web pages in GoLive, you can also use other applications, such as Adobe Photoshop, Adobe ImageReady®, Adobe Illustrator, Adobe InDesign, and Adobe LiveMotion to create images for rollovers and graphics, and even to build entire Web pages.

• To create a design that is mostly graphics, consider using Photoshop to create graphics and lay out pages.

• To create a design that is mostly HTML with some graphics, consider using Photoshop to create graphics and GoLive to lay out the Web pages.

In GoLive CS you can place non-optimized images (Photoshop and Illustrator files) directly on a Web page and let GoLive automatically convert them into Web-formatted graphics. See Lesson 7, "Using Smart Objects."

• To create images for complex rollovers and animations, consider using ImageReady.

• To create Macromedia Flash navigation elements, consider using LiveMotion for authoring in the SWF file format. There are benefits—such as adding interactivity—to creating navigational elements in LiveMotion even if the output is GIF or JPEG.

• To create a page based on sliced images, consider using ImageReady or Photoshop.

Working with text

You can type directly onto a Web page; you can type in a text box, a table cell, a layer; and you can paste or drag text onto a page from another application. You can apply formatting—color, font, type size, and alignment, for example—to individual words or blocks of text. You can format text into lists and indented paragraphs.

GoLive provides three ways for formatting text on your Web page:

• You can apply HTML text attributes using the toolbar and the Type menu. The toolbar includes attributes for headings, paragraphs, bold, italic, teletype, alignment, text size and color, and numbered and bulleted lists. This is an easy way to apply formatting to small chunks of text.

• You can save HTML text attributes applied using the toolbar and Type menu in the HTML Style palette, so that you can quickly and easily apply the same formatting to other text on other pages. HTML Styles are not linked to the text, however, so changing a style does not automatically update any text that the style has already been applied to.

• You can use cascading style sheets (CSS) to obtain the greatest consistency and control over text formatting and presentation. Cascading style sheets let you define text-formatting attributes on a style sheet that instructs Web browsers to reuse these attributes whenever text refers to them. Because the code is written once as an internal style sheet or as an external style sheet, CSS also saves download time. When you change a style in a cascading style sheet, all pages containing text that refers to the style are updated automatically.

Consider structuring text first with HTML elements so you can be sure that a page will still look good in older browsers that don't support CSS. Use the Paragraph Format pop-up menu on the toolbar to add structure to text by applying HTML headings and other structural elements. Then create a style sheet and use the CSS Selector and Properties tab to set up tag selector styles that build upon the structure elements, adding color, fonts, and so on to each style. Because different browsers support CSS attributes differently, it is important to check your pages in various browsers. Remember also that users can turn off support for cascading style sheets or override the styles of a page with their own CSS file.

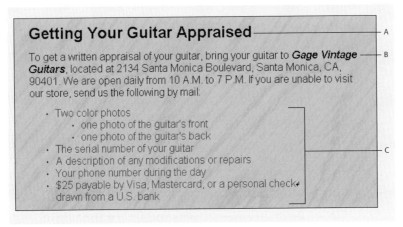

Text formatted using HTML structure elements
A. *Heading 1* **B.** *Emphasis attribute for inline text* **C.** *Bulleted list*

Adding interactivity to pages

You can add images, sound, movies, and animations to liven up Web pages.

• Rollovers and image maps are easy to create. Use an approved naming convention for the image files, and after you link the first rollover image, GoLive automatically links the remaining image files.

• Movies are easily added with the QuickTime movie editor included with GoLive.

• Place nonoptimized source files for images or animations directly on your pages using Smart Objects, and GoLive converts the files into Web-formatted graphics. When you resize or make other changes to the graphic on your page, GoLive uses the original source file to generate a new Web-formatted version.

Adding links

As you build pages, you'll add resource links to connect images and media in the pages to their source files, and you'll add navigational links to move within pages, between pages, or to URLs. Not only is it easy to create links, but GoLive continually checks the integrity of links and helps resolve broken links. See Lesson 6, "Creating Navigational Links."

Previewing pages

When you've finished with a page or a site, or when you just want to see how something is working out, you can preview pages using the Layout Preview in the GoLive document window, or you can preview pages in your favorite browsers using the GoLive Preview in Browser button on the GoLive toolbar. GoLive also gives you access to browser profiles that simulate different browsers on different platforms—you can even see how your work will look on wireless devices.

Managing a site

Once you have built a site, site management and maintenance is easy in the site window. Whenever you use the site window to move a page to a new folder, rename a page, add a new page to the site, or change an image file, GoLive automatically updates the paths between every related file, URL, or object on a page. GoLive checks the link integrity in HTML pages, with PDF files, QuickTime movies, SWF files, and embedded JavaScript source code in a site, as well as alerts you to pages that contain empty or incorrect reference links. See Lesson 13, "Managing Web Sites."

Publishing a site

After you have set up Internet preferences and Publish Server settings, transferring your site files to the FTP server is only a button click away. Files and folders can be uploaded automatically. See Lesson 13, "Managing Web Sites."

Getting started

Now that you have an understanding of the tasks involved in building a Web site, you'll build a simple Web site for a fictional company called First Strike Matches. First you'll view the finished site in a Web browser.

1 Open a Web browser (Netscape® Communicator or Microsoft® Internet Explorer, for example). From the File menu of your Web browser, open the *index.html* file in Lessons/Lesson02/02End/matchbox folder/matchbox/ on your hard drive. (The command used to open a page depends on the browser you use, but it is usually File > Open or File > Open File.)

Note: As you work through the lessons in this book, make sure that your operating system is set to display file extensions. Working without file extensions turned on will be difficult.

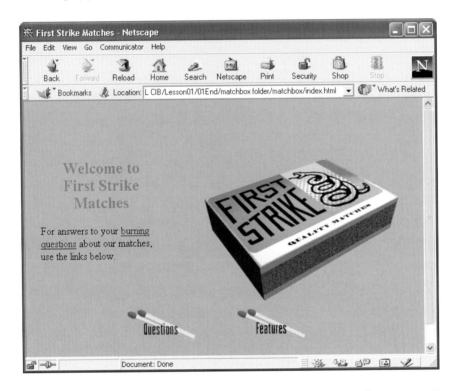

Some features of the Web pages you'll view require browsers that support JavaScript and Dynamic Hypertext Markup Language (DHTML). If you don't have an appropriate browser, you can use GoLive to preview some elements of the site, as described in "Previewing a Web page" on page 80.

2 Click the links in the Web page, and explore the site. You must have QuickTime 5.0 or later loaded in order to see the video at the bottom of the Questions page (questions.html).

3 When you have finished viewing the Web site, close your browser.

Creating a new site

Now you'll begin creating your own version of the First Strike Matches Web site.

If as you work through this lesson, you find you're having difficulty with the GoLive interface, move on to Lesson 3, "Getting to Know the Work Area," and return to this lesson later.

1 Start Adobe GoLive.

When GoLive first launches you can choose one of the following options from the GoLive Welcome dialog box:

• New Page to create a new untitled HTML page.

• New Site to open the Site Wizard for creating a new site.

• Open to open an existing Web page or an existing site project file.

Note: If you have set your preferences for the introductory screen to not appear when you start GoLive, choose File > New Site and go to step 3.

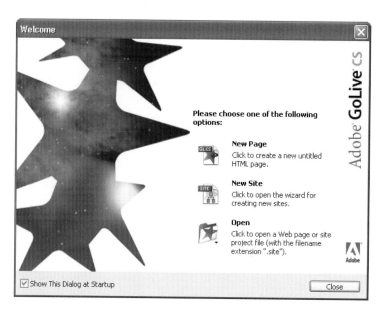

2 Click New Site.

The Site Wizard helps you through the process of creating a new Web site.

3 Select the Single User option, and click Next.

4 In the next screen, select Blank Site, and then click Next.

5 Enter **matchbox** in the Site Name text box. This will be the name of the folder that contains the site.

6 Specify the site's new location.

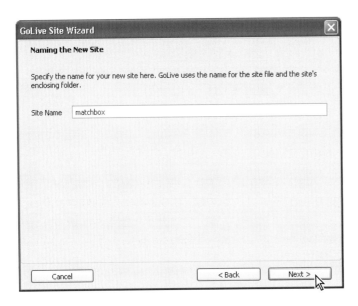

7 Click the Browse button, select the Lesson02 folder, and click OK (Windows) or Choose (Mac OS).

8 Click Finish in the Site Wizard to create the new site. That's all there is to creating a new site.

GoLive displays a site window, with a blank home page file, called index.html, already in the Files tab. Traditionally the home page of a Web site is named index.html. This is the page displayed when a viewer views the site without entering the filename of a specific page in the site. For example, if you upload the contents of the folder matchbox to the Web location www.FirstStrikeMatches.com, a viewer who uses a browser to go to http://www.FirstStrikeMatches.com sees the file index.html.

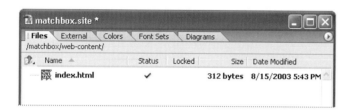

Adding files and folders

The site window is where you add pages, images, and other media files to a site—either by dragging or importing the files into the Files tab, or creating new pages. When you drag or import HTML and image files from other locations on your hard disk into the site window, GoLive creates a copy in the site's root folder on your hard drive and leaves the source files in their original locations.

Importing files and folders

You are now ready to add some elements to the site. First you'll import a folder of images and other media files that you'll add to the Web pages.

1 Click the Files tab of the site window to make sure it is selected.

2 Choose File > Import > Files to Site from the GoLive command bar.

3 In the Add to Site dialog box, navigate to Lessons/Lesson01/01Start/. Select the media folder (but don't open it) in the 01Start folder, click Add Folder (Windows) or Add (Mac OS), and then click Done.

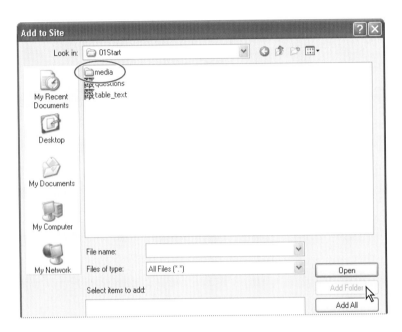

4 In the site window, click the plus sign (Windows) or the triangle (Mac OS) next to the media folder to display the folder's contents. These are the images you'll use to build your Web pages. Click the symbol next to the media folder again to close the folder.

Creating a new folder

Next you'll add a new folder to the site to hold some of the pages you'll create.

1 Be sure to click the title bar of the site window to make the site window active.

2 To create a new folder, click the Create New Folder button( ) on the GoLive toolbar.

3 Rename the new untitled folder **pages**.

Most Web servers are case-sensitive and restrict the characters you can use in filenames and folder names. When naming files and folders, avoid using a forward slash (/), space, or ampersand (&). Avoid using a period (.) except as part of an extension (for example, index.html), and avoid using the hyphen (-) as the first character in a filename or folder name. Your Web server may have additional requirements.

The site now consists of a file named index.html (the home page of the site) and two folders—the media folder that you imported, which contains several image files, and the pages folder that you created, which is currently empty.

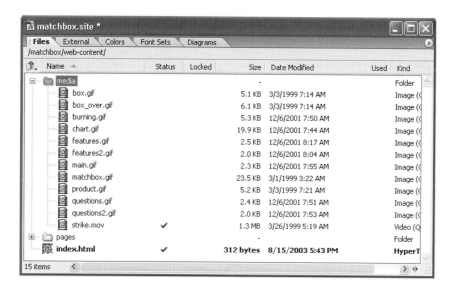

Designing a first Web page

Now that you've added some folder structure to the site, you'll begin designing your first Web page.

In the next lesson, Lesson 3, "Getting to Know the Work Area," you'll learn how to customize your desktop in GoLive. For the moment, you'll simply move your site window to the bottom of your monitor display, and position the document window above it.

1 To reposition your site window, drag it by its title bar to the bottom left of the screen.

2 In the Files tab of the site window, double click the index.html file to open the home page in its own document window.

3 Drag the document window by its title bar and position it above the site window.

If you need to resize either the site window or document window, do so.

4 To resize a window, drag the lower right corner.

If needed, you can toggle between the site window and the document window by clicking the Select Window button (🗔) (🗔) on the toolbar.

To avoid clutter, you'll close any palettes that are open. You can easily re-open palettes as they are needed.

5 To close all open palettes, choose Window > Workspace > Hide Palettes.

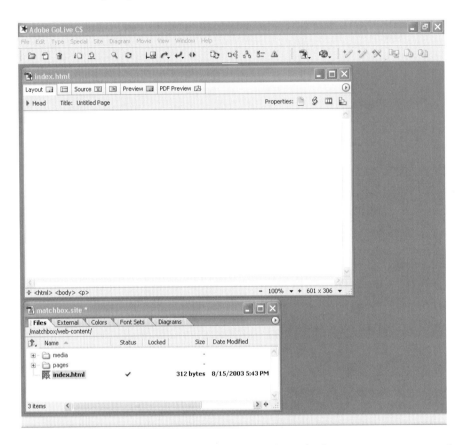

First you'll change the title of the Web page. The title that you enter appears in the title bar of a Web browser when your page is viewed. The title is also used, together with keywords, by Internet search engines and browsers to identify content in your pages. The title is not the same as the file name.

6 Click the text "untitled page" located next to the word "title" at the top of the document window to make the text editable. Replace this text with the new title, **First Strike Matches**. You can use the Backspace button to erase the existing text, or you can drag to select the text and type over it.

To add text or apply a value that you enter in the GoLive work area, you can either press Enter or Return or change the focus by clicking elsewhere in the work area.

For this lesson, you'll use the default page size.

When designing Web pages, you'll usually want to make them no wider than your viewer's screen. You can choose 720 from the menu at the bottom right of the document window to display the current page at 720 pixels wide, the standard default width for 17-inch monitors. This helps prevent you from adding objects, such as large graphic banners, that are too wide to display on a standard page. If you know the monitor size of your target audience, consider subtracting 60 pixels from the width and 120 pixels from the height of the monitor resolution to get the optimal size for your page without scrolling.

Adding text

When you're adding content to your Web pages, you'll often use the layout grid. Creating a layout using GoLive layout grids is generally easier than creating a layout using HTML tables. Layout grids let you create table-based designs without having to deal with cells, rows, and columns. And when you're finished, you can easily convert a layout grid to a table. The layout grid automatically lengthens to accommodate objects you place on it. The layout grid is one of the many objects available in the Objects palette that allow you to add elements to Web pages.

For more information on the layout grid, see Lesson 4, "Designing Web Pages."

1 Choose Window> Objects to display the Objects palette. Make sure the Basic button (■) is selected at the top of the Objects palette. Notice the tooltips that appear as your mouse pauses over the buttons at the top of the palette. Notice also that the names of the objects in the palette appear at the bottom of the palette as your mouse passes over them.

2 Drag the Layout Grid icon from the Basic set of the Objects palette to your Web page.

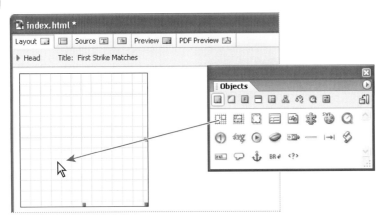

You can type directly onto a Web page in GoLive, but because you've added a layout grid, you'll need to place a container called a layout text box onto the layout grid before you can add text. After you add the layout text box, you can resize the box and move it around the grid to easily position text on your page.

3 Drag the Layout Text Box icon from the Basic set of the Objects palette to the top left corner of the layout grid on the Web page.

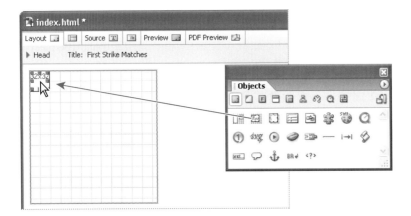

You can reposition the layout text box (or any object) by selecting it and moving the mouse pointer to any of its edges. When the pointer turns into a side-ways hand, drag the layout text box to where you want it. You can move any selected object one pixel at a time by holding down Ctrl+Alt (Windows) or Option (Mac OS) and pressing an arrow key.

4 Click inside the layout text box to create an insertion point, and type **Welcome to First Strike Matches**.

5 Press Enter to create a second paragraph, and type **For answers to your burning questions about our matches, use the links below.**

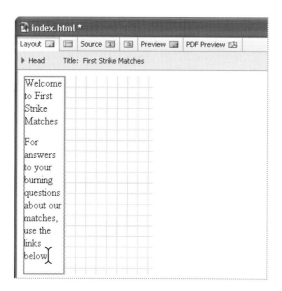

You can edit and format the text as easily as in a word processor.

6 Place the cursor at the beginning of the text you just entered, and drag to select the text "Welcome to First Strike Matches".

7 On the toolbar, click the Align Center (☰) and Bold (**B**) buttons and choose Header 2 from the Paragraph Format menu. (To show the toolbar, choose Window > Main Toolbar.)

8 Resize the layout text box (or any object) by selecting it. Move the pointer over the edge of the text box until the pointer changes into a left-pointing hand, and then click to select the text box. Move the pointer to one of the box handles. When the pointer turns into a double sided arrow, drag the handle until the box is the size you want.

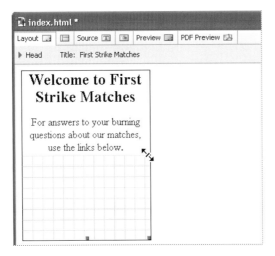

9 Choose File > Save.

It is good practice to save your project regularly as you work. Save both the document window and the site window.

10 Click in the site window to activate it, and choose File > Save.

Adding color to text

Now you'll add color to the text you entered and to the background of the page.

1 In the document window, place the cursor at the beginning or end of the text "Welcome to First Strike Matches", and drag to select the text.

2 Choose Window > Color to display the Color palette.

The Color palette has several color sets representing different color spaces. The color set you'll use most often is the Web-safe (also called "browser-safe") color set. It's a good idea to use Web-safe colors because they keep your colors from dithering (shifting) when viewed on monitors that can't display more than 256 colors.

3 In the Color palette, click the arrow at the top right of the Color palette and select Only Web Colors.

4 With the RGB sliders selected, choose a color by entering a value in the Hex Value text box and pressing Enter or Return. (We chose the color value #CC6600.)

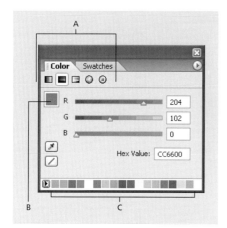

*A. Color space icons **B.** Preview pane
C. Recent Color Swatches*

As with many features in GoLive, there are several ways to set the color of text. You can set text color using cascading style sheets or you can use the HTML Styles palette. Consider using cascading style sheets if you are likely to be making global changes to text styles; consider using HTML styles if you are more likely to be making only localized changes.

Changing the background color of a page

Now you'll change the background color of your page.

1 Select the page properties icon next to the word properties in the upper right hand side of the layout screen. In the page inspector, check the background color box and then click the mouse on the box to the right of the word color. In the color palette enter 66CCCC as the hex value. The background color changes.

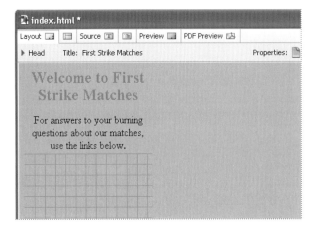

2 Choose File > Save.

Adding images

To make your Web page more visually appealing, you can use images in your design. In this part of the lesson, you'll add three images to the page. You'll add each image by putting an image placeholder on the page and then linking the placeholder to an image file.

The standard image formats for the Web are Graphical Interchange Format (GIF) and Joint Photographic Experts Group (JPEG). GIF images are typically used for line art, and JPEGs are typically used for photographs and other images with more than 256 colors. In this lesson, you'll use GIF images. Portable Network Graphics (PNG) images are not a fully supported format, but have combined qualities of GIF and JPEG.

You'll begin by enlarging the grid.

1 Click anywhere on the edge of the layout grid to select it. Blue handles appear when the grid is selected. Position your cursor over the blue square handle on the right side of the layout grid, and when the cursor changes to a double- headed arrow () drag about two inches to the right to widen the layout grid. You need to widen the layout grid to have enough space to add the image placeholder.

2 Click the Objects tab to bring the Objects palette to the front and hide the Color palette.

3 Drag the Image icon from the Basic set of the Objects palette, and place it on the layout grid to the right of the layout text box on your Web page.

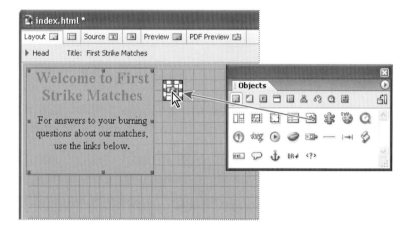

GoLive provides a context-sensitive Inspector that lets you quickly customize objects without using commands in the menu bar. You'll use the Inspector now to work with the image placeholder.

4 Choose Window > Inspector to display the Inspector.

Because an image placeholder is selected, the Inspector appears as the Image Inspector. The Source text box in the Basic tab of the Image Inspector contains the text (Empty Reference!) because the image placeholder in your Web page does not refer to an image yet.

Now you'll drag the pick whip to connect the placeholder on the Web page with an image file in the site window.

5 Make sure you can see the matchbox.gif file in the Files tab of the site window. Expand the media folder if necessary by clicking the plus sign or triangle next to the folder.

6 Select the image placeholder in the document window, and drag from the Pick Whip button (🖼) in the Basic tab of the Image Inspector to the file matchbox.gif in the media folder in the site window.

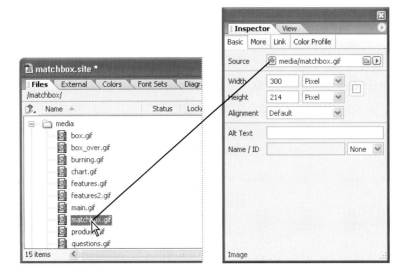

You have successfully made the connection when the line from the Pick Whip button connects with and highlights the filename in the site window. At this point, you can release the mouse button.

The GIF image appears on the Web page, and the Source text box in the Basic tab of the Image Inspector shows the relative path of the image (media/matchbox.gif). That's all there is to placing an image on your Web page.

7 To lengthen the layout grid so that you can place more images, click the edge of the grid so that the Inspector changes to the Layout Grid Inspector. In the Layout Grid Inspector, enter **360** for Height, and press Enter or Return.

8 If necessary, scroll down the document window. Drag two more Image icons from the Basic set of the Objects palette and place them next to each other near the bottom of the layout grid on the page. Make your page look like the following.

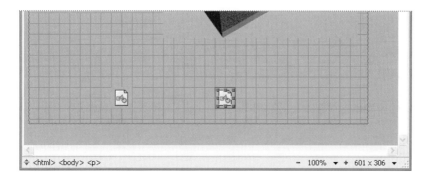

9 Select the empty image placeholder on the left and use the Pick Whip button in the Basic tab of the Image Inspector to link it to the file features.gif in the site window. Review the procedure in steps 5 and 6 if necessary.

10 Select the remaining image placeholder and use the same procedure to link it from the Basic tab of the Image Inspector to the file questions.gif.

Note: If you drag from the Pick Whip button and the target image file isn't visible, you can hold the mouse over a folder to open that folder. If the target image file name is off the bottom of the window, you can hold the mouse at the bottom of the site window (below the visible file names) to scroll down the window.

To keep this lesson manageable, you'll not take time to align the images perfectly. You'll learn how to do this in Lesson 4, "Designing Web Pages."

11 Choose File > Save to save your work.

12 In the site window, click the icon next to the media folder to hide the contents of the folder.

Previewing a Web page

You have just completed your first Web page built with GoLive. You can preview your page within GoLive or by using your browser. Not all objects on a Web page can be previewed in GoLive. For example, GoLive cannot show certain JavaScript actions, anchors, and animations. For this reason, it is always a good idea to preview pages using a browser as well as GoLive.

First you'll check your preferences for previewing the home page in GoLive. You'll need to make sure that the Preview Mode is activated in the Modules preferences.

1 Choose Edit > Preferences (PC) or GoLive > Preferences (Mac).

2 To display the Modules preferences, click Modules in the left pane of the dialog box.

You can use the Modules preferences to activate or deactivate modules. By deactivating unused modules, you can reduce the program's memory requirements, which can improve the program's launch time and responsiveness.

3 To read a description of the Preview Mode module, select Preview Mode in the right pane of the dialog box. Then click the triangle next to Show Item Information. To hide the description, click the triangle again.

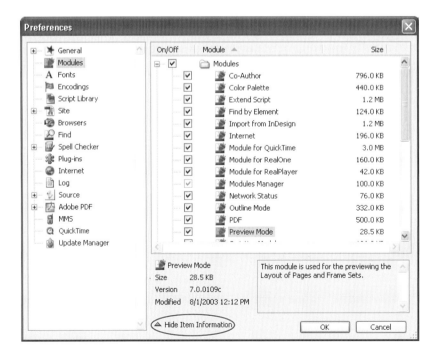

4 To activate the Preview Mode module, make sure that the checkbox next to Preview Mode is selected.

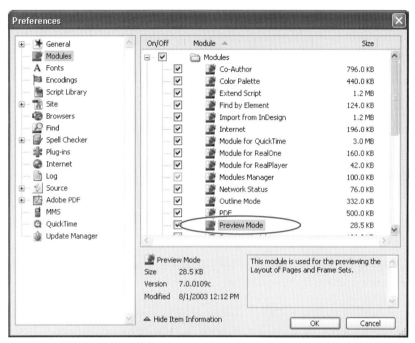

Preview Mode module activated

5 Click OK to close the Preferences dialog box.

6 In the document window, click the Preview tab ( ) to preview the document in Layout Preview.

The Layout Preview shows you what your page will look like in a generic browser. Remember, though, that the Layout Preview is not a substitute for viewing your pages in actual browsers.

7 When you've finished, click the Layout tab to return to the Layout Editor.

Now you'll set up your preferences for viewing pages in a Web browser.

To preview the home page in a browser, you need to have installed a browser on your hard disk. You'll also need to set preferences for browsers in GoLive, which you'll do now.

8 In GoLive, choose Edit > Preferences (PC) or GoLive > Preferences (Mac), and click the Browsers icon in the left pane of the Preferences dialog box.

Displaying Browsers preferences

9 Do one of the following:

• To add all browsers on your hard disk to the browser list, click Find All. (Recommended.)

• To add a single browser, click Add. Then select the browser, and click Open (Windows), or click Add (Mac OS) and then click Done.

10 In the scrolling window, click in the box next to the name of the browser that you want to be launched when you either click the Preview in Browser button ( )( ) on the toolbar or choose File > Preview In > Default Browser.

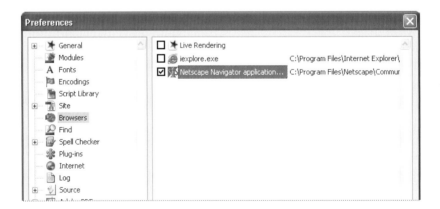

Important: GoLive lets you select multiple browsers to be launched at the same time when previewing. However, it's recommended that you only select a single browser to be launched to reduce memory requirements. Other browsers listed in the Preferences (but not checked) can be launched on demand by clicking the arrow to the right of the Show in Browser button and then selecting the required browser.

11 Click OK to save your preferences.

Now you can see what your Web page looks like in your browser of choice.

12 Open your Web page in your browser by clicking the Show in Browser button on the toolbar. The browser displays the current page, index.html.

13 Close your browser. In GoLive, click in the document window to activate it, and choose File > Close to close the index.html page.

Creating a second Web page

You're now ready to create a second Web page for the site. When you are finished, this page will contain formatted text, a rollover, a table, and a QuickTime movie.

Importing a Web page

You'll create this second page by importing a page that has been partly built for you and then adding to the content of the page.

1 In the Files tab of the site window, click the pages folder to select it. Selecting the pages folder, ensures that the page you are about to add will be added inside the pages folder.

2 Choose File > Import > Files to Site.

3 In the Add to Site dialog box, navigate to the folder /Lessons/Lesson02/02Start/, and select the file questions.html. Click Add and then Done.

4 Click the plus sign or triangle next to the pages folder to expand the folder. You've added the questions.html page to your site, but as you can see, its status shows that the page has broken links ( ).

You'll fix that shortly as you link the empty placeholders to images.

5 Open the questions.html page by double clicking it in the site window.

Your new page already has a title, "Burning Questions for First Strike Matches," and the background color has been added, as have a layout grid and several image placeholders.

Before you link the placeholders to images, you'll open the media folder in your site window.

6 In the site window, click the plus sign or triangle next to the media folder to show its contents.

7 Scroll to the top of the document window if necessary, and click to select the image placeholder at the top left of the page.

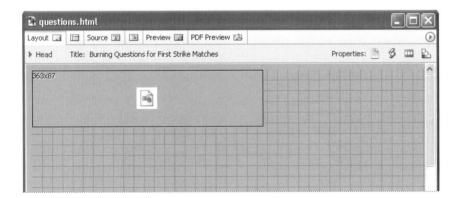

8 With the image placeholder selected, drag from the Pick Whip button ( ) in the Basic tab of the Image Inspector to the file burning.gif in the media folder in the site window. Remember that if the media file is closed, you can drag from the Pick Whip button and hold the pointer over a folder to open that folder. You can also hold the pointer at the bottom of the site window (below the visible file names) to scroll down the window.

Now you'll link the three image placeholders at the bottom of the page. Later you'll use these images to create navigation buttons for the site.

9 Scroll to the bottom of the document window.

10 Select the leftmost image placeholder. In the Basic tab of the Image Inspector, drag from the Pick Whip button and link it to the file questions2.gif, using the same procedure that you used in Step 8. Select the center image placeholder and link it to the file features.gif. Select the rightmost image placeholder and link it to the file main.gif.

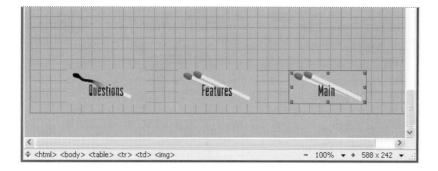

11 Choose File > Save to save the page.

Creating a rollover

Now you'll make a rollover on the page. Rollovers are images that change in appearance when you roll the mouse pointer over them or hold the mouse button down on them. GoLive rollovers use the Detect Rollover Images feature, which automatically assigns over and down images in one step if you used the appropriate naming convention. You'll learn more about this in Lesson 9, "Creating Rollovers."

1 Scroll to the top of the questions.html document window.

 2 Click the Basic button (📄) at the top of the Objects palette, and drag the Image icon from the Basic set of the Objects palette to the top right side of the layout grid on the questions.html page.

3 With the newly added Image placeholder selected, select Window>Rollovers and Actions, to make the Rollovers and Actions palette appear, make sure that the Normal Image icon is selected in the Rollovers tab.

4 Drag from the top Pick Whip button—the text box contains the words (EmptyReference!)—in the Rollovers tab to the file named box.gif in the media folder in the site window. The box.gif image appears in the page.

Because your files are correctly named and saved in the same folder, the box_over.gif is automatically referenced for the over state in the Rollovers tab of the Rollovers and Actions palette.

If you don't like the position of your new rollover, simply select it and drag it to a new position. You'll learn how to precisely position objects in later lessons.

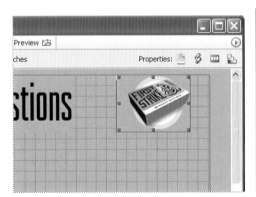

Because you are in the Layout Editor, the Web page shows the Normal image for the rollover. Now you'll check the Over image using the GoLive Preview Editor.

5 Choose File > Save.

It is always a good idea to save a page before previewing it.

6 Click the Preview tab in the document window, and roll your mouse over the matchbox at the top right of the page. You should see both states of the rollover button—that is, the matchbox will open and close.

When you are finished, click the Layout tab to return to the Layout Editor.

7 Choose File > Close to close the questions.html file.

If you check the Files tab in the site window, you'll see that GoLive has added a GeneratedItems folder. This folder contains JavaScript code for the rollover.

Creating stationery

Because you're going to use this same page design to create a third page for your site, you'll save the page you've just created as stationery by copying the questions.html page to the Stationery folder in the Extras tab of the site window.

1 Click the double-headed arrow (⊞) in the lower-right corner of the site window to open up the right pane and an additional set of tabs if the Site window is not already in split view mode. The Extras tab contains folders (created automatically by GoLive) for special resource files that save you time creating Web pages and help you maintain consistency from page to page. All of the files shown in the Extras tab can be reused in your site.

You can drag the vertical bar between the two panes in the site window to resize the panes if you wish.

2 In the Files tab of the site window, click the plus sign or the triangle next to the media folder to hide the contents.

3 Select the questions.html file in the pages folder, and Ctrl-drag (Windows) or Option-drag (Mac OS) the file to the Stationery folder in the Extras tab to copy it from the Files tab to the Stationery folder. You can also drag a file from the Files tab of the Site window to the Stationery tab of the Library palette.

4 If a Move Files dialog box appears, click OK.

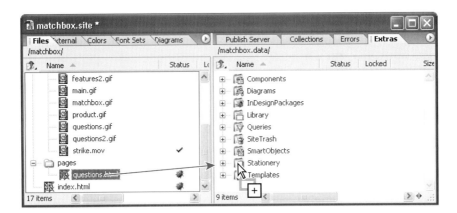

5 Click the plus sign (Windows) or the triangle (Mac OS) next to the Stationery folder to show its contents. Select the questions.html file you just copied, and rename it fs_stationery.html.

Later in this lesson, you'll use this stationery to create a third Web page. But first you'll add a table to your Web page.

Formatting a table

Instead of using a layout text box to add text as you did on the first page, you'll use a table to place text on this page. This will give you more control over the spacing between paragraphs. For this lesson, we've already created the table and text for you. In later lessons, you'll learn how to add tables to the layout grid and how to import or copy and paste text into tables.

1 Double-click the questions.html file in the Files tab of the document window to open the file.

2 Scroll up in the questions.html document window if necessary so you can see the Burning Questions image at the top of the page.

3 Choose File > Open from the GoLive command bar, and open the file table_text.html in the folder Lessons/Lesson02/02Start/.

This file contains the table and text that you will add to the questions.html page.

4 Move your pointer over the top left corner of the table until the pointer turns into this (), then click to select the table. A border appears around the table when it is selected, and the Inspector becomes the Table Inspector.

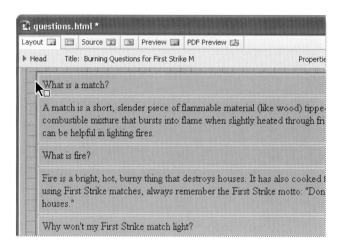

5 Choose Edit > Copy.

6 Choose File > Close to close the file table_text.html.

7 Click the title bar of the questions.html document window to make the window active, and choose Edit > Paste to paste the table into the document.

8 If you don't like the position of the table, select the table as you did in step 4, and then drag it to the preferred position. You can also select the table and click the Align Center button ( ) on the toolbar to center the table on the layout grid.

Now you'll format the table to improve the spacing of the text on the page.

9 With the table still selected, in the Table Inspector, enter **0** for Border to remove the table border. When viewers look at the page in a browser, they won't see a table outline. You'll check this in the Layout Preview shortly.

10 Enter **5** for Cell Pad to reduce the space around text in the table cells. Press Enter or Return.

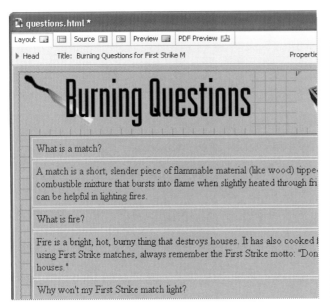

11 Select the text "What is a match?" in the first row of the table. You can triple click in the text to select the entire row. Then choose 5 from the Font Size menu (None ⬍) on the toolbar so that the text looks like a heading. You'll learn more about formatting text using the Font Size menu in Lesson 4, "Working with Text and Tables."

12 Select the text "What is Fire?" and "Why won't my First Strike match light?" in turn and change their font size to 5 as well. Click outside the text to deselect it.

13 To see how the finished text looks, click the Preview tab in the document window. Because you have turned off the table borders, the text displays without revealing the table structure—the text looks attractively and evenly spaced.

14 Click the Layout tab to return to the Layout Editor.

15 Choose File > Save to save your work.

Adding a QuickTime movie

You can place any multimedia element that Netscape Communicator or Microsoft Internet Explorer supports into a Web page you are creating with GoLive. Here you'll add a QuickTime movie to the page to show viewers how to strike a match.

 1 If necessary, scroll to display the area below the table and above the match images on the Web page. Then drag the QuickTime icon from the Basic set of the Objects palette to this area. If you don't have enough space to add the QuickTime icon, select the table and use the arrow key on your keyboard to move the table further up on the page.

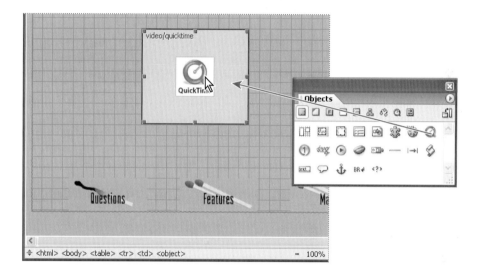

The Inspector changes to the Plug-in Inspector. Now you'll connect the Plug-in placeholder on the Web page to a QuickTime file in the site window.

Note: You loaded the QuickTime 5 plug-in when you installed GoLive CS.

2 With the placeholder selected on the Web page, drag from the Pick Whip button in the Basic tab of the Plug-in Inspector to the QuickTime file strike.mov in the media folder in the site window.

The first frame of the strike movie appears on the Web page.

3 Click the QuickTime tab of the Plug-in Inspector.

4 Select Show Controller to display a movie control bar when viewers play the movie.

5 Deselect Autoplay so the movie doesn't start until a viewer chooses to play it.

6 With the Plug-in placeholder still selected, click the Align Center button (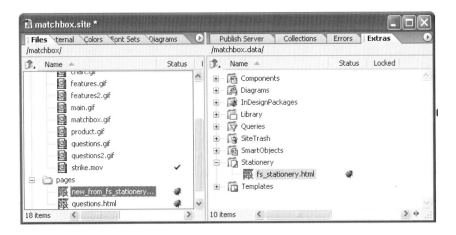) on the toolbar to center align the movie to the layout grid. (This button is dimmed if the movie is already aligned to the center.)

7 Choose File > Save.

Now you'll preview the movie in your browser.

8 Click the Preview in Browser button on the toolbar. The browser displays the questions.html page. Click the Play button at the bottom left of the movie to play the movie.

9 Close your browser, and in GoLive, close the page questions.html.

Creating a third Web page

To finish your site, you'll create a third Web page based on the stationery that you created in the previous section, and you'll add an image to the page.

1 In the Site window, click the Extras tab and make sure that Stationery folder is selected from the pop-up menu at the bottom of the palette. An icon representing the stationery that you created earlier is displayed.

2 Drag the fs_stationery.html icon from the Stationery folder in the Site window's Extras tab to the pages folder in the Files tab of the site window. The new file is named new_from_fs_stationery.html.

3 Rename the file **features.html**.

4 Double click features.html to open the file.

First you'll change the page title.

5 Select the text "Burning Questions for First Strike Matches" at the top of the document window. Replace this text with the new title "**Product Features for First Strike Matches.**"

Now you'll replace the Burning Questions image at the top of the page with the Product Features image (product.gif).

6 Click in the area of the Burning Questions image on the features.html page to select the image.

7 In the Basic tab of the Image Inspector, drag from the Pick Whip button ( ) to the product.gif image in the media folder in the Files tab of the site window.

8 Choose File > Save to save your work.

Next you'll add a pre-prepared graphic that outlines the features of First Strike Matches.

9 Drag an image icon from the Basic set of the Objects palette, and place it on the layout grid below the Product Features image on the left side of the page.

10 With the image placeholder selected, in the Basic tab of the Image Inspector, drag from the Pick Whip button to the chart.gif file in the media folder in the Files tab of the site window.

11 Use the arrow keys on your keyboard to reposition the image that you've just added until you are pleased with the vertical spacing on the page. You can also click the Align Center button ( ) on the toolbar to center the image between the left and right margins of the layout grid.

12 Choose File > Save to save the page.

13 Choose File > Close to close the page.

Creating links

You now have three pages with varying amounts of content. But as yet, there is no way viewers can get from one page to another. You'll link the text in the index.html page so that viewers can click there to go to the other two pages.

1 Double-click the index.html file in the site window to open that page for editing.

2 In the document window, drag to select the text "burning questions" under the heading "Welcome to First Strike Matches."

The Inspector changes to the Text Inspector.

3 Click the Create Link button (🔗) in the Text Inspector.

4 Drag from the Pick Whip button (🔘) in the Text Inspector to questions.html in the pages folder in the site window. Then click away from the text to deselect it.

The text in index.html is now blue and underlined to indicate it is a link. You have just created your first link in GoLive.

5 Choose File > Save.

Linking from images

In addition to linking from text, you can also link from a graphic. Now you'll link the buttons you created on the index.html page to the features.html and questions.html pages.

1 In the Layout view of index.html, select the Features image (features.gif) at the bottom left of the page.

The Inspector changes to the Image Inspector.

2 Click the Link tab in the Image Inspector, and click the Create Link button (🔗).

3 Drag from the Pick Whip button () in the Link tab of the Image Inspector to the Features page, features.html, in the pages folder in the site window. If the features.html file isn't visible, position the pointer over the icon to the left of the pages folder until the folder opens, and then drag to select the file.

Notice that the link you make on the Basic tab of the Inspector is to an image or graphic that appears on the page, whereas the link you make on the Link tab is a navigational link. You'll learn more about links, including setting e-mail links, in Lesson 6, "Creating Navigational Links."

4 Select the Questions image (questions.gif) at the bottom right of the index.html page. Create a link using the same steps that you used for the Features image, but this time link the Questions image to the Questions page, questions.html, in the pages folder of the site window.

5 Choose File > Save.

If you wish, you can repeat these steps to link the navigation images on the features.html page and the questions.html page. In each case, the main.gif image links to the home page, index.html.

You're now ready to test your links in the browser.

6 Click the Preview in Browser button (🌐)(🦊) on the toolbar to preview your page in the browser you selected in the GoLive preferences.

You can also preview your site by starting a Web browser outside of GoLive.

Note: If you don't have enough memory to run the browser and GoLive at the same time, exit or quit GoLive. Launch your browser, and locate and open the index.html file in Lesson02/matchbox folder/matchbox/.

Test the links you have created. If you created links only on the home page, index.html, you'll need to use the Back button on your browser to return to the home page as you test the links.

7 When you are finished, close your browser. Close any files open in GoLive and minimize the GoLive window.

Comparing the files on your desktop with the site files

Now that you've created a site and previewed it, you can see how the files in your site window relate to the files on your hard drive.

1 On your desktop, look at the structure GoLive created for your site. Use Windows Explorer (Windows) or the Finder (Mac OS) to open the Lesson02 folder or the folder where you saved the site you just created.

When you create a site using the Site Wizard, GoLive creates a site project file and three additional folders—the site's web-content folder, the web-data folder, and the web-settings folder. GoLive also offers you the option of creating a project folder that makes it easier to keep your site project file and related folders together. Matchbox is the name of the project folder.

2 Open the Matchbox folder in Lesson02/02start to view the site project file and the three related folders.

• *matchbox* is your site project file. This site project file is a special GoLive document that opens up the GoLive site window to display an exact replica of the files and folder structure on your desktop. The site project file is used by GoLive to record the structure of your site and manage the contents of the site. This file is not uploaded as part of the Web site.

• The web-content folder holds the Web pages and media files that make up your site. Every time you create a new site, GoLive automatically adds a blank home page, whose filename is index.html, in the Files tab. When you upload your site to a Web server, you upload the contents of this root folder.

• The web-data folder holds all of the reusable site design elements and site asset files. The folder contains the Components, Diagrams, Library, Site Trash, SmartObjects, Stationery, and Templates folders. Elements stored in these folders are used in building and maintaining your site, but they need not be uploaded as part of the site.

• The web-settings holds automatically generated information about your site's settings. These are XML files that GoLive uses to transfer information about your site's project file settings.

Managing sites

Now you'll examine the correspondence between the contents of the GoLive site window and the contents of your hard drive in more detail and see how important it is to work in the site window.

1 Double click the matchbox site project file to open the site window in GoLive. Be sure the Files tab is selected.

The files and folders you see listed in the Files tab in the site window are the same files and folders that are in the site's web-content folder on the hard disk. When you move a file, rename it, add a page, or create a new folder in the Files tab, GoLive automatically makes the change in the site's web-content folder and updates all link references in the site.

Now you'll test the value of always working in the site window.

2 In the Files tab of the matchbook site window, click the plus sign or triangle next to the pages folder to show its contents, and select the file features.html. Rename the file advantages.html and press Enter or Return.

Because changing the name of a file would normally break the links from any pages that were connected to it under its old name, GoLive displays a dialog box that lets you update all the links affected by the name change.

3 Click OK, and GoLive will automatically update necessary links.

This simple name change gives you a glimpse of the powerful management capabilities of the site window in GoLive.

4 Minimize the GoLive window, and use Windows Explorer (Windows) or the Finder (Mac OS) to see that the file is renamed on your hard drive within a few seconds. GoLive has automatically updated the files on your hard drive based on the change you made in the site window.

5 In GoLive, drag any file from your desktop into the Files tab of the site window. Again, notice that GoLive automatically adds the file to the matchbox folder on your hard drive.

Now you'll reverse your actions, this time working on your desktop.

6 Using Windows Explorer (Windows) or the Finder (Mac OS), drag the file just added to the folder matchbox back onto your desktop. Notice that the file is still present in the Files tab of the GoLive site window.

7 Using Windows Explorer (Windows) or the Finder (Mac OS), select the file advantages.html (in Lessons/Lesson02/matchbox folder/matchbox/pages/). Rename the file features.html. Press Enter or Return. Notice that the file is not renamed in the Files tab of the GoLive site window.

GoLive does not automatically manage changes made outside the site window. Now you'll synchronize the changes you make outside the site window and update your site window.

8 Click inside the matchbox site window to activate it. Then click the Refresh View button (🔄) on the GoLive toolbar. GoLive updates your site project file.

Although synchronizing your site project file with the files on your hard drive is easy, it is always better to work from the site window to avoid potential problems. To better understand the site management capabilities of GoLive, be sure to work through Lesson 13, "Managing Web Sites."

9 Close any open files in GoLive, and exit or quit GoLive.

GoLive has a rich palette of tools, and this lesson has only given you a taste of some of the more commonly used ones. As you work through the subsequent lessons, you'll look at some of the tasks you have already accomplished in more detail and you'll learn about new features. When you are finished working through this book, you should have the confidence to find the GoLive tools and workflow that best fit your needs.

Review questions

1 What is the GoLive site project file, and why is it important?

2 What are some of the ways you can add existing pages and folders to your site window?

3 What is a layout grid used for?

4 What are the standard image formats used on Web pages?

5 How does GoLive manage file name changes, links, and file synchronization?

Review answers

1 The GoLive site project file, named *yoursitename*, is a special document that GoLive creates to help you work with all of your pages, media files, and resources. The site project file opens up the site window, displaying an exact replica of the files and folder structure on your desktop. It is from the site window that you build and restructure your site, link pages and images, store reusable site assets (like page templates), and transfer and synchronize the site files with your server.

2 You can add pages and folders to your site window in a number of ways:

• Drag a Generic Page icon or a Folder icon from the Site set of the Objects palette into the site window.

• Import files into the site window using the File > Import > Files to Site command.

• Drag files into the site window from the desktop.

3 A layout grid is used for laying out Web pages. You can drag text boxes, images, and other objects onto the layout grid to lay out a page precisely without having to work with HTML tables. The layout grid is an HTML table that GoLive formats for you.

4 The standard image formats for the Web are Graphical Interchange Format (GIF) and Joint Photographic Experts Group (JPEG). GIF files are typically used for line art; JPEG files are typically used for photographs and images with more than 256 colors.

Portable Network Graphics (PNG) images are not a fully supported format, but have combined qualities of GIF and JPEG.

5 Name changes, link updates, and file synchronization are managed automatically by GoLive in the site window. If you do change file names or add files to your site outside the site window, you should always refresh the site window to synchronize the files on your hard drive with those in the site window. Changing a file name outside the site project file can break the links if the page contains any references.

3 Getting to Know the Work Area

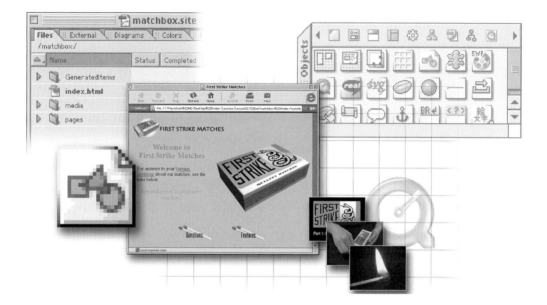

In this lesson, you'll practice using the site window, document window, context-sensitive toolbar, and most commonly used palettes. You'll also arrange and save the positions of palettes on the screen as a custom workspace for use throughout the lessons in this book.

About this lesson

In this lesson, you'll learn how to do the following:

• Open an existing Web site in Adobe GoLive.

• Display graphical site views that let you look at the site hierarchy.

• Discover unreferenced Web pages and media files using the scratch pane of a site view.

• Locate a file in the site window using the context-sensitive toolbar.

• Display, rearrange, collapse, and expand palettes.

• Save the current sizes and positions of palettes on the screen to create a custom workspace.

• Add a Web-formatted image to a page.

• Display context menus to choose commonly used commands quickly.

• Set preferences.

• Select different browser profiles for reviewing a Web page in GoLive.

• Get information quickly using Hints.

This lesson takes approximately 60 minutes to complete.

If needed, copy the Lessons/Lesson03/ folder onto your hard drive. As you work on this lesson, you'll overwrite the start files. If you need to restore the start files, copy them from the *Adobe GoLive CS Classroom in a Book* CD.

Note: *Windows users need to unlock the lesson files before using them. For more information, see "Copying the Classroom in a Book files" on page 2.*

Getting started

In this lesson, you'll open, view, and modify the fictional Web site for First Strike Matches that you created in Lesson 2, *"Developing Web Sites with Adobe GoLive CS."* Don't worry if you didn't do Lesson 2; we placed a copy of the site in the Lesson03 folder for you. As you work through this lesson, you'll learn more about the basic features of GoLive, including the site window, document window, context-sensitive toolbar, and most commonly used palettes. You'll also learn time-saving techniques for all of your GoLive projects, including creating a custom workspace, displaying context menus, and setting preferences.

First you'll view the finished site in your Web browser.

1 Start your Web browser.

2 From your browser, open the *index.html* file, the home page for the site, located in Lessons/Lesson03/03End/matchbox folder/matchbox/. (The command to open a file from the browser varies with the browser but is usually File > Open, File > Open Page, or File > Open File.)

To work with a site created in GoLive 6.0, open the site directly in GoLive CS. To work with a site created in an older version of GoLive (4.0 or earlier) or another Web authoring application, import it into a new GoLive CS site.

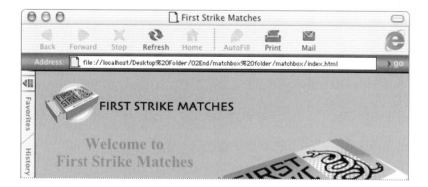

Notice the new logo and company name in the upper left corner of the page. You'll add these elements during this lesson.

3 Explore the site by clicking links on the home page and other pages of the site.

4 When you have finished viewing the site, close it and exit or quit your browser.

Opening and viewing a site

You'll begin this lesson by opening the First Strike Matches Web site in GoLive. To open an existing site created in GoLive, you open its site project file (the file with the .site filename extension), which opens up the site window. First you'll view the site in the site window, and then you'll look at graphical site views that let you see the site hierarchy in different representations.

Using the site window

As you learned in the previous lesson, you use the site window to build and manage the resources for a site. Resources for a site can include files (HTML, media, and other resource files), external URLs and e-mail addresses referenced by site files, design diagrams of possible site implementations, custom site colors, custom site font sets, a library of frequently used site objects, and reusable site objects such as page templates. The site window is organized into several tabs, which are used to handle different aspects of site management.

Now you'll open the First Strike Matches Web site in GoLive, so that you can learn more about the site window.

1 Start Adobe GoLive.

By default, an introductory screen appears prompting you to create a new page, create a new site, or open an existing file.

Note: You can set preferences for the introductory screen to not appear when you start GoLive. If the introductory screen doesn't appear, choose File > Open and go to step 3.

2 Click Open to open an existing file.

3 Navigate to the *matchbox* file in Lessons/Lesson03/03Start/matchbox folder/, and click Open.

When you open the matchbox file, the site window appears with the Files tab selected. The Files tab displays the contents of the site's web-content folder, which includes the HTML, media, and other resource files used to create the site, as well as folders to organize the files.

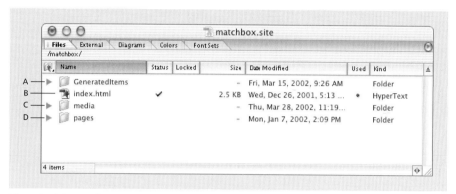

Files tab of site window **A.** *GeneratedItems folder where GoLive stores JavaScript it creates*
B. *Index.html, home page for site* **C.** *Media folder where you store images and other media files*
D. *Pages folder where you store HTML files for additional pages*

The web-content folder for the First Strike Matches Web site contains three folders—two that you added in Lesson 2 and one that GoLive generated automatically. (GoLive generated the GeneratedItems folder when you added the rollovers in Lesson 2.) You'll open the media and pages folders that you added to see their contents using two different methods.

4 Click the symbol next to the media folder to expand the folder.

The media folder contains the media files used on the pages for the site. It contains Web-formatted image files in GIF format and a QuickTime movie.

5 Click the symbol next to the media folder again to close the folder.

6 Double-click the pages folder to display only its contents in the Files tab. Notice that the path displayed at the top of the Files tab changed from /matchbox/ to /matchbox/pages/, indicating that you've gone down one level in the file hierarchy.

The pages folder contains the HTML files for the site with the exception of the site's home page, index.html.

7 Click the Upwards button (▣)(Windows) or (▣) (Mac OS) at the top of the Files tab. Notice that you've gone up one level in the file hierarchy to return to the root folder.

When you start GoLive, several palettes appear by default. Because you won't be using any of these palettes for now, you'll hide them in one easy step so your work area isn't cluttered.

8 To hide all palettes, choose Window > Workspace > Hide Palettes.

It's important to remember that the folders and files displayed in the site window reflect actual folders and files on your hard disk, as described in Lesson 2, "Developing Web Sites with Adobe GoLive CS."

It's highly recommended that you use the site window (as opposed to a system tool such as Explorer or Finder) to build and manage the resources for a site. Using the site window, it's easy to add, open, edit, link, and organize files. When you add files to a site by dragging files from the desktop to the site window, GoLive copies the files to the site without moving the original files. In addition, when you use the site window to move, rename, or delete site files, GoLive automatically updates link and reference information.

Important: If you do use a system tool (such as Explorer or Finder) to move, rename, or delete site files, make sure that you refresh the site window in GoLive so that it reflects the contents of the site on your hard drive. To refresh the contents of the Files, Diagrams, Library, or Extras tab in the site window, click the desired tab, and then click the Refresh View button ( ) on the toolbar or choose Site > Refresh View.

Now you'll display the contents of another tab in the site window.

9 Click the Colors tab to bring it to the front. (You can also click the triangle in the upper right corner of the site window to display the site window menu, and choose Colors from the menu.)

The Colors tab contains colors that you can save and reuse on pages for a site, as well as folders to organize the colors. By default, the Colors tab contains a New Colors folder that contains a color named white, which is the default background color of the home page, index.html. Site colors remain linked to the pages they're used on, so you can change a site color and update any page that uses the color. For more information on using custom site colors, see "Creating a custom color palette and adding color to text" on page 174 in Lesson 4, "Designing Web Pages."

Now you'll display the right pane of the site window, which contains an additional set of tabs.

10 To display the right pane, click the double-headed arrow (⟨⟩) in the lower right corner of the window.

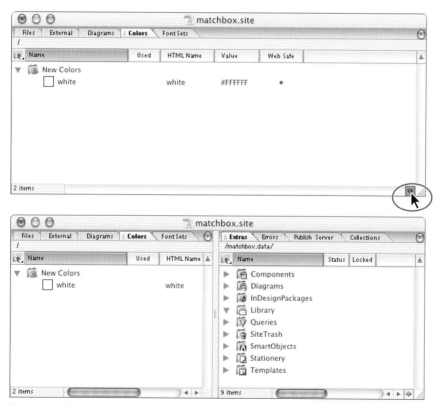

Right pane of site window with Extras tab selected

The right pane appears with the Extras tab selected. The Extras tab displays the contents of the site's web-data folder, which includes folders for storing objects that you can create and reuse in a site. For information on creating reusable site objects, see "Creating a component to be used as a navigation bar" on page 154 in Lesson 4, "Designing Web Pages."

The Extras tab also displays folders for storing design diagrams, smart objects, and files moved to the site trash. A design diagram lets you lay out the structure of a site before you create real pages and helps you manage the site creation process (see Lesson 1, "Creating Design Diagrams" for more information). Smart objects revolutionize the way you incorporate images and media from other applications, saving you time and effort (see Lesson 7, "Using Smart Objects" for more information). The site trash holds files and folders you discard from the site window. You can easily retrieve items from the site trash and return them to your site.

Although a site contains several folders and files, it's important to understand that only the contents of the web-content folder (displayed in the Files tab of the site window) get uploaded to the Web. For example, reusable site objects don't get uploaded to the Web as separate files. Instead, they automatically become part of the source code for the pages that reference them.

You can easily hide the right pane of the site window when you aren't using it.

11 To hide the right pane, click the double-headed arrow below the scroll bar for the right pane.

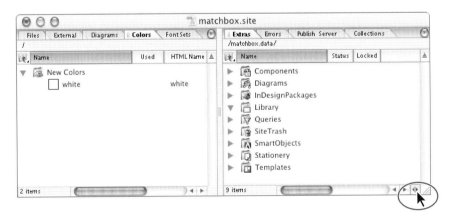

Click the double-headed arrow to hide right pane

To make room for other windows and palettes that you'll use during this lesson, you'll position the site window at the bottom of your work area.

12 If needed, reposition the site window by dragging its title bar, and resize the window by dragging its lower right corner.

Using graphical site views

GoLive provides site views that are graphical representations of a site's pages and the links that connect them. You can use the site views with the site window to display the content and structure of a site and to examine the links and relationships between pages.

Now you'll display the Navigation view of the First Strike Matches Web site. The Navigation view shows a hierarchy of pages in the site beginning with the home page.

1 Click the Open Navigation View button (▦) on the GoLive toolbar. If your toolbar is hidden, choose Window > Main Toolbar to display it.

In the Navigation view, the home page (index.html) appears at the top of the hierarchy.

2 To expand the view click the Expand button (⊞) for a page.

3 If you're unable to view the site completely, resize the window containing the Navigation view by dragging its lower right corner.

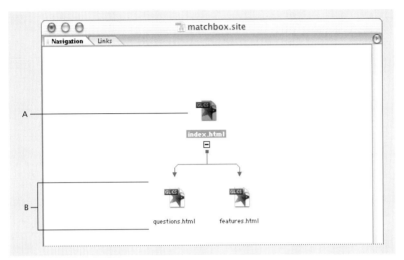

Navigation view **A.** *Home page* **B.** *Children of home page.*

Using the View palette, you can modify a site view by spotlighting specific pages or links, changing its orientation, and displaying peripheral panes. Spotlighting lets you focus the view on specific pages or links without removing pages from the view. Now you'll spotlight any pages with an incoming link to the Features page (features.html).

4 Choose Window > View to display the View palette.

To make room for other windows and palettes, you'll position the View palette and any other palettes on the right side of your work area.

5 If needed, reposition the View palette by dragging the title bar of its group window.

6 Click the Features page in the Navigation view to select it. In the Navigation tab of the View palette, select Incoming.

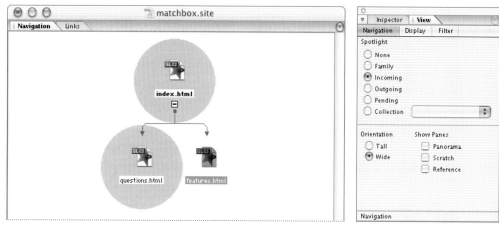

Pages containing an incoming link to the selected page are spotlighted.

Pages with incoming links to the Features page are spotlighted. You can also choose to spotlight a family of pages, pages with outgoing links to a selected page, and pending links in a site.

7 To remove the spotlighting, select None in the View palette.

In addition to the main pane, you can display several peripheral panes in the Navigation view—a panorama pane that lets you adjust the view, a reference pane showing media files referenced by selected pages in the main pane, and a scratch pane showing unreferenced Web pages and media files in the site. Now you'll display the scratch pane in the Navigation view. (A file is unreferenced if no page in the site contains a resource link to the file or the file has not been added to any page.)

8 In the View palette, under Show Panes, select Scratch to display the scratch pane.

The first_strike_logo.gif file appears in the scratch pane, indicating that it hasn't been referenced on any page in the site. Later in this lesson, you'll use this file to add a company logo to the home page.

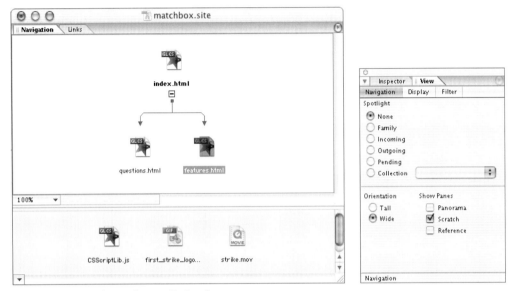

Navigation view with scratch pane displayed

9 To hide the scratch pane, deselect Scratch in the View palette.

Now that you have finished using the View palette, you'll hide it.

10 Choose Window > View to hide the View palette and any palettes in its group. (In Mac OS X, you may need to close the palette by clicking the Close button at the top left of the palette.)

You can move a site view to the site window, so that it's more accessible. To try this out, you'll move the Navigation tab from the window it shares with the Links tab to the site window.

11 If needed, reposition or resize the Navigation view so that it doesn't overlap the site window. Then drag the Navigation tab to the site window.

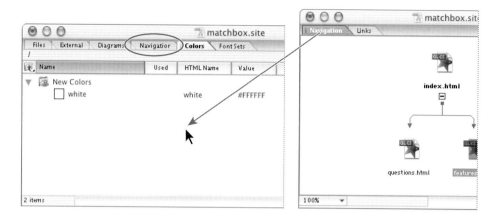

Now you can display the Navigation view from within the site window.

12 Click the Navigation tab to bring it to the front of the site window.

You can also move a tab outside of a site window, so that it appears in its own window. To try this out, you'll move the Navigation tab outside of the site window.

13 Drag the Navigation tab from the site window to an empty space in your work area.

When you move two tabs to two separate windows, you can sometimes use them in conjunction. For example, when the Navigation tab and Links tab are in separate windows, you can select a page in the Navigation tab as a way of locating the same page in the Links tab.

The Links tab displays the Links view, another graphical site view. In the Links view, you can expand the home page to show incoming links to the page in one direction and outgoing links from the page in another direction. Now you'll expand the home page to show outgoing links from the page.

14 If needed, reposition the windows containing the Navigation and Links tabs, so that they don't overlap and can be viewed in a side-by-side comparison.

15 In the Links view, click the Expand button (⊞) to the right of the home page. Make sure that the Features page is selected in the Navigation view. Notice that the Features page also appears selected in the Links view as one of the outgoing links for the home page.

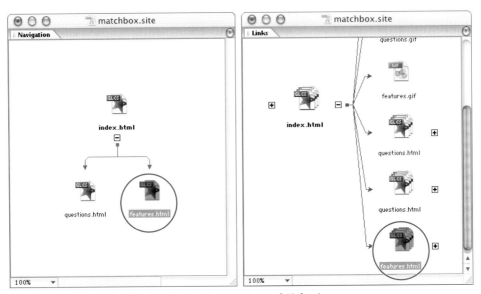

Features page (features.html) selected in Navigation view and Links view

You can easily return the tabs to their default configuration.

16 Choose Default Configuration from the site window menu. You open the site window menu by clicking the arrow at the top right of the site window.

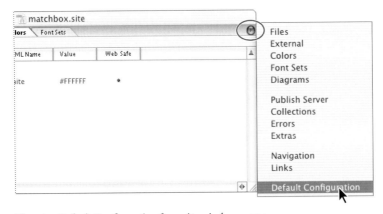

Choosing Default Configuration from site window menu

The Navigation view and Links view close, just as they were closed when you first opened the site.

17 Click the Open Navigation View button (🔲) on the toolbar. Notice that the Navigation view now appears in its default configuration (in conjunction with the Links view in a single window).

18 To close the Navigation view, click the close box in the upper right (Windows) or left (Mac OS) corner of the window.

Using the document window

After you create a Web site in GoLive and have set up its file structure, you can begin designing its Web pages.

In Lesson 2, you worked on the design of the home page for the First Strike Matches Web site. Now you'll open the home page from the site window, so that you can learn more about the document window. You can open an existing page in a site directly from the site window.

1 In the site window, click the Files tab to bring it to the front. Then double-click the index.html file, the home page, to open it.

The home page opens in the document window with the Layout tab selected. The Layout tab displays the Layout Editor, which is where you visually lay out the content of a page. The home page currently has several objects that you added to it in Lesson 2, including a layout grid, layout text box, and two images linked to additional pages in the site.

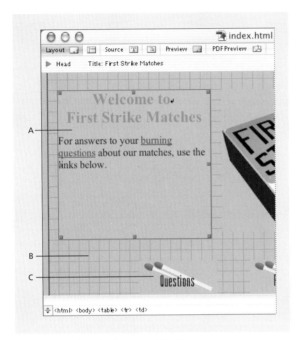

*A. Layout text box **B.** Layout grid **C.** Image*

The document window has several other tabs which you can use to lay out a frame set, work with the page's source code, and preview a browser simulation of the page in the Layout Preview. If you're using GoLive for Mac OS, you also have an additional tab for previewing frame sets in the Frame Preview.

To make room for other windows and palettes, you'll position the document window at the top of your work area.

2 If needed, reposition the document window by dragging its title bar, and resize the window by dragging its lower right corner.

To change the view in the document window, you simply select another tab. When you have text or an object selected in the Layout Editor, it automatically becomes selected in the Source Code Editor, making it easy for you to locate its source code. First you'll select text in the Layout Editor and then you'll view your selection in the Source Code Editor.

3 In the document window, select the text "Welcome to" in the headline "Welcome to First Strike Matches." Then click the Source tab to bring it to the front. Notice how the text is also selected in the page's source code. Depending on how you resized your document window, you may need to scroll down in the Source Code Editor window to see the selected text.

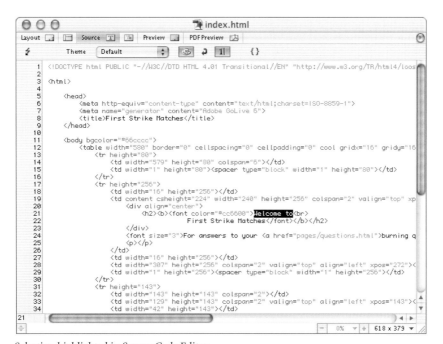

Selection highlighted in Source Code Editor

Besides viewing a document's source code, HTML programmers can also use the Source Code Editor to check syntax, fine-tune the source code, and even build pages from scratch. If you don't want to change the view of the document window to work with the source code, you can also display the source code in a pane in the Layout Editor, which you'll do now.

4 In the document window, click the Layout tab to bring it to the front. Then click the double-headed arrow (⬍) in the lower left corner of the document window.

Displaying source code pane

The source code pane appears at the bottom of the document window. Now you'll change the position of the pane so that it displays on one of the sides or the top of the window.

5 Alt-click (Windows) or Option-click (Mac OS) the double-headed arrow in the lower left corner of the document window. Continue to click until the source code pane is in the desired position.

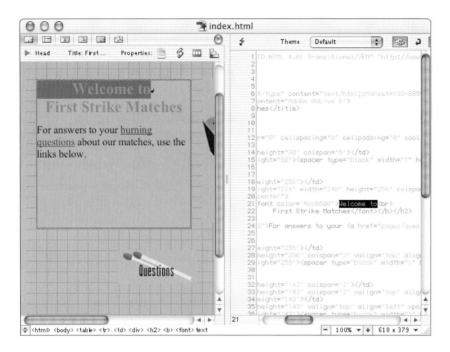

Now you'll resize the pane to customize your work area.

6 Move the pointer to the edge shared by the main pane of the document window and the source code pane. When the pointer changes to a double-headed arrow, drag to resize the source code pane in proportion to the main pane.

7 To close the source code pane, click the double-headed arrow in the lower left corner of the document window again.

○ *If you prefer to see the source code in a separate window, choose Window > Source Code to open the Source Code palette.*

The Layout Editor also has a head section pane where you can store page information, including the page title and keywords, used by Web browsers. The head section of each page already contains a Title element for the page title that appears in the upper-left corner of the document window. Now you'll display the head section pane for the home page.

8 Click the triangle in the upper left corner of the Layout Editor.

Displaying head section pane

The head section pane appears at the top of the Layout Editor. It contains several elements, including the default Title element. For more information on adding elements to the head section pane, see Lesson 4, "Designing Web Pages."

9 Click the triangle in the upper left corner again to close the head section pane.

To arrange the windows on your desktop, you can cascade, horizontally tile, or vertically tile any open document windows, site windows, and graphical site view windows. GoLive stacks the windows on top of each other with just their edges showing or fits the windows side by side. Now you'll horizontally tile the open windows for the First Strike Matches Web site.

10 Make sure that you only have the document window for the home page and the site window for the First Strike Matches Web site open. Then choose Window > Cascade and Tile > Tile Horizontally.

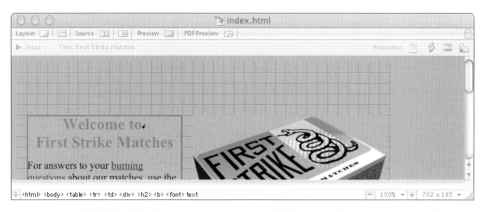

Open windows tiled horizontally

You can easily return to your original desktop configuration by resizing and repositioning windows. (To resize a window, drag its lower right corner. To reposition a window, drag its title bar.)

Using the toolbar

GoLive features several toolbars, which you can use to quickly access menus and commands. You use the main toolbar when working with a document in the Layout Editor or with files or site assets in the site window. The main toolbar is context-sensitive, which means that its contents change depending on what you have selected in the work area. You use additional toolbars when working with source code. To show or hide a toolbar, choose the name of the toolbar from the Window menu. To reposition a toolbar, drag its title bar (Windows) or lower left corner (Mac OS). (The source code toolbar appears below the Source tab in the document window when the Source tab is selected, and is toggled on and off from the context menu.)

Now you'll use the toolbar to locate a file in the Files tab of the site window. Using the toolbar to locate files within a site can save you time when working with unfamiliar or larger sites. You'll locate the first_strike_logo.gif file, which you'll use later in this lesson to add a company logo to the home page. The first_strike_logo.gif file appeared in the scratch pane of the Navigation view as an unreferenced file.

First you'll make the site window active, so that the contents of the toolbar change to provide you with options for working in the site window.

1 To make the site window active, click its title bar or click the Select Window button (![icon]) on the toolbar. Notice how the contents of the toolbar change.

With the site window activated, you can use the toolbar to create new folders, open pages, delete files, display file information, find site assets, and more. Now you'll display the Find window and instruct GoLive to search for items in the active tab of the site window with names that begin with "first."

2 In the site window, make sure that the Files tab is selected. Then click the Find Site Assets button (![icon]) on the toolbar.

3 In the Find window, enter **first** in the text box. For the Find Items Whose pop-up menus, make sure that Name and Begins With are selected. Click Find.

Entering search criteria in Find window

GoLive automatically opens the media folder and selects the first_strike_logo.gif file, the first item it found with the search criteria. Keep the location of this file in mind for use later in this lesson.

4 Select the Find window, and click its close box in the upper right (Windows) or left (Mac OS) corner of the window to close it.

When you have a file selected in the site window, you can easily display information about it using the toolbar. Now you'll display information about the first_strike_logo.gif file.

5 Click the Show Information in Explorer (Windows) or Show Information in Finder (Mac OS) button () on the toolbar.

Displaying system information about first_strike_logo.gif file in Mac OS

Your operating system displays information about the file, such as its file type, size, location on the hard drive, and creation date. You can also display file information by selecting a file in the site window and using the File Inspector.

6 Close the information window.

Creating a custom workspace

GoLive features several palettes that make it easy to perform a variety of tasks involved in building and maintaining a Web site. Using palettes, you can easily add objects to a page layout, add color to text and objects, set attributes for selections in document and site windows, display a simulated view of your pages in a variety of Web browsers, and more.

Because you'll be using a variety of palettes as you work in GoLive, it's important to know how to display, rearrange, collapse, and expand palettes. To save you time and effort as you work on different types of pages, you can even save the current sizes and positions of palettes on the screen as a custom workspace. Now you'll arrange palettes to create a custom workspace that you can use throughout the lessons in this book.

1 To display the palettes that appear by default when you start GoLive, choose Window > Workspace > Default Workspace.

Several groups of palettes appear in the work area in their default positions. The palettes used most often throughout the lessons in this book are the default palettes.

So that you have room in your work area for document and site windows, you'll collapse the palettes into tabs on the screen. You can collapse palettes on the left side and right side of the screen. Now you'll collapse each of the palettes on the right side of the screen.

2 If you're using GoLive for Windows, maximize the application window.

3 To collapse each of the palettes, position the pointer over the palette's name and drag the palette to the right side of the screen. Make sure that you drag each palette to an empty area on the right side of the screen, so that tabs don't overlap and become hidden when an adjacent palette is open. (Note: If object palette is horizontal, click the (🔳) to change its orientation)

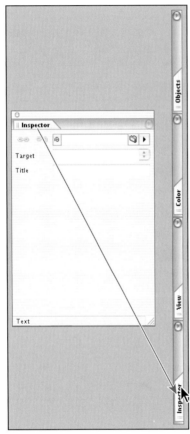

Collapsing palettes into tabs on right side of screen

Once a palette is collapsed into a tab, you can adjust the tab's position by dragging the tab along the edge of the screen. To expand a palette, simply click its tab. Now you'll try expanding the Objects palette.

4 Click the Objects palette tab to expand the palette.

*Expanding Objects palette from
side tab*

The Objects palette expands by appearing to slide out from the edge of the screen. Most palettes have a palette menu that you use to change the contents of the palette or choose commonly used commands. To display a palette menu for a collapsed palette, first click the palette's tab to display the palette and then right-click (Windows) or Control-click (Mac OS) the palette's tab.

The method for displaying a palette menu is different when the palette appears in a window. In this case, click the triangle in the upper right corner of the palette to display the palette menu.

Now you'll try displaying the Objects palette menu.

5 Click the triangle by the Objects palette to display the Objects palette menu.

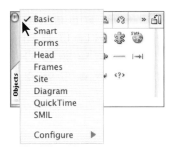

Displaying Objects palette menu

To collapse a palette menu, simply click its tab again.

6 Click the Objects palette tab to collapse the palette.

Now that you've arranged the palettes on the screen, you'll save their current sizes and positions as a custom workspace. Custom workspaces prevent you from having to rearrange palettes when working on different types of pages. Once you've created a custom workspace, you can select its name from the Window > Workspace menu to implement it.

7 Choose Window > Workspace > Save Workspace.

8 Enter **GoLive CIB** in the text box to name the new workspace, and click OK.

To illustrate how easy it is to implement your new workspace, you'll display the palettes as they appear in their default workspace. Then you'll display the palettes as they appear in the custom workspace you just created.

9 Choose Window > Workspace > Default Workspace to implement the default workspace.

10 Choose Window > Workspace > GoLive CIB to implement your custom workspace.

When you start each lesson in this book, we recommend that you implement the GoLive CIB custom workspace to save you time and effort. At any time, you can separate a palette from the screen edge by dragging its tab out to the center of the screen or into a palette group.

Setting up your work area

We recommend that you set up your work area as shown in the following illustration. Place the document window at the top, the site window at the bottom, and commonly used palettes collapsed on the right side of the screen. To move a window, drag its title bar.

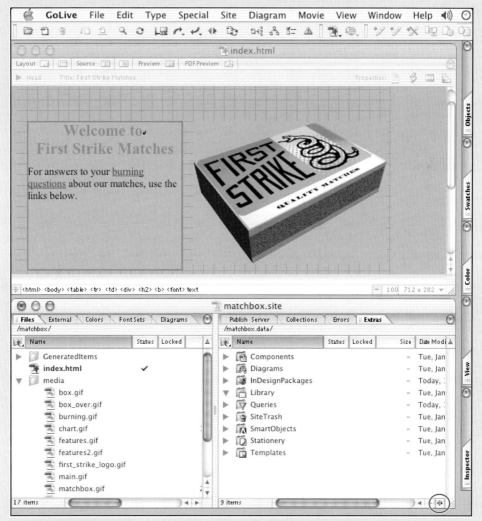

To show or hide the right pane of the site window, click the double-headed arrow in the lower right corner of the left pane of the window.

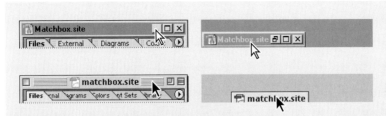

To collapse a document window, site window, or graphical site view window into a tab, drag its title bar to the bottom of the screen. (In Windows, first maximize the application window.) You can also click its Minimize button (Windows) or Control-click its title bar (Mac OS other than OS X).

To expand one of these windows, click its Restore button (Windows) or click the tab at the bottom of the screen (Mac OS).

To collapse a palette into a tab, select the palette's name and drag it to the left side or right side of the screen. To expand the palette, click the tab on the edge of the screen. To separate the palette from the screen edge, drag the tab out to the center of the screen or into a palette group.

To view the palette menu when a collapsed palette is expanded, click the triangle by the tab.

If your work area is limited, you can keep the site window collapsed and still connect files to placeholders on the page using the Pick Whip button in the Inspector. Drag from the Pick Whip button to the site window, and continue to hold down the mouse button. The site window expands, and you can drag to the desired file in the window.

Using the Objects palette

The Objects palette contains several sets of related icons, organized according to general tasks that you perform when building and maintaining a Web site. You use the Basic or default set of icons to add objects, such as layout grids, layout text boxes, layers, tables, and images, to your pages. Other sets make it easy for you to add smart objects, create forms, add meta information, lay out frames, add dynamic content, add generic site objects, add reusable site objects, and create site design diagrams.

Across the top of the Objects palette are several buttons, which you click to display the different sets. Now you'll learn how to view the names of buttons in the Objects palette.

1 To expand the Objects palette, click the Objects palette tab.

2 To view the name of a button in the Objects palette, position the pointer on top of it. The name of the button appears below it as a tooltip. Notice that the Basic button (▣) is highlighted, indicating that its set of icons appears in the palette.

To change the set of icons that appear in the palette, you click a button in the Objects palette or choose the name of the desired set from the Objects palette menu.

Note: *At its default size, the Objects palette may have too many buttons to display along the top of the palette. To view hidden buttons, click the arrow in the upper right or upper left of the palette.*

Now you'll learn how to view the names of icons in the Objects palette.

3 To view the name of an icon, position the pointer on top of it. The name of the icon appears at the bottom of the palette.

💡 *If the names of the icons don't appear at the bottom of the palette, drag the palette away from the edge of the screen and then collapse it again.*

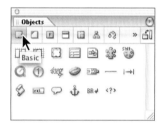

Viewing name of button   *Viewing name of icon*

To add an object to your page, you drag the icon from the Objects palette to the document window or double-click the icon. Now you'll use the Objects palette to add an image placeholder to the home page. You'll use this placeholder to add a company logo.

4 If it isn't already open, open the home page (index.html) by double-clicking its filename in the Files tab of the site window.

5 Drag the Image icon from the Basic set of the Objects palette to the blank space in the upper left corner of the home page.

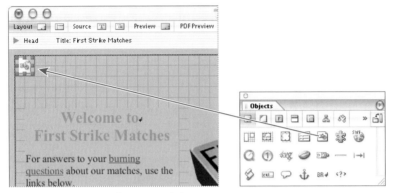

Dragging Image icon to document window

Now you'll use the toolbar to precisely position the image placeholder on the layout grid. You can also reposition a placeholder on a layout grid by dragging it.

6 Make sure that the image placeholder is selected. On the toolbar, make sure that **0** is entered in the Horizontal Position text box and in the Vertical Position text box. If you need to apply an entry, press Enter or Return, or change the focus by clicking inside the document window.

Entering values on toolbar

7 Click the Objects palette tab to collapse the palette.

Next you'll use the Inspector to link the image placeholder to the first_strike_logo.gif file located in the site's media folder.

Using the Inspector

The Inspector is a context-sensitive palette with contents that change depending on your selection in the work area. You use the Inspector to set attributes for text and objects on your page, files and site assets in the site window, styles in a cascading style sheet, and more. The name of the Inspector is based on your selection. For example, when you select a table on your page, the Inspector changes to the Table Inspector and displays options for setting table attributes.

Now you'll use the Inspector to link the image placeholder on the home page to the first_strike_logo.gif file.

1 In the document window, make sure that the image placeholder is selected. Then click the Inspector tab to expand the palette.

Because you have the image placeholder selected, the Inspector changes to the Image Inspector with the Basic tab selected. Notice that the word Image appears at the bottom of the Inspector, indicating the name of the Inspector.

2 In the site window, make sure that the media folder is open and that the first_strike_logo.gif file is visible in the window.

3 If necessary, reselect the image placeholder in the document window, and drag from the Pick Whip button (⊚) in the Basic tab of the Inspector to the first_strike_logo.gif file in the Files tab of the site window.

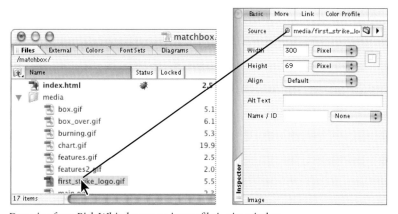

Dragging from Pick Whip button to image file in site window

When the link has been successfully created, the image appears on the page and the path to the file (/media/first_strike_logo.gif) appears in the Source text box in the Image Inspector. It's important to understand that the type of link you just created is a resource link that references an image file as opposed to a navigation link the user clicks to go to a new location (such as another page in the site). For information on creating navigation links, see Lesson 6, "Creating Navigational Links."

4 Click the Inspector tab to collapse the palette.

Next you'll save the index.html file using a context menu.

Using context menus

GoLive contains several context-sensitive menus that display commands relating to the active window or selection. You use context menus as a quick way to choose commonly used commands. Now you'll use a context menu to save the changes you've made to the home page.

1 To display a context menu, position the pointer over the active window or selection—in this case, the page icon (📄) in the upper left corner of the document window.

2 Then do one of the following:

• In Windows, click with the right mouse button.

• In Mac OS, hold down Control and click with the mouse button.

3 In the context menu that appears, choose Save or Save As to save the page.

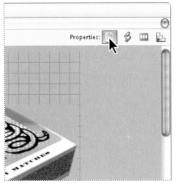 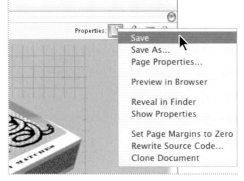

Using context menu to save page

Setting GoLive preferences

You can change most of the program settings using the Preferences dialog box, giving you control over the way GoLive looks and behaves.

In this section you'll learn about two important preferences that control how GoLive behaves when it launches and where files are stored when they're removed from the site.

1 Choose Edit > Preferences (Windows) or choose GoLive> Preferences (Mac OS).

The Preferences dialog box appears with General preferences shown by default. (If General preferences don't appear, click General in the left pane of the dialog box.) Using the General preferences, you can specify how GoLive behaves when it launches so that GoLive shows an introductory screen, creates a new page, or does nothing.

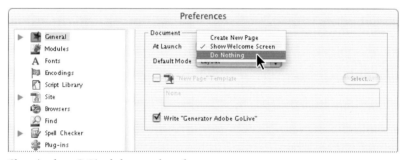

Changing how GoLive behaves at launch

To see more General preferences, click the plus sign (Win) or arrow (Mac) next to General in the left pane of the dialog box, and select a name from the list that appears below it. Now you'll display the Site preferences, which you use to specify where files are stored when they're removed.

2 Click Site in the left pane of the dialog box. Notice the setting in the right pane of the dialog box that specifies for files to be removed to the site trash (instead of the system trash).

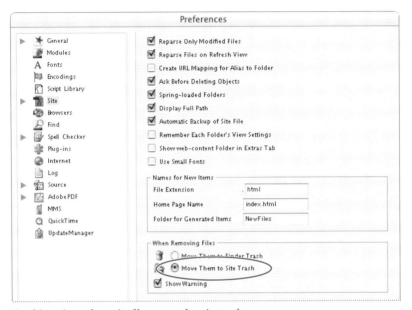

Use this option to have site files removed to site trash.

3 Click Cancel to close the Preferences dialog box without making any changes.

When files are removed to the site trash, they're stored in the Site Trash folder in the Extras tab of the site window. Unlike the system trash, the site trash makes it easy for you to store unwanted files temporarily and retrieve them later as needed.

Previewing in GoLive

You can preview your Web pages directly in GoLive. In Layout Preview, you can test navigation links, play QuickTime movies, and view animated GIFs and any other plug-in media items that GoLive supports. Now you'll preview the home page in GoLive.

1 In the document window, click the Preview tab ( ) to view the document in the Layout Preview.

The Layout Preview displays an approximation of what your page looks like when it's finally published on the Web. You can also preview a page using the Live Rendering window to preview changes you make in the Layout editor on the fly. (File> Preview In> Live Rendering)

2 Test the navigation links on the home page and on the other pages of the site.

You can also view a browser simulation of your page in the Layout Editor by choosing the profile of a specific browser in the View palette, which you'll do now.

3 Click the Layout tab to return the document view to the Layout Editor.

4 Click the View palette tab to expand the palette.

5 In the View palette, choose "Explorer 5 Mac" from the Profile menu to see how your page appears in Microsoft Internet Explorer 5 for Mac OS. Try the different menu options and observe how your page changes in the preview. Be sure you can see some of the text on the page, other than in a graphic.

Choosing option from Profile menu

6 When you have finished, click the View palette tab to collapse the palette.

Previewing in a Web browser

In addition to previewing your page in GoLive, you should always preview it using a variety of browsers, browser versions, and platforms. You'll need to use browsers to determine potential browser differences and to preview items for which GoLive doesn't provide native support.

Now you'll preview the home page in a Web browser.

1 Do one of the following:

• If you selected a single browser in the Browsers preferences as described in "Previewing a Web page" on page 80, click the Preview in Browser button on the toolbar. When a single browser is selected, the button appears as the program icon of the selected browser.

• If you selected multiple browsers in the Browsers preferences, click on the Preview in Browser button to launch all selected browsers. Alternatively hold down the mouse button on the triangle to the right of the Preview in Browser button, and then drag to the desired browser from the pop-up menu. When two or more types of browsers are selected in the Preferences (such as Netscape and Explorer), the button appears as a generic browser icon.

2 When you have finished viewing the site, exit or quit your browser.

It's good practice to always save your pages before previewing them. In addition, always use GoLive to bring up the preview in a browser (using the Preview in Browser button, for example), so that any changes you've made to the pages appear in the browser. (If you don't launch the browser from GoLive, an older version of the page may be cached in the browser memory.)

Review questions

1 How do you open an existing Web site in GoLive?

2 How do you display a graphical view of a site?

3 What's the recommended way to set up your work area in GoLive?

4 How do you both collapse and expand a palette?

5 What's a custom workspace? How do you implement one?

6 What palette do you use to add an image placeholder to your page? What palette do you use to link an image placeholder to an image file?

7 What's the recommended way to preview a site or page that you've created in GoLive?

Review answers

1 To open an existing Web site in GoLive, choose File > Open, select the file (with the .site extension) in the site's project folder, and click Open.

2 To display a graphical view of a site, click the Open Navigation View button (🔲) on the toolbar.

3 It's recommended that you set up your work area by placing the document window at the top, the site window at the bottom, and commonly used palettes collapsed on the right side of the screen.

4 To collapse a palette into a tab, drag the palette's name tab to the left side or right side of the screen. To expand a palette, click the tab at the edge of the screen.

5 You can arrange and save the positions of palettes on the screen as a custom workspace, which you implement to save time and effort on different projects. To save a custom workspace, choose Window > Workspace > Save Workspace. To implement a custom workspace, choose its name from the Window > Workspace menu.

6 You use the Basic set of the Objects palette to add an image placeholder to your page and the Inspector to link the placeholder to an image file.

7 In addition to previewing your site or page in GoLive, you should always preview it using a variety of browsers, browser versions, and platforms. You'll need to use browsers to determine potential browser differences and to preview items for which GoLive doesn't provide native support.

4 Designing Web Pages

Adobe GoLive provides you with a variety
of tools for laying out your Web pages,
including tables, layout grids, floating
boxes, and frame sets. It also provides you
with several ways to quickly add objects
and apply colors frequently used in your
Web site, saving you both time and effort.
In this lesson, you'll explore the various
tools for page layout as you work on the
design of three Web pages.

About this lesson

In this lesson, you'll learn how to do the following:

• Create a new Web site and add files to it.

• Create a component that stores frequently used page content, such as a navigation bar, and add the component to each page in a site.

• Use a layout grid to precisely place text, images, and other objects on a page.

• Add Web-formatted images to a page using a variety of methods.

• Align, distribute, and move multiple objects on a layout grid.

• Add a background image, keywords, comments, and a date and time stamp to a page.

• Add text to a page using layout text boxes on a layout grid, and copy and paste text into a table.

• Create a custom color palette that stores frequently used site colors, and apply the colors to pages in a site.

• Extract color from an image or other element on the screen, and add it to a custom color palette.

• Use layers to place overlapping objects on a page.

• Edit a component's source file to have GoLive automatically update each page that contains it.

This lesson takes approximately 60 minutes to complete.

If needed, copy the Lessons/Lesson04/ folder onto your hard drive. As you work on this lesson, you'll overwrite the start files. If you need to restore the start files, copy them from the *Adobe GoLive CS Classroom in a Book* CD.

Note: Windows users need to unlock the lesson files before using them. For more information, see "Copying the Classroom in a Book files" on page 2.

Getting started

In this lesson, you'll review and build on the skills you learned in Lessons 2 and 3. You'll create a new Web site for the fictional company called Gage Vintage Guitars and work on the design of three Web pages for the site. You'll learn more about how to lay out pages using tables, layout grids, and layers. You'll also learn more about reusable site objects (components, stationery pages, and page templates) that can save you both time and effort. In addition, you'll learn how to add a background image, keywords, comments, and a date and time stamp to a Web page.

First you'll view the finished pages in your Web browser. Currently the pages don't contain any navigation links, so you'll need to open each page individually. You'll add navigational links to these pages in Lesson 6, "Creating Navigational Links."

1 Start your Web browser.

2 In your Web browser, open the *index.html* file in Lessons/Lesson04/04End/gage folder/gage/.

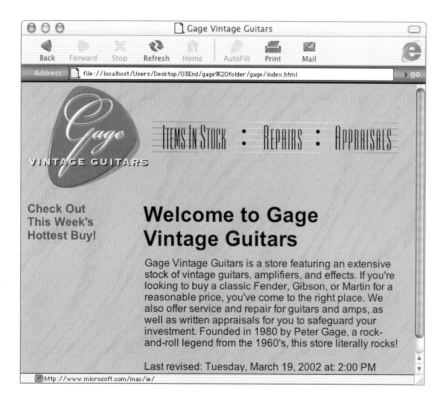

3 Open the *appraise.html* file in Lessons/Lesson04/04End/gage folder/gage/pages/.

4 Open the *hottest.html* file in Lessons/Lesson04/04End/gage folder/gage/pages/.

5 When you have finished viewing the pages, close them and exit or quit your browser.

Creating a new Web site

You'll begin this lesson by creating a new Web site for Gage Vintage Guitars. You'll create a blank, single-user site.

1 Start Adobe GoLive.

By default, an introductory screen appears prompting you to create a new Web page, create a new site, or open an existing file.

Note: You can set preferences for the introductory screen to not appear when you start GoLive. If the introductory screen doesn't appear, choose File > New Site to display the GoLive Site Wizard, and go to step 3.

2 Click New Site to display the GoLive Site Wizard.

3 Make sure that Single User is selected, and click Next.

4 Make sure that Blank Site is selected, and click Next.

5 In the Site Name text box, enter **gage** as the name of the new site. Click Next.

6 Click Browse, and then use the dialog box to select the Lesson04 folder, located in the Lessons folder on your hard drive, and click OK (Windows) or Choose (Mac OS).

7 Click Finish in the Site Wizard.

Creating new site

GoLive creates a site project folder named gage folder within the Lesson04 folder. This folder contains a site project file (gage) to manage the site contents; a web-content folder, which by default contains a blank home page called index.html; a web-data folder, where you store different types of reusable site objects and other resources; and a web-settings folder, where GoLive stores settings you make in the site window and the Site Settings dialog box.

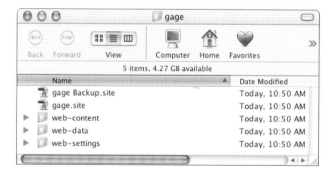

The site window appears with the Files tab selected. The Files tab displays the contents of the site's web-content folder. Remember, all of the folders and files displayed in the site window reflect actual folders and files on your hard disk.

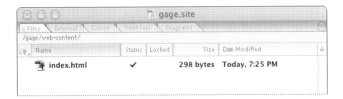

Now you're ready to add files to the site.

Adding files to the Web site

You can add Web pages, media files, and other resource files to an existing Web site. To add files from other locations to your site, it's recommended that you use the GoLive Import command or drag the files into the Files tab of the site window. With either of these methods, GoLive copies the files to the site without removing the original files.

Now you'll import a folder of image files into the site.

1 If it isn't already selected, select the site window. Also, make sure that the Files tab of the site window is selected.

2 Choose File > Import > Files to Site.

3 Select the images folder in Lessons/Lesson04/04Start/. Click Add or Choose, and then click Done.

Importing images folder to site

The images folder is copied to the site's root folder and appears in the Files tab of the site window.

Note: You can also drag folders and files from another location into the Files tab of the site window. Using a system tool (such as Windows Explorer or the Mac OS Finder), simply select the desired folder or files, and drag them to the site window.

4 In the site window, click the plus sign (Win) or the arrow (Mac) next to the images folder to display the folder's contents.

The images folder contains several Web-formatted images in GIF that are ready to be added to pages.

Now you'll add a new folder to the site for storing additional pages.

5 Choose Site > New > Folder.

A new folder is added to the site's root folder and appears in the Files tab of the site window. Now you'll rename the folder.

6 Type **pages** to rename the folder, and click in the blank space outside the folder to deselect it.

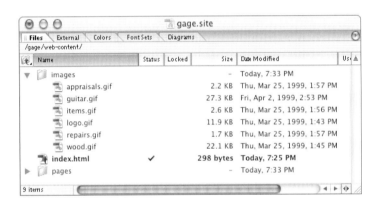

Note: *To apply text or a value that you've entered in GoLive, you need to press Enter or Return, or change the focus by clicking elsewhere in the work area. Keep this in mind whenever you're working in GoLive.*

Now you'll import an existing page to the site. Later in this lesson, you'll update the design of the page.

7 Make sure that no folders are selected in the site window, and choose File > Import > Files to Site. (If you accidentally import a file while a folder is selected in the site window, the file will be imported to that folder rather than being imported at the root level.) The Import Files to Site command isn't available unless the Files tab in the site window is active.

8 Select the file appraise.html in Lessons/Lesson04/04Start/. Click Add (Win) or Choose (Mac), and then click Done.

9 In the Copy Files dialog box, click OK to copy the file and update the site.

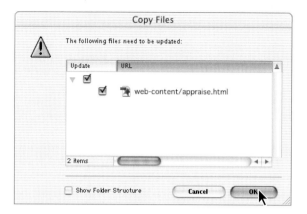

The appraise.html file is added to the site's root folder and appears in the Files tab of the site window. Now you'll move the appraise.html file to the pages folder.

10 In the site window, select the appraise.html file, and drag it to the pages folder. Click OK in the Move Files dialog box.

11 Click the plus sign (Win) or the arrow (Mac) next to the pages folder in the site window to display the folder's contents.

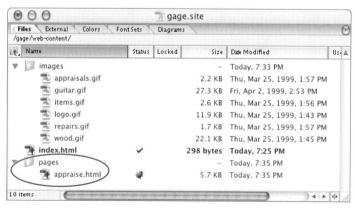

Displaying folder's contents

Now that you have finished adding files to the site, you can begin designing its pages. You'll start by creating a component for a navigation bar that you'll later add to each page in the site.

Creating a component to be used as a navigation bar

A component is an HTML source file that stores text and objects, such as a navigation bar, that you want to add to multiple pages in a site. When a component is added to a page, it's added as a single object and remains linked to its source file. To update a component, you simply update its source file to have GoLive automatically update all pages containing it.

At the top of each page in the Gage Vintage Guitars site, you'll place the company logo and a navigation bar for the site. Instead of creating this page content multiple times, you'll create it once and save it as a component that you can quickly add to each page. Now you'll create a new page that you'll store as a component. You store components in the Components folder, located in the site's web-data folder.

1 To display the right pane of the site window, click the double-headed arrow (⬚) in the lower right corner of the window.

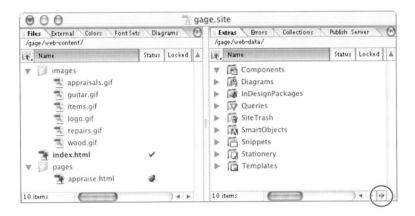

The right pane of the site window appears with the Extras tab selected. The Extras tab displays the contents of the site's web-data folder, which includes the Components folder.

2 Place the site window at the bottom of your work area, so that the window is visible when you create a new page. To move a window, drag its title bar.

3 Choose Window > Objects, or click the tab if the Objects palette is collapsed.

For more information on working with palettes, see "Creating a custom workspace" on page 126. For detailed information on using the Objects palette, see "Using the Objects palette" on page 132.

4 In the Objects palette, click the Site button (⊞)to display the Site set of icons in the palette. (You can also choose Site from the Objects palette menu.)

 5 Drag the Generic Page icon from the Site set in the Objects palette and drop it on the Components folder in the Extras tab of the site window.

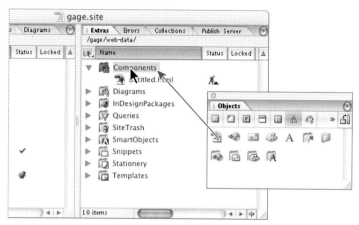

Adding new page to site's Components folder

A new page, untitled.html, is added to the Components folder and appears in the Extras tab of the site window.

6 Enter **navbar.html** to rename the file.

Note: To add a new page to a site, you can also choose File > New Page. If you use this method, make sure that you save the page to the appropriate folder on your hard drive.

Now you'll open the navbar.html file.

7 Double-click the navbar.html file to open it.

The navbar.html file opens in the Layout Editor of the document window.

Note that the default window size for new pages is 619. You'll use this default size in this lesson.

Now you'll change the title of the page. Page titles, together with keywords, are used by Internet search engines and browsers to identify content in your pages.

8 Select the default page title (Untitled Page).

9 Enter **Navigation Bar** as the new title.

10 Choose File > Save.

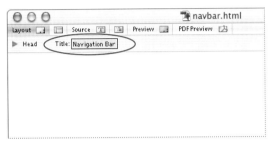

Changing page title

You can check that a file is saved as a component by selecting the Extras tab in the site window and choosing the Components folder. Your navbar.html file should now be saved in the Site Extras set, ready to be added to any page.

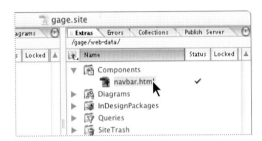

Now you'll begin designing the component by adding a layout grid to the page.

Adding a layout grid

GoLive layout grids make it easy for you to create table-based designs in your pages. Instead of setting up multiple table cells, you can add a single layout grid to a page and position objects anywhere on the grid with 1-pixel accuracy. You can easily add text to a grid by dragging a layout text box onto the grid and entering text into the layout text box.

1 Click the navbar.html window to make it active.

2 Drag the Layout Grid icon from the Basic set ( ) in the Objects palette to the page. (You can also double-click the Layout Grid icon to place a layout grid at the insertion point on the page.)

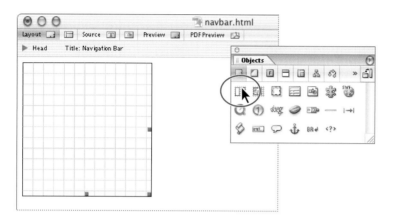

A layout grid is added to the page. Now you'll specify a width for the layout grid.

3 Choose Window > Inspector to open the Inspector, or click the tab if the Inspector is collapsed.

4 In the Layout Grid Inspector, enter **600** for Width. Press Enter or Return.

To resize a layout grid, you can also select it and drag one of its handles.

Now that you've added a layout grid to the page, you can add objects, such as images, to it.

Adding an image using the Pick Whip button

Traditionally when you create an image for use on the Web, you work in a program such as Illustrator or Photoshop, and then save the image in a Web-safe format such as GIF or JPEG. It's also a good idea to maintain the source file in its original format and resolution, in case you need to make changes to the image in the future. In GoLive, you can add Web-formatted images to the page using a variety of methods.

💡 *You can also add images to a page using GoLive Smart Objects, which can save you both time and effort. Using Smart Objects, you can drag an image's source file (such as an .ai or a .psd file) to a page and optimize the image for the Web directly in GoLive. GoLive creates a Web-formatted version of the image in a target file that it adds to the page. When you update the source file, GoLive automatically regenerates the target file to update the image on the page (see Lesson 7, "Using Smart Objects").*

Now you'll add four Web-formatted images to the page using different methods. First you'll add a company logo using the Pick Whip button in the Image Inspector.

1 Drag the Image icon from the Basic set (🖾) in the Objects palette to the upper left corner of the layout grid. Don't worry about the exact placement of the placeholder; you'll precisely position each image later in this lesson.

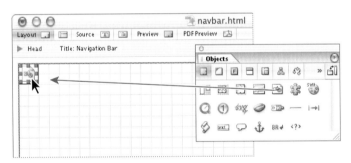

Adding image placeholder to page

An image placeholder appears on the layout grid, and the Inspector changes to the Image Inspector. If needed, you can adjust the position of the placeholder, as well as any other object on the grid, by dragging it.

2 In the Basic tab of the Image Inspector, notice that the Source text box shows "Empty Reference!" This indicates that the image placeholder doesn't reference an image file yet.

Now you'll use the Pick Whip button to link an image file in the site window with the placeholder on the page.

3 In the Files tab of the site window, make sure that the images folder is open and the logo.gif file is visible.

4 Drag from the Pick Whip button (📷) in the Image Inspector to logo.gif in the images folder within the site window.

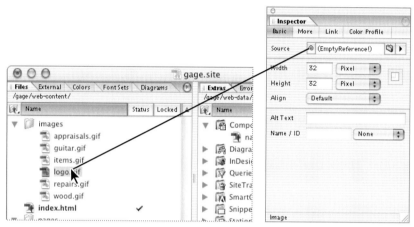

Using Point and Shoot button to specify image

The company logo is added to the page, and the path to the logo.gif file appears in the Source text box in the Image Inspector.

GoLive supports the use of low-resolution images that appear in the browser while high-resolution images are loading. You can generate low-resolution images quickly using GoLive, which you'll do now.

5 In the More tab of the Image Inspector, click Generate. The image must be selected in the document window for this tab to be available.

A low-resolution (low-source) image file named logols.gif appears in the images folder in the site window in addition to the logo.gif file, and the Low option in the Image Inspector is automatically selected.

Now you'll add alternative text for the image. In browsers that don't support images or have image loading turned off, the text is displayed instead of the image. This text may also be used by text reading machines for the visually impaired.

6 In the Basic tab of the Image Inspector, enter **Gage Vintage Guitars Logo** in the Alt Text box.

7 Choose File > Save to save navbar.html.

Adding an image using a keyboard shortcut

Now you'll add a second image to the page using a keyboard shortcut. This image is part of the navigation bar for the site.

1 Drag the Image icon from the Basic set (▥) in the Objects palette to the right of the company logo on the page.

2 Hold down Alt (Windows) or Command (Mac OS), and drag from the image place-holder on the page to items.gif in the images folder within the site window.

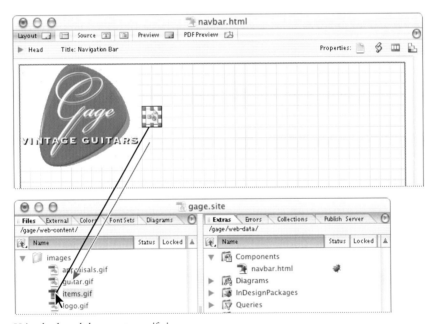

Using keyboard shortcut to specify image

3 In the Basic tab of the Image Inspector, enter **Items In Stock** in the Alt Text box to add alternative text for the image you just added.

Because items.gif is small in file size (1K), you don't need to create a low-source (low-resolution) image.

Adding images by dragging

Now you'll add a third and then a fourth image to the page by dragging. These images also are part of the navigation bar for the site. You don't need to worry about aligning these images perfectly; you'll do that in a later section of the lesson.

 1 Drag the Image icon from the Basic set (▣) in the Objects palette to the right of the Items In Stock image on the page.

2 Drag repairs.gif from the images folder in the site window to the image placeholder on the page.

3 Click the newly added image in the document window to select it.

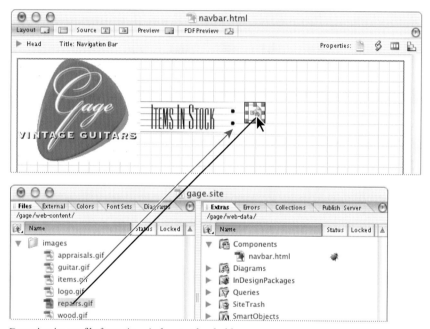

Dragging image file from site window to placeholder

4 In the Basic tab of the Image Inspector, enter **Repairs** in the Alt text box.

Now you'll add the fourth image to the page.

5 Drag the Image icon from the Basic set in the Objects palette to the right of the Repairs image on the page.

6 Drag appraisals.gif from the images folder in the site window to the image placeholder on the page.

7 Click the newly added image to select it.

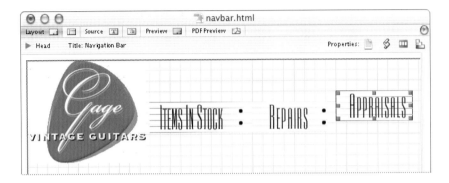

8 In the Basic tab of the Image Inspector, enter **Appraisals** in the Alt text box.

9 Choose File > Save to save navbar.html.

To add an image to a page, you can also drag the image file from the site window to the page, without using an image placeholder. Using a placeholder, however, gives you more control over the placement of the image.

Creating Web pages using Photoshop-based designs

The majority of Web design firms and professionals create their Web page layouts in Adobe Photoshop, including rollovers and animated GIFs, and then bring the designs into their Web pages. When you design a page layout in Photoshop, you can slice it into a table of individual images and GoLive will automatically put the slices into a custom HTML table in your page. When you save the Photoshop image for the Web, you can reformat the HTML and JavaScript code so that any rollovers are fully editable in GoLive. You can use any of these methods to add your Photoshop designs to your Web pages in GoLive:

• Dragging a Photoshop image file from the site window into the page automatically creates a Smart Object link between Photoshop and GoLive. If the image is sliced, GoLive places the slices into a new table and saves each slice as a separate Web image. You can continue to update the design in Photoshop and GoLive automatically optimizes the sliced images for the Web. (See the Adobe GoLive CS online Help.)

• *If you want to preserve multiple layers of a Photoshop design, you can import the layers of the image as individual Web images in layers (DHTML layers). Because the Web images are displayed in layers, you can completely reposition them, overlap them, and apply other actions to them such as the Show Hide action. (See the Adobe GoLive CS online Help for information on hiding and showing layers.)*

• *You can use your Photoshop-based design as a tracing image and save individual cutouts as Web images in layers. If you want, you can create a duplicate page that places the tracings in a table-based design by converting the layers to a layout grid. (See the Adobe GoLive CS online Help for more information.)*

Aligning and distributing multiple objects

Now that you've added all of the images, you're ready to align and distribute them. You'll align the tops of the three images for the navigation bar using the Align palette.

1 To display the Align palette, choose Window > Align.

 The toolbar lets you align objects relative to a layout grid, while the Align palette lets you align and distribute objects relative to each other or their parent.

2 Click the Items In Stock image to select it. Then Shift-click the Repairs image and the Appraisals image to add them to the selection.

3 In the Align palette, click the Vertical Align Top button ( ) under Align Objects. (If the tops of the selected objects are already aligned, this button is dimmed.)

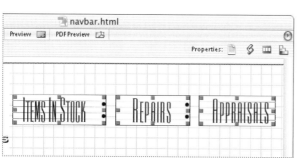

The tops of the selected images are aligned.

4 With the three images still selected, click the Vertical Align Top button ( ) under Align to Parent.

The three images are aligned with the top of the layout grid.

5 Choose Window > Align to close the Align palette.

Now you'll move the three images together using a keyboard shortcut.

6 Click away from the three images to deselect them, and select only the Items In Stock image on the page. Then hold down Ctrl+Alt (Windows) or Option (Mac OS), and press the Left Arrow key until the image moves no further.

7 Select only the Repairs image on the page, and use the same method to move it to the left until it moves no further. Then select only the Appraisals image, and move it to the left until it moves no further.

The selected objects are moved horizontally on the page so that their edges touch each other.

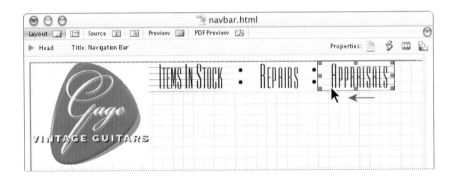

Note: By default, a layout grid has options set to snap objects to the grid. To move a selected object 16 pixels (the default spacing between the horizontal and vertical lines of the grid), press an arrow key. To move a selected object 1 pixel, hold down Ctrl+Alt (Windows) or Option (Mac OS), and press an arrow key.

When you have finished placing objects on a grid, it's a good idea to optimize the grid, which you'll do now. Optimizing a grid reduces its size, so that it takes up less space on the page.

8 Click the layout grid to select it. Then click Optimize in the Layout Grid Inspector.

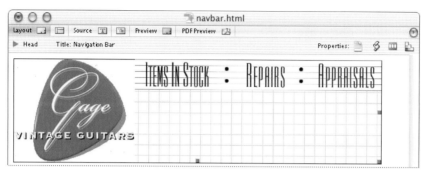

Optimized layout grid

For the purposes of this lesson, you won't add navigation links to the images. You'll add these links later in Lesson 6, "Creating Navigational Links."

9 Choose File > Save to save navbar.html. Then choose File > Close to close it.

Designing the home page

Now that you have finished creating the component for a navigation bar, you're ready to design the home page for the Web site. The home page will provide information that introduces users to Gage Vintage Guitars. First you'll open the home page and change its title.

1 In the Files tab of the site window, double-click index.html to open it.

2 Change the title of the page to **Gage Vintage Guitars**. Select the default title and enter the new title.

Applying a background image

You can apply an image or color to the background of your page to visually enhance it. You can also apply an image or color to the background of a container on the page, such as a layout grid. When choosing an image for the page background, keep in mind that GoLive and browsers treat the image as a tile that's repeated to cover the page.

Now you'll add a background image to the home page. First you'll preview the image using the File Inspector.

1 In the Files tab of the site window, select the wood.gif file in the images folder.

The Inspector changes to the File Inspector and displays detailed information about the selected file.

2 Click the Content tab of the File Inspector, and notice that a preview of wood.gif appears.

Now you'll use the wood.gif file to add a background image to the page.

3 Click the Page icon (▤) in the upper right corner of the document window, so that the Inspector changes to the Page Inspector.

4 In the Page tab of the Page Inspector, select (or check) the Image option under Background.

5 Drag from the Pick Whip button (⬛) in the Page Inspector to wood.gif in the images folder within the site window.

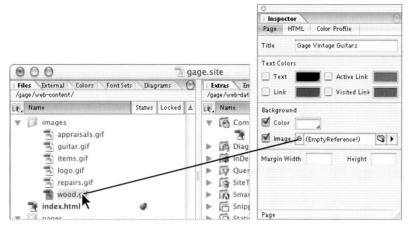

Specifying image to tile for page's background

Result

The image of the wood is tiled to cover the page.

6 Choose File > Save to save your work.

Adding a component using a placeholder

Now you'll add the navigation bar to the home page using the component that you created earlier in this lesson. First you'll add a component placeholder to the page, and then you'll link the placeholder to a file in the site's Components folder.

1 Drag the Component icon from the Smart set ( ) in the Objects palette to the upper left corner of the page.

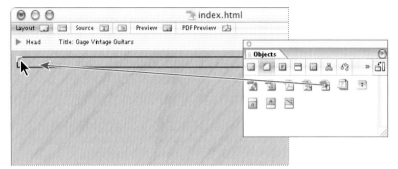

Adding component placeholder to page

A component placeholder is added to the page.

2 Select the component placeholder, and the Inspector changes to the Component Inspector. Drag from the Pick Whip button ( ) in the Component Inspector to navbar.html in the Components folder in the site window. (Remember that the Components folder is displayed in the Extras tab in the right pane of the site window.)

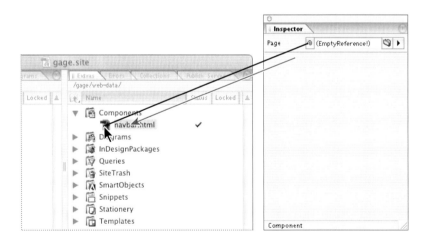

The navigation bar is added to the top of the page.

3 Choose File > Save to save the home page.

Adding text using layout text boxes

When you add text to a page using layout text boxes on a layout grid, you can easily rearrange the location of the text by moving or aligning the boxes. You can also add images and other objects to layout text boxes, so that you can align objects within the text or wrap text around objects.

Now you'll add text to the home page using layout text boxes on a layout grid. First you'll add a layout grid to the page.

 1 Drag the Layout Grid icon from the Basic set () in the Objects palette to the empty area below the component on the page.

Now you'll specify a width and height for the grid.

2 In the Layout Grid Inspector, enter **600** for Width, press Tab to jump to the next text box, and enter **300** for Height. Press Enter or Return.

Now you're ready to add the first layout text box to the layout grid. You'll use this box to add a main heading to the page.

 3 Drag the Layout Text Box icon from the Basic set in the Objects palette to the upper center area of the layout grid.

A layout text box is added to the grid. If needed, you can adjust the position of the box by moving the pointer to an edge of the box so that it turns into a hand, and then dragging the box.

4 Click inside the layout text box to create an insertion point, and type **Welcome to Gage Vintage Guitars**. Then choose Header 1 from the Paragraph Format menu on the toolbar.

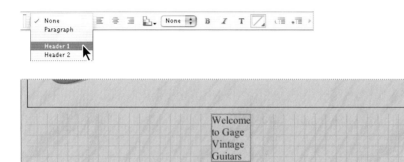

Text in layout text box, reformatted as Header 1

You can use the toolbar to position selected objects precisely on a layout grid. Now you'll use the toolbar to reposition the layout text box.

5 Click an edge of the layout text box to select it. Be sure to select the layout text box and not the layout grid box.

6 On the toolbar, enter **179** in the Horizontal Position text box, press Tab to jump to the next text box, and enter **0** in the Vertical Position text box. Press Enter or Return.

The layout text box is repositioned 179 pixels from the left edge of the layout grid and 0 pixels from the top of the grid.

You can also use the toolbar to resize a selected object. Now you'll use the toolbar to resize the layout text box.

7 On the toolbar, enter **400** in the Width text box, press Tab to jump to the next text box, and enter **80** in the Height text box. Press Enter or Return.

Note: *If the values used in this section don't work on your system, you can adjust them as necessary. Use the values given as a guide.*

Entering values to reposition and resize selected object

The layout text box is resized to 400 pixels in width and 80 pixels in height.

Note: *In a browser, a layout text box automatically adjusts its size in relation to its content, which resizes according to the platform that the browser is using (for example, to accommodate fonts that appear larger in Windows and smaller in Mac OS). This can affect the size of the layout grid, as well as the position of other items on the layout grid, altering the intended design. So that text size appears more consistently across platforms, you can assign a pixel size definition for all text using a cascading style sheet.*

Now you'll add a second layout text box to the layout grid. You'll use this box to add a subheading to the page.

8 Drag the Layout Text Box icon from the Basic set in the Objects palette to the upper left area of the grid.

9 Click inside the second layout text box to create an insertion point, and type **Check Out This Week's Hottest Buy!** Then drag to select the text that you just typed, click the Bold button (**B**) on the toolbar, and choose 4 from the Font Size menu on the toolbar.

After applying individual HTML attributes to text using the toolbar, you can save them as a group in the HTML Style palette, and then use the palette to reapply the group of attributes to other text in your site (see Lesson 5, "Working with Text and Tables," for more information). You can also use cascading style sheets to define text formatting once and then instruct browsers to reuse the definitions whenever text on a page refers to them (see Lesson 12, "Using Cascading Style Sheets," for more information).

10 To resize the second layout text box, click an edge of the box to select it, and drag one of its handles.

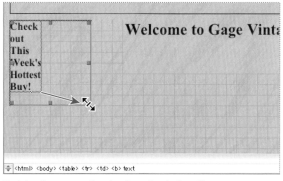

Resizing layout text box by dragging its handles

11 Choose File > Save to save index.html.

Adding text using a table

In addition to displaying information in rows and columns, tables can be used to lay out text and objects on a page. To add text to a table, you can type directly in a table cell, copy and paste text from GoLive or another application, and import text from a text-only file created in a word-processing or spreadsheet application, for example.

Now you'll use a table to add text that introduces Gage Vintage Guitars to the home page. Currently, the text resides in a text-only file. To save time, you'll copy and paste the text from the file into a single-cell table that you'll add to the page. You can place a table directly on the page or on a layout grid, which gives you more control over its placement but may result in more complex HTML code.

 1 Drag the Table icon from the Basic set (▣) in the Objects palette to the area below the main heading on the layout grid.

Adding table to layout grid

A table is added to the grid, and the Inspector changes to the Table Inspector. By default, the table has three rows and three columns. You'll change the number of rows and columns using the Table Inspector.

2 In the Table tab of the Table Inspector, enter **1** for Rows, press Tab to jump to the next text box, and enter **1** for Columns. Press Enter or Return.

Now you'll specify the width of the table. You'll also set the table's border width to 0, so that the borders appear as a solid or dashed outline in the Layout Editor but don't appear in the browser.

3 In the Table tab of the Table Inspector, enter **400** for Width. If it isn't already chosen, choose Pixel from the menu to the right of the Width text box. Enter **0** for Border. Press Enter or Return.

Now you'll copy and paste text from a text-only file into the table.

4 Navigate to the folder Lessons/Lesson04/04Start, and double-click the intro.txt file to open it in a text editor.

5 Create an insertion point anywhere in the text, and choose Edit > Select All to select all the text. Choose Edit > Copy to copy the text, and then choose File > Close to close the text file without saving any changes.

6 In the index.html document window in GoLive, click in the newly added table to create an insertion point, and choose Edit > Paste.

Text from the intro.txt file is added to the table.

Now you'll precisely position the table using the toolbar.

7 Move the pointer over the top left of the table until it turns into this ( ), and then click to select the table in the document window.

8 On the toolbar, enter **179** in the Horizontal Position text box, press Tab to jump to the next text box, and enter **80** in the Vertical Position text box. Press Enter or Return.

Now you'll optimize the layout grid to reduce its size.

9 Click the layout grid to select it. Then click Optimize in the Layout Grid Inspector.

10 Choose File > Save to save index.html.

Creating a custom color palette and adding color to text

You can collect and organize colors for a site in the Colors tab of the site window. The colors appear in both the Colors tab and the Site Colors in the Swatches palette, either of which you can use as a custom color palette to color text and objects on a page. (In the Swatches palette, click the triangle in the upper right side and choose Site Colors to display colors used in the site.) When you change a site color in the Colors tab, GoLive automatically updates every occurrence of the color in the site on pages that are closed.

As an alternative to applying color using the Colors tab or the Swatches palette, you can create a cascading style sheet to apply color to text and objects. Cascading style sheets simplify the maintenance of text and other attributes on a page and throughout a site.

Now you'll add color to emphasize text on the page.

1 In the site window, click the Colors tab to bring it to the front. So that you can see all the information listed in the Colors tab, close the right pane of the site window by clicking the double-headed arrow (⬌) next to the scroll bar for the right pane.

Colors tab in site window

Notice that the Colors tab contains a Scanned Colors folder that contains a site color named white, which is used as the default background color for the home page. Select the Scanned Colors text and change the name to Gage Colors.

2 With the Gage Colors folder selected, choose Site>New>Color. An untitled color is added to the Color tab. Now you'll rename the color according to how you'll use it in the site. Because you'll use the color to emphasize text, you'll name the color "emphasis."

3 In the Colors tab of the site window, click the untitled color text to select it. Enter **emphasis** to rename the color.

4 Choose Window > Color, or click the Color tab to open the Color palette.

5 In the Color palette, click the triangle in the upper right of the color palette and select Only Web Colors. Make sure the RGB sliders tab is selected and in the Hex Value text box, enter **990000**. Press Enter or Return.

6 In the document window, drag to select the text "Check Out This Week's Hottest Buy!"

7 Drag the emphasis color from the Colors tab of the site window to the selected text on the page. Then click in the blank area outside the selected text to deselect it.

The color of the selected text changes to red.

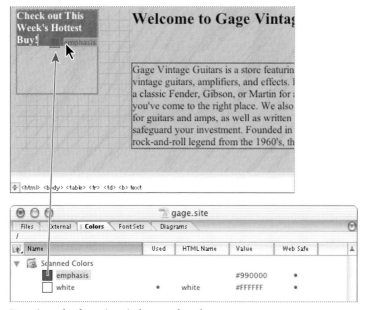

Dragging color from site window to selected text

You can use the Color palette's eyedropper to extract a color from an image or other element on the screen. Then you can find the closest Web-safe approximation of the color in the Only Web Colors List and add the color to the Colors tab. This feature is useful when you want to match the color of two objects on a page, such as an image and page background.

Now you'll add another untitled color to the Colors tab, extract a color from the company logo in the component on the page, and add a Web-safe approximation of it to the Colors tab.

8 With the Gage Colors folder selected, choose Site>New>Color. A new color named untitled color appears.

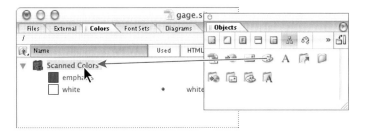

Now you'll extract a color from the company logo.

9 Choose the untitled color and click the eyedropper in the Color palette, so that the pointer turns into an eyedropper.

10 Move the eyedropper from the Color palette to the shadow of the guitar pick on the page. Notice that the color changes in the preview pane of the Color palette as you drag the eyedropper.

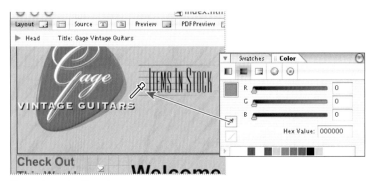

Extracting color from image on page

When you click the mouse, the extracted color appears in the preview pane and in the untitled color preview pane. Ours was 999966.

11 In the Colors tab of the site window, click the name of the untitled color in the Scanned Colors folder to select it. Enter **shadow** to rename the color.

If desired, you can now match the color of text or an object on the page with the shadow color.

12 Choose File > Save to save index.html.

Now you'll add keywords, comments, and a date and time stamp to the home page.

Specifying keywords

You specify keywords for a page so that Internet search engines and browsers can identify content in the page. To specify keywords, you add a Keywords element to the head section pane of the document window, and then use the Keywords Inspector to add a list of keywords for the element.

Now you'll specify keywords for the home page.

1 To display the head section pane, click the triangle next to the word Head in the upper left corner of the document window.

2 Drag the Keywords icon from the Head set (⊟) in the Objects palette to the head section pane.

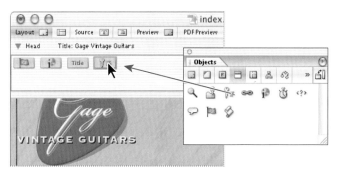

Adding Keywords element to head section

A Keywords element is added to the head section of the page, and the Inspector changes to the Keywords Inspector.

To add an element to the head section pane, you can also drag it to the body of the page to have GoLive automatically open the head section pane and add the element to it.

3 In the Keywords Inspector, click the Create New Item icon a the bottom right side of the Inspector to add a new keyword to the list. Then enter a word or phrase that you want to use as a keyword in the text box at the bottom of the Inspector. (We used the phrase "Gage Vintage Guitars.") Press Enter or Return. The new keyword is listed in the Inspector pane and added to the document head pane.

Adding keywords using Keywords Inspector

4 Click the Source tab in the document window to check that the keyword is added correctly. Click the Layout tab to return to the Layout Editor.

5 Click the triangle next to the word Head to close the head section pane.

6 Choose File > Save to save index.html.

Adding comments

As you lay out content on a page, you may want to add hidden comments about its design for future reference. Comments appear in GoLive in the Comment Inspector and the source code and other HTML editors, but they don't appear in browsers. You can add comments to the head section or the body of a page.

Now you'll add comments to the body of the home page.

 1 Drag the Comment icon from the Basic set (▪) in the Objects palette to an area nearby the "Check Out This Week's Hottest Buy!" text.

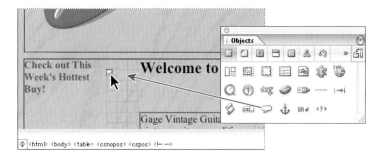

A symbol appears on the page to indicate the comment's location, and the Inspector changes to the Comment Inspector. You enter comments in the Comment Inspector.

2 In the Comment Inspector, delete the text "your comment here," enter the following text: **Remember to add navigation links to this page.**

Now you'll view the comment.

3 Click elsewhere in the work area to have the Inspector change from the Comment Inspector. For example, we clicked on the text block, "Check Out This Week's Hottest Buy."

4 Click the Comment icon on the page to select it, and then view your comments in the Comment Inspector.

5 Click the Source tab in the document window to view your comment in the source code. Click the Layout tab to return to the Layout Editor.

6 Choose File > Save to save your work.

Adding a date and time stamp

You can add a date or time stamp to a page, so that viewers can tell when you last updated the page. GoLive reads the current date or time from your computer's built-in clock and writes the result in a custom tag. It then updates the information dynamically whenever you save the page.

Now you'll add a date and time stamp to the home page. First you'll add descriptive text before the date and time stamp.

1 In the table that contains the descriptive paragraph about Gage Vintage Guitars, click after the last character (!) to insert a cursor, and press Enter or Return to begin a new line of text. Then type **Last revised:** with a space after it.

Now you'll add a date stamp to the page.

 2 Drag the Modified Date icon from the Smart set (⬜) in the Objects palette to the cursor on the page, or double-click the icon.

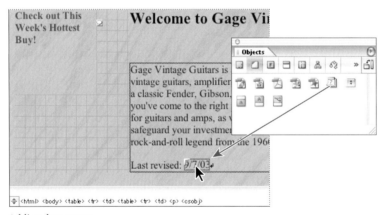

Adding date stamp

A date in a default format is added to the page, and the Inspector changes to the Modified Date Inspector.

Now you'll specify a format for the date.

3 In the Modified Date Inspector, choose a country from the Format menu, and select a date format from the list of options for the specific country. We chose U.S. (United States) and the long date form (day, date, year).

Now you'll add a time stamp with the text "at" preceding it.

4 In the document window, after the date stamp, type **at** with a space before and after it.

5 Drag another Modified Date icon from the Smart set in the Objects palette to the cursor on the page, or double-click the icon.

6 In the Modified Date Inspector, choose a country from the Format menu, and select a time format from the list. We chose U.S. (United States) and the hours:minutes form.

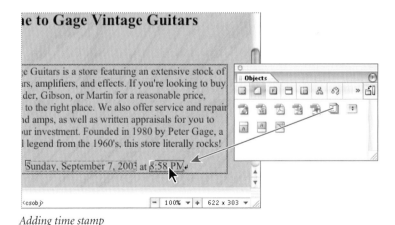

Adding time stamp

7 Choose File > Save to save index.html.

8 Click the Preview tab to preview the page. Notice that the comment does not appear in the preview. Click the Layout tab to return to the Layout Editor.

9 Then choose File > Close to close the page.

Now you're ready to design two other pages for the site.

Adding a component to an existing Web page

Now you'll update the design of an existing Web page that you've already added to the Web site. The page provides information on how viewers can get their guitars appraised by Gage Vintage Guitars. First you'll add the navigation bar to the top of the page, and then you'll update the site's Colors tab with colors used on the page.

Currently the Appraisal page doesn't contain the navigation bar for the site. You'll add the navigation bar using the component you created earlier in this lesson. You've already learned how to add a component by first adding a component placeholder to the page. Now you'll learn how to add a component without using a placeholder.

1 In the Files tab of the site window, double-click appraise.html in the pages folder to open it.

2 In the Extras tab in the site window, click the plus sign (Win) or the arrow (Mac) next to the Components folder. Navbar.html appears under the Components folder.

3 Drag the icon of navbar.html to the upper left corner of the page. Be sure to drop it above the image in the background.

Using icon in Objects palette to add component

4 If necessary, scroll up to bring the beginning of the document into view.

The navigation bar is added to the top of the page, and the Inspector changes to the Component Inspector.

5 In the Component Inspector, notice that the Page text box shows the path to navbar.html.

6 Choose File > Save to save appraise.html.

Updating the custom color palette

If you scroll down the appraise.html page you just added, you'll notice the colors that have been applied to the background of the page, and the first and second columns of the table on the page. (You'll learn how to do this in the next lesson.) Now you'll update the Colors tab in the site window with colors used in the site that aren't already listed. To update the Colors tab, you first need to close any pages in the site.

1 Make sure that you close any pages that are open.

2 In the site window, click the Colors tab to bring it to the front. Then choose Site > Get Colors Used.

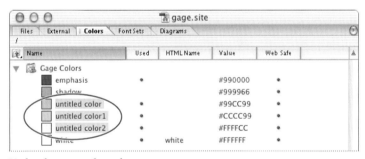

Updated custom color palette

New site colors are added to the Gage Colors folder in the Colors tab as untitled colors. The site colors that have been added are ones used on the Appraisal page.

Now you'll name each of the new untitled site colors according to how they're used on the Appraisal page.

3 Click in the blank space outside the selected colors to deselect them.

4 Click the name of the green untitled color to select it. Enter **column2** to rename the color. This is the color used in the second column of the table.

5 Change the name of the khaki untitled color to **page** (the background page color), and change the name of the cream untitled color to **column1** (the color used in the first column of the table).

6 Choose File > Save to save your work.

Designing a Web page using layers

Layers let you divide a Web page into rectangles that can be formatted and positioned individually. They represent DHTML layers, which means you can overlap, hide and show, and animate them on the page. They can contain any HTML element that a page can contain, such as text, an image, or another layer. However, some Web browsers may have problems with layers that contain tables or layout grids. If you embed a layer within another layer, the embedded box inherits any cascading style sheet information from the parent box.

Note: To display properly, layers require Web browser version 4.0 or later. To see what a layer would look like in a browser that doesn't support cascading style sheets (layers are built with cascading style sheets), turn off CSS Support in the browser's settings, as described in "Exploring style sheets" on page 432. Be sure to turn CSS support back on when you are finished.

Now you'll design a new page for the site using layers. This page will provide users with information on this week's hottest buy at Gage Vintage Guitars. First you'll create a new page.

1 In the site window, click the Files tab.

2 Drag the Page icon from the Site set (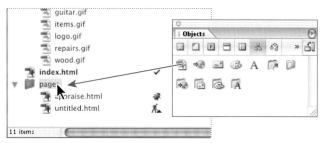)in the Objects palette to the pages folder in the Files tab of the site window.

Adding new page to pages folder

A new page is added to the pages folder and appears in the Files tab of the site window. Note the empty-page alert icon that indicates the status of the new page.

3 Enter **hottest.html** to rename the file, and then double-click the hottest.html file to open it.

The hottest.html file opens in the Layout Editor of the document window. First you'll change the title of the page.

4 Enter **Hottest Buy** as the new title. Select the default title next to the word Title in the upper left corner of the document window, and enter the new title.

Now you'll change the background color of the page. Using the custom color palette, you can easily match the background color of the Hottest Buy page with the background color of the Appraisal page. You've already learned how to add a site color using the Colors tab in the site window. Now you'll learn how to add a site color using the Site Color list in the Swatch palette.

5 Select the Swatch palette. Click the triangle at the upper right side of the Swatch palette and choose Site Colors.

6 Select the page properties icon for hottest.html. The Inspector changes to Page Inspector.

7 Click the Color Field on the right side of the word color in the Page Inspector.

8 In the Site Color list in the Swatch palette, select the color named "page" so that it appears in the preview pane.

9 The background color of the page changes to khaki.

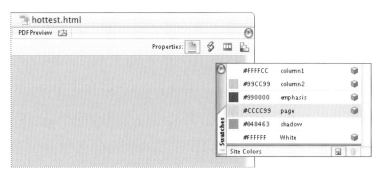

Changing page's background color

Now you'll add the navigation bar to the page, as you did with the other pages for the site.

10 In the Extras tab in the site window, make sure that navbar.html is selected from the Components folder.

11 Drag the navbar.html icon from the Components tab to the upper left corner of the page.

The navigation bar is added to the top of the page, and the Inspector changes to the Component Inspector.

12 Choose File > Save to save hottest.html.

Adding the first layer

Now you'll add a layer to the page. You'll use this layer to add an image of a guitar to the page.

1 Drag the Layer icon from the Basic set ( ) in the Objects palette to the area below the component on the page. (You can also double-click the Layer icon to place a layer at the insertion point on the page.)

A layer appears on the page in the upper left corner below the component, and the Inspector changes to the Layer Inspector. When you add a single layer to a page, GoLive inserts a small yellow marker labeled SB, which stays at the original point of insertion even after you move the layer.

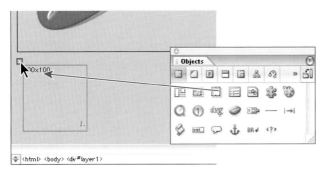

Adding a layer to page

It's important to name layers, so that you can differentiate them from one another. GoLive displays their names in the Layers palette and in lists that you choose from when applying actions to them or animating them. Now you'll name the layer according to the contents that you'll add to it.

2 In the Layers Inspector, enter **Image** in the Name text box.

Now you'll add the guitar image to the layer.

3 Drag guitar.gif from the images folder in the Files tab of the site window to the layer on the page.

The guitar image appears in the layer.

4 Click in the blank space outside the image to deselect it.

💡 *You can convert non-overlapping layers and their contents into objects on a layout grid in a new untitled page. This is useful if you need a table-based design for the page in addition to your DHTML layers-based design. If the layer contains text, it converts into a layout text box on the grid. The position, size, and background color attributes of the layer are retained. GoLive creates a new page to contain the converted objects, keeping the original page of layer intact.*

Adding the second layer

Now you'll add a second layer to the page that will contain a description of the guitar shown on the page.

1 Position the pointer immediately to the right or immediately below the yellow layer marker.

2 Double-click the Layers icon in the Objects palette.

The second layer appears.

3 In the Layers Inspector, enter **Description** in the Name text box to name the second layer.

For now you'll move the Description layer to an empty area of the page.

4 Move the pointer over an edge of the Description layer, so that the pointer turns into a hand pointing left. Then drag the Description layer to the right of the Image layers.

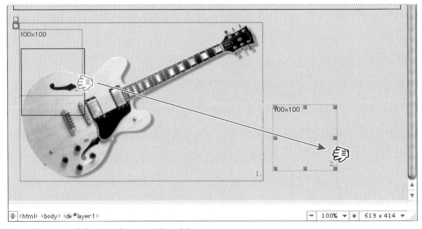

Dragging second floating box to right of first one

Now you'll add text to the Description layers. You'll enter a description of the guitar shown on the page.

5 Click inside the Description layer, and type **1981 Gibson ES-347**. Then drag to select the text you've just typed, click the Bold button (**B**) on the toolbar, and choose 5 from the Font Size menu on the toolbar. If you have difficulty selecting the text, enlarge the layer slightly.

Now you'll add color to the selected text using the emphasis color stored in the custom color palette.

6 In the Gage Color folder in the site window, select the emphasis color, so that it appears in the preview pane.

7 Drag the color from the preview pane to the selected text on the page.

The color of the text changes to red.

8 Click in the blank space outside the selected text to deselect it.

Now you'll precisely position the Description layer using the Layer Inspector.

Note: If the values used in this section don't work for you, you can adjust them as necessary. Use the values given as a guide.

9 Move the pointer over an edge of the Description layer, so that the pointer turns into a hand pointed to the left. Then click an edge of the layer to select it.

10 In the Layers Inspector, enter **250** for Left, and enter **300** for Top. Press Enter or Return.

The layer is repositioned 250 pixels from the left edge and 300 pixels from the top of the page.

Now you'll resize the layer using the Layer Inspector.

11 In the Layer Inspector, enter **200** for Width, press Tab to jump to the next text box, and enter **100** for Height. Press Enter or Return.

The layer is resized to 200 pixels in width and 100 pixels in height.

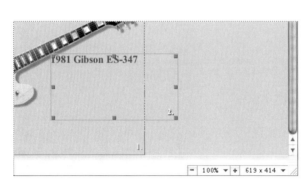

Repositioning and resizing layer

 You can also resize a layer by selecting it and dragging one of its handles.

12 Choose File > Save to save hottest.html.

Laying out pages with layers

Layers can be positioned precisely, because they are implemented using the DIV element. The DIV element, formatted with a CSS ID style for the width, visibility, and absolute position of the layer, instructs the browser to create a subdivision that is not part of the normal flow of HTML within the page.

Layers can contain background images or color, and they can inherit properties from the page's cascading style sheet (see "Using Cascading Style Sheets" in the Adobe GoLive CS online Help). For table-based designs, you can convert non-overlapping layers and their contents to a new page with the contents duplicated on a layout grid (see the Adobe GoLive CS online Help for more information).

Resizing and positioning layers

You can position layers accurately using the Layer Inspector and a page grid that you define in the Grid Settings dialog box. By assigning a z-index to each layer, you can control the order that the boxes are stacked on top of each other (for example, a layer with a z-index of 2 appears in front of a box with a z-index of 1).

You can also use the Transform and Align palettes to position, resize, and align multiple layers in the same way as other objects (see the Adobe GoLive CS online Help for more information).

💡 *Visitors using older Web browsers may not see a Web page correctly if it contains features and technology such as JavaScript, frames, and layers. Also, not all browsers and browser versions support these features equally. You can use a browser-switch script to direct visitors to separate pages if your page contains elements that are not supported equally by older browsers or all browser versions. For more information, see "Creating a browser switch action" on page 364.*

Editing a component

An additional benefit of using a component to place frequently used page content throughout your site is that you only need to edit a single file to make changes to it. When you save your changes to the component, GoLive automatically updates all pages containing it.

Now you'll edit the component for the navigation bar. You'll move the images in the navigation bar down so that they're vertically centered on the layout grid.

1 In the document window, notice that the Items In Stock, Repairs, and Appraisals images are aligned to the top of the layout grid. Try to click the Items In Stock image to select it for editing. Notice that you selected the entire component instead.

You can't edit the objects in the component from this page. Instead, you must edit them in the source file in which you created them.

2 Double-click the component on the page to open the component's source file. (You can also double-click navbar.html in the Components folder, located in the Extras tab in the right pane of the site window.)

3 In the navbar.html window, click the Items In Stock image to select it. Then Shift-click the Repairs image and the Appraisals image to add them to the selection.

4 Click the Align Center button ( ) on the toolbar to center the images vertically on the grid.

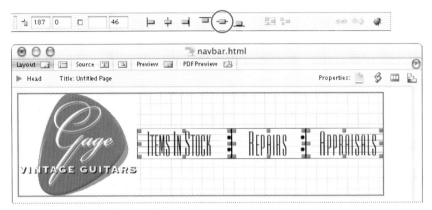

Images centered vertically on grid

5 Choose File > Save to save navbar.html.

6 Click OK for GoLive to automatically update the pages that use navbar.html as a component. When the update is finished, click OK to close the dialog box.

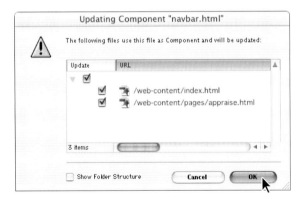

7 Choose File > Close to close navbar.html.

8 Make the hottest.html window active, and notice that the component has been updated automatically.

9 Save and close the file.

Previewing in GoLive

To preview each Web page, do the following:

1 In the site window, double-click index.html, appraise.html, or hottest.html to open the page. Remember, the appraise.html and hottest.html files are located in the pages folder.

2 In the document window, click the Preview tab to view the page in Layout Preview.

GoLive displays a preview of the page. Notice the change in the navigation bar that reflects the change you made to the component.

Note: *You haven't linked the pages yet, so you will have to view them separately. You'll link pages in Lesson 6, "Creating Navigational Links."*

3 When you have finished viewing the pages, close any open pages and the site window.

Review questions

1 After you create a new Web site in GoLive, what folder and files appear in the Files tab of the site window?

2 Name two benefits of using a component.

3 When do you use a layout grid to design a page?

4 Name two ways that you can specify an image for an image placeholder on a page.

5 Name a way in which you can add text to a table.

6 What is a custom color palette, and how do you add a color to a custom color palette?

7 Can you extract color from an image that you've added to a page? If so, how?

8 When do you use layers to design a page?

Review answers

1 The Files tab displays the contents of the site's root folder, which contains a blank home page called index.html.

2 A component lets you store frequently used page content, such as a navigation bar. You can quickly add the component to multiple pages in a site. To edit a component, you only need to edit a single file (its source file) to have GoLive automatically update each page that contains it.

3 You use a layout grid to create table-based designs in your pages. Instead of setting up multiple table cells, you can add a single layout grid to a page and position objects on the grid with 1-pixel accuracy.

4 To specify an image for an image placeholder, do one of the following:

• Drag from the Pick Whip button in the Image Inspector to an image file in the site window.

• Hold down Alt (Windows) or Command (Mac OS), and drag from the image placeholder to an image file in the site window.

• Drag an image file from the site window to the image placeholder.

5 To add text to a table, you can type directly in a table cell, copy and paste text from GoLive or another application, and import text from a text-only file created in a word-processing or spreadsheet application, for example.

6 You can collect and organize colors for a site in the Colors tab of the site window. The colors appear in both the Colors tab and the Site Color list in the Swatches palette, either of which you can use as a custom color palette. To add a color to a custom color palette, drag the Color icon from the Site set in the Objects palette to the Colors tab of the site window. Select a color in the Color palette, and then drag the color from the Color Field to the untitled color in the Colors tab. Finally, rename the color according to its use in the site.

7 Yes, you can extract color from an image that you've added to a page. To do so, move the pointer to any color swatch in the Swatch palette, so that the pointer turns into an eyedropper. Drag the eyedropper from the Color palette to the image whose color you want to copy, and click the mouse. The extracted color appears in the preview pane of the Color palette.

8 You use layers to divide a page into rectangles that can be formatted and positioned individually. You can also overlap, hide and show, and animate them on the page.

Lesson 5

5 Working with Text and Tables

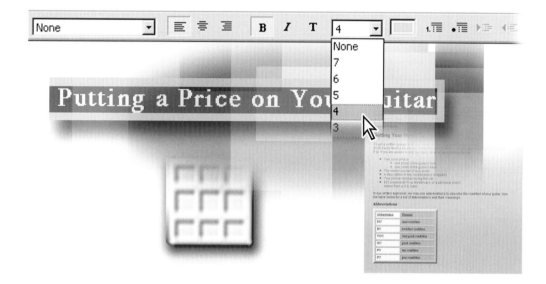

With Adobe GoLive, you can add text to a Web page using a variety of methods. Once the text is added, you can easily format and color it. When you've completed your page design, you can convert the layout grid to a table to reduce the amount of code.

About this lesson

In this lesson, you'll learn how to do the following:

- Add text to a Web page.

- Apply paragraph and physical styles to text.

- Spell check text.

- Create numbered and unnumbered lists.

- Add a line break.

- Change the color of text.

- Use a table to present spreadsheet data.

- Copy and paste data into a table from another application.

- Format a table by specifying options, applying a predefined table style, and sorting the contents of a table.

- Capture a table style so that you can reuse it later.

- Convert a layout grid to an HTML table.

This lesson takes approximately 45 minutes to complete.

If needed, copy the Lessons/Lesson05/ folder onto your hard drive. As you work on this lesson, you'll overwrite the start files. If you need to restore the start files, copy them from the *Adobe GoLive CS Classroom in a Book* CD.

Note: *Windows users need to unlock the lesson files before using them. For more information, see "Copying the Classroom in a Book files" on page 2.*

Getting started

In this lesson, you'll learn how to create the Appraisals page for the Gage Vintage Guitars Web site that we provided for you in Lesson 4, "Designing Web Pages." The page provides information on how viewers can get their guitars appraised by the company. First you'll add text to the page using layout text boxes on a layout grid, and a table to present information in rows and columns. You'll learn a variety of methods for formatting both text and tables. When you've completed the page design, you'll convert the grid to a table to reduce the amount of code used on the page.

First you'll view the finished page in Adobe GoLive.

1 Start Adobe GoLive.

By default, an introductory screen appears prompting you to create a new page, create a new site, or open an existing file.

Note: You can set preferences for the introductory screen to not appear when you start GoLive. If the introductory screen doesn't appear, choose File > Open and go to step 3.

2 Click Open to open an existing file.

3 Open the *appraise.html* file in Lessons/Lesson05/05End/.

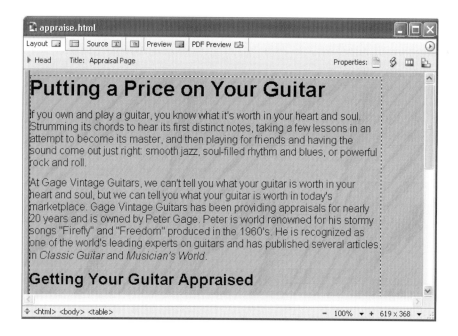

4 Choose Window > Inspector to open the Inspector, or click the Inspector tab if the palette is collapsed.

5 Click on the border around the text. Notice that the Inspector becomes the Table Inspector, indicating that the page is formatted as a table rather than a layout grid. Although text and objects were originally placed on the page using a layout grid, the grid was converted to a table as a final step in the page design.

6 Scroll downward in the document window, so that you can view all of the contents of the page.

7 Click in the upper left of the two-color table titled Abbreviations. Again notice that the Inspector becomes the Table Inspector. This table is nested in the larger table that contains the entire page.

8 When you have finished viewing the page, close the appraise.html file.

About converting layout grids to tables

The GoLive layout grid is a valuable tool for laying out Web pages. It offers great flexibility for moving design elements around on a page and for placing elements with pixel precision. It lets you group items, align and distribute objects, and layer elements using layers. However, it does use a fixed width (which may or may not be desirable), it uses a spacer tag which may not be supported in the same way in all browsers, and it can add extra code.

Designing with HTML tables is generally more difficult than designing with a layout grid. Because you are working with rows and cells, you need to have planned your page layout ahead of time and understand exactly where every element is going to be placed on the page.

In GoLive, you can use the flexibility and convenience of the layout grid to develop your Web page, and when you have finalized your design, you can convert the layout grid to a table, stripping out the extra code and eliminating potential problems with different browsers interpreting the layout grid differently. If you need to adjust the layout at any point after you have converted the layout grid to a table, you can convert the table back to a layout grid.

[?] For more information on converting layout grids to tables, see "Converting a layout grid to a table" in the Adobe GoLive CS online Help.

Creating a new Web page

In this lesson you'll create a new version of the appraise.html page you just looked at.

1 In GoLive, choose File > New Page.

2 Choose File > Save As, and save the untitled.html document as appraise.html. Save the document in the Lessons/Lesson05/05Start/ folder.

Note: *To keep this lesson simple, you'll work in a page outside the site window. This isn't normally recommended, however.*

Now you're ready to begin designing the page. First you'll change the title of the page. When viewed in a Web browser, the title of the page appears in the title bar of the browser.

3 Select the page title, "Untitled Page."

4 Enter **Appraisal Page** as the new title.

Selecting default page title   *New page title*

Now you'll select a window size for the page. The window size is valid only in GoLive, not browsers. However, it can help you limit the design of your page to fit within a desired window size. For the lessons in this book, we've generally used a window size of 580 pixels to accommodate users with 14-inch monitors.

5 Choose 580 from the Window Size menu in the lower right corner of the document window.

6 Choose File > Save to save your work.

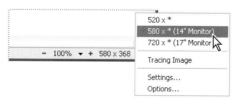

Choosing window size

Changing the background color and image

Now you'll change the background color of the page from white to khaki and add a background image.

1 Choose the Page Properties icon and check the Color box if it is not already checked.

2 Click the Color Field next to the right of the word color to select it.

3 Choose Window > Color to display the Color palette, or click the Color tab if the palette is collapsed.

4 In the Color palette, click the triangle in the upper right side and choose Only Web Colors.

5 With the RGB slider tab selected, type **CCCC99** in the Hex Value text box and press Enter or Return.

The selected color appears in the preview pane of the Color palette.

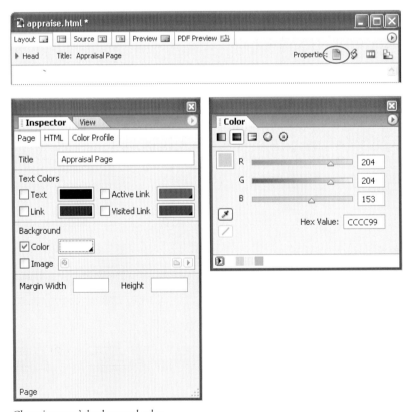

Changing page's background color

The background color of the page changes to khaki. Now you'll add the background image.

6 Choose Window > Inspector to open the Inspector, or click the Inspector tab if the Inspector is collapsed.

7 Click the page icon of the appraise.html file.

8 In the Page Inspector, select the Image option and click the Browse button (🖼).

9 Select the file wood.gif in Lessons/Lesson05/05Start/, and click Open.

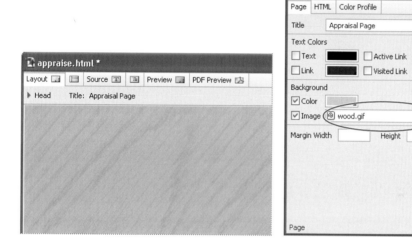

You now have the background color and image for your page.

10 Choose File > Save.

Adding a layout grid

As you did in earlier lessons, you'll initially use a layout grid in the design of the Web page. Later in the lesson, when the design is final, you'll convert the layout grid to an HTML table.

1 Choose Window > Objects to open the Objects palette, or click the Objects tab if the palette is collapsed.

2 Drag the Layout Grid icon from the Basic set ( ) of the Objects palette to the appraise.html page.

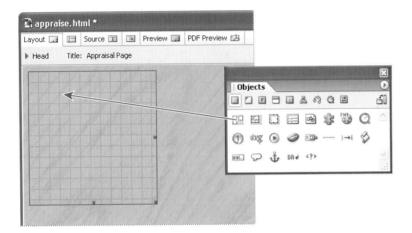

3 Select the layout grid that you just added, and in the Layout Grid Inspector, enter **573** for Width, and press Enter or Return. This is the width of the navbar.html component you created in Lesson4, "Designing Web Pages." By making the content of this page the same width as the navigation bar component, the design of the page will be unified if you add the component later.

4 Choose File > Save to save your work.

Adding text

GoLive provides a variety of methods for adding text to your documents:

• You can add text to a GoLive document by typing directly in the document window.

• You can import text from another application into a table.

• You can add text to a page using layout text boxes and layers.

• You can copy text from a document created in another application, such as Microsoft Word, and paste the text into a GoLive document.

• You can drag text clips, created from SimpleText or Note Pad documents, from the desktop to GoLive documents.

For more information about adding text to GoLive documents, see "Adding text to Web pages" in the Adobe GoLive CS online Help.

Now you'll add text to the page using a layout text box. You'll add a heading to the page.

1 Drag a Layout Text Box icon from the Basic set (▢) of the Objects palette to the top left corner of the layout grid.

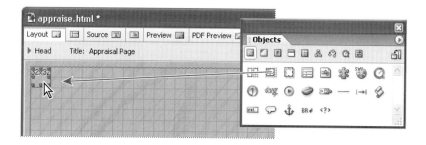

2 Select the layout text box, and drag it by the bottom corner handle until it is almost the width of the layout grid. (Make sure you don't make the layout text box the same size as the grid. You don't want to completely cover the grid.)

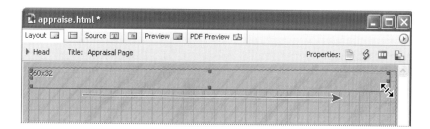

3 Click inside the layout text box to create an insertion point, and type **Putting a Price on Your Guitar**. Press Enter or Return to create a new paragraph.

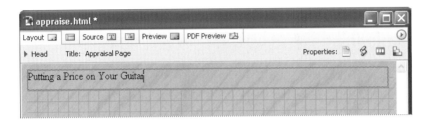

You'll copy additional text for the page from another HTML document that we've provided for you, and then paste it into the layout text box.

4 Choose File > Open, and open the appraisetext.html file in the Lessons/Lesson05/05Start/ folder.

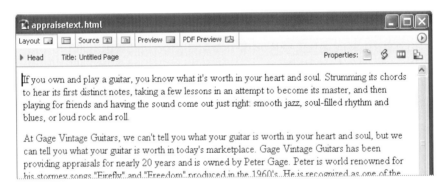

5 Click to create an insertion point anywhere in the appraisetext.html document, and choose Edit > Select All. Then choose Edit > Copy.

6 Choose File > Close to close the appraisetext.html document. You don't need to save any changes.

7 Return to the appraise.html document, and click to create an insertion point one line below the text "Putting a Price on Your Guitar." Choose Edit > Paste to insert the copied text into the layout text box.

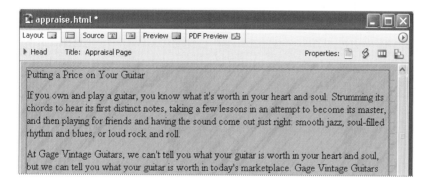

Notice how the layout text box expands to hold the newly added text.

8 Choose File > Save to save your work.

Now you're ready to format the text you've added.

Formatting text

GoLive lets you format text in a variety of ways. You use paragraph styles, such as Header 1 and Header 2, to format paragraphs. You use physical styles, such as Bold and Italic, to emphasize text. And you use structural styles, such as Emphasis and Strong, to both emphasize and classify text.

Note: You can apply fonts, type sizes, and color to selected text using CSS styles or HTML text formatting attributes. Font sets (groups of font choices for Web browsers) that you create appear in the CSS Selector Inspector and the Type > Font menu. When you use the Type > Font menu or the toolbar to apply font sets, relative sizes, or color attributes to selected text, GoLive places the information inside the font element. Because the font element is known to cause problems with browsers interpreting style sheets, you may want to avoid mixing your methods for applying these attributes. (For information on applying these attributes to text using CSS styles, see "Setting Font properties" in the Adobe GoLive CS online Help.)

Now you'll apply paragraph styles to format the headings in the document.

1 Click anywhere in the "Putting a Price on Your Guitar" heading on the page.

2 Choose Header 1 from the Paragraph Format menu on the toolbar to format the text as a heading.

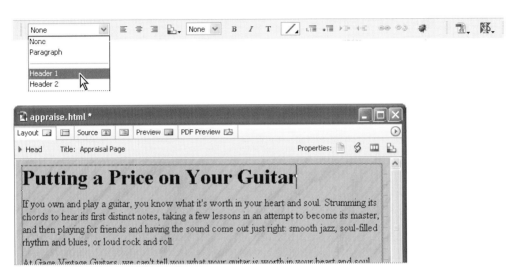

3 Click in the "Getting Your Guitar Appraised" line of text, and choose Header 2 from the Paragraph Format menu to format the text as a subheading.

Now you'll apply physical styles to some of the text in the document.

4 Select the words "Classic Guitar" near the end of the paragraph before the "Getting Your Guitar Appraised" subheading.

5 Click the Bold button (**B**) on the toolbar to make the selected text bold.

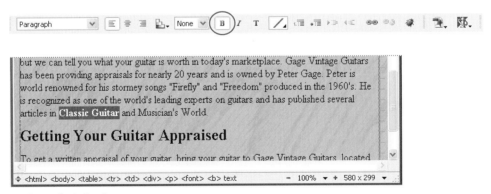

Applying physical style to text

You can easily remove a physical style and apply a new one.

6 Click the Bold button again to remove the bold style from the selected text.

7 Click the Italic button (I) on the toolbar to italicize the selected text, and click in the blank space outside the text to deselect it.

8 Apply the italic style to the words "Musician's World" at the end of the same sentence.

You can also apply a structural style to selected text, by choosing an option from the Type > Structure menu.

Applying HTML structural attributes to inline text

Structural text attributes (also known as HTML content-based styles) let you define selected text in meaningful categories, such as text that needs special emphasis or a strong pronouncement. Web browsers vary in their interpretations for structural attributes as appropriate for their users. For example, one browser may use italics for the Emphasis attribute, while another browser may use bold face. Another browser used by the visually impaired may use a loud voice.

Using CSS styles in your style sheets, you can build upon these structural attributes. For example, to emphasize a word, use the Emphasis element to apply HTML structure to the text and then use a CSS style to make the word big and bold.

• The Emphasis attribute is most commonly used to emphasize text. In most browsers, the selected text appears italicized.

• The Strong attribute is used for strongly emphasizing text. In most browsers, it makes the selected text bold.

• The Quotation (cite) attribute is used to identify the selected text as content taken from another source. Most browsers display quotations using a smaller font size and italics.

• The Sample attribute is used to place special emphasis on small character sequences taken out of their normal context. Most browsers display samples using a monospaced font.

• The Definition (dfn) attribute is used to define special terms or phrases, and to assist in creating a page index or glossary. Most browsers display definitions as plain text.

• The Variable (var) attribute is used most often in conjunction with the Code attribute to represent variable names or user-supplied values within the code. Most browsers display variables with an italicized monospaced font.

• The Code attribute is used for text that represents computer source code or other machine-readable content. Most browsers display code using a monospaced, teletype style font such as Courier.

• The Keyboard (kbd) attribute is used to identify the selected text as text that is typed on the keyboard. Most browsers display keyboard entries using a monospaced font.

Creating lists

You can use GoLive to quickly format paragraphs as numbered or unnumbered lists. Now you'll create a numbered list from some of the text on the page.

1 Scroll downward in the document window, so that you can view the entire "Getting Your Guitar Appraised" section.

2 Select the seven paragraphs below the first paragraph in the section. (Your selection should begin with "Two color photos" and end with "$25 payable by Visa, Mastercard, or a personal check drawn from a U.S. bank.")

3 Click the Numbered List button (▦) on the toolbar to format the seven paragraphs as a numbered list.

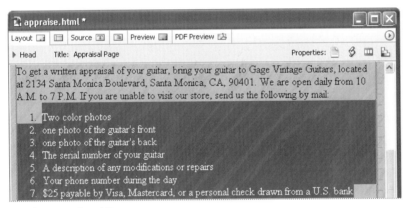

Creating a numbered list

By default, GoLive creates a numbered list with Arabic numerals. You can choose from several options to change the numbering style of the list.

4 Choose Type > List > Upper Roman to change the leading characters to uppercase Roman numerals.

Now you'll change the numbered list into an unnumbered list.

5 Click the Unnumbered List button (▦) on the toolbar to change the leading characters from numbers to bullets.

6 Click in the blank space outside the list to deselect it.

GoLive lets you easily create a hierarchical list with different numbering styles or leading characters.

7 Select the second and third items in the list.

8 Click the Increase List Level button ( ) on the toolbar to further indent the selected items and change their leading characters from bullets to circles.

9 Click in a blank space to deselect the two items.

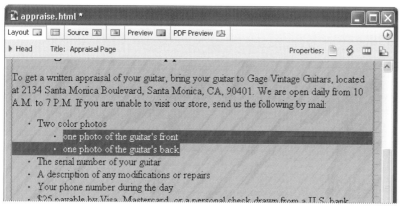

Indenting list items

Adding a line break

Notice that the last item in the unnumbered list is longer than the other items. You can use a line break to make the last item flow onto two lines, rather than one.

1 Click before the word "drawn" in the last item to insert a cursor.

2 Double-click the Line Break icon in the Basic set ( ) of the Objects palette, or drag the Line Break icon from the Objects palette to the cursor on the page.

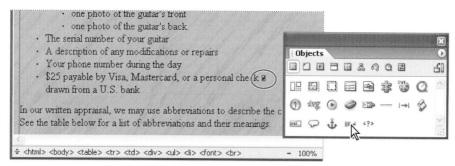

Adding line break by double-clicking

The line breaks, and the text beginning with "drawn" is moved to the following line.

💡 *You can also add a line break by clicking inside a paragraph to insert a cursor and pressing Shift+Enter or Shift+Return.*

Changing the color of text

Now you'll change the color of the unnumbered list to red.

1 Select the text in the unnumbered list, including the leading character of the first item in the list.

2 Click the Text Color field on the toolbar to display the Color palette.

Text Color field

3 In the Color palette and with the RGB slider selected, enter **990000** in the Hex Value text box, and press Enter or Return.

The selected color appears in the preview pane of the Color palette.

4 The color of the selected text changes to red.

5 Click in the blank space outside the selected text to deselect it.

6 Choose File > Save.

Saving a text style

To save you both time and effort, you can save individual HTML formatting attributes that you've applied to text as a group in the HTML Styles palette. Then you can use the palette to reapply the group of attributes to other text in your site. Now that you've created a red text style, you can easily save this style and apply it to text on this page or anywhere else throughout the site.

1 Select a portion of the list text that is colored red.

2 Choose Window > HTML Styles to open the HTML Styles palette.

3 Click the New Style button ( ) at the bottom of the palette.

4 In the New Style dialog box, enter a name for the new style, and press Enter or Return. We chose "Red Text" as the name.

Notice that the color of the text is already recorded in the color box.

5 Click the inline icon so that you can apply this style to individual letters and words, as well as to entire paragraphs.

Inline icon selected

6 Click OK to add the style to the HTML Styles palette.

You can now select any text on the page and click the Apply Style button ( ) in the HTML Styles palette to color the selected text red. To remove a style, choose Edit > Undo Apply HTML Style.

7 Close the HTML Styles palette, and choose File > Save to save your work.

Reverting and restoring changes to pages

When designing your Web page, you can use the History palette or menu commands to revert to a previous state of a page or site. The History palette records the changes that you make to a page in the Layout Editor or Source Code Editor and changes you make to files in the site window. Each time that you make a change, the new state of the page or site is added to the History palette. You can revert to a previous state of the page or site by selecting any state in the History palette. Once you've reverted to a previous state, you can restore changes that you made to that state by choosing a newer state in the History palette.

–From the Adobe GoLive CS online Help.

Adding a table

GoLive lets you quickly add tables to your documents. Tables are often used to control how text wraps on a Web page and to position text, images, and other media on a Web page. They are also used to present information in rows and columns. In this lesson, you'll add a table to present tab-separated information.

In its written appraisals, Gage Vintage Guitars uses abbreviations to describe the condition of a guitar. You'll add a table to the page that will contain a list of abbreviations and their meanings used by the company. Then you'll copy and paste data into the table from a text-only file.

1 Scroll downward in the document window, so that you can view the end of the document. Click after the last word in the paragraph beginning with "In our written appraisal," and press Enter or Return.

 2 Drag the Table icon from the Basic set of the Objects palette to the cursor on the page.

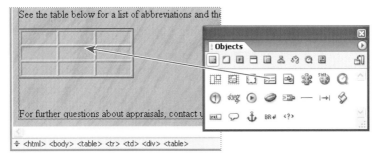

An empty table appears at the cursor location, and the Inspector changes to the Table Inspector.

Now you'll copy and paste data into the table from a text-only file. The data in the text-only file is formatted so that each line represents the contents of a row, with tabs separating the data between the columns.

3 Start any word-processing application, or use the File > Open command from GoLive.

4 Open the table.txt file In Lessons/Lesson05/05Start/.

5 Click in the document to create an insertion point, and choose Edit > Select All or drag to select all the text in the file. Then choose Edit > Copy or an equivalent command, depending on your word-processing application, to copy all the text in the file. Close the table.txt file without saving any changes.

You can import data into a table from a text-only file in which the data is separated with tabs using the Import button on the Table Inspector. You can also copy data from cells in another application and paste the copied material into a GoLive table. Rows and columns will be added to the GoLive table as needed. See "Adding text to tables" in the Adobe GoLive CS online Help.

6 In the appraise.html document window, select all the cells in the newly added table by creating an insertion point in the first cell of the table and Shift-dragging across the rows and down the columns of the table.

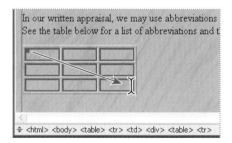

7 Choose Edit > Paste.

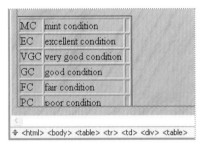

Text pasted into table cells

GoLive adds extra columns and rows to the table as necessary to accommodate the copied and pasted data.

If you were not able to copy and paste the contents of table.txt into appraise.html, you can open the file table.html in GoLive and copy and paste the finished table into your document. You will need to delete the empty table you placed in appraise.html first.

Note: *Most spreadsheet applications can export data to a text-only file. For more information, see the documentation of your spreadsheet application.*

Making selections within tables

As you design a table and add images and other content to it, selecting cells or nested tables can become difficult. GoLive provides you with a variety of ways to select cells, rows, columns, and nested tables to suit your needs. You can make selections directly in the document window, in the markup tree bar, or in an outline of the table in the Select tab of the Table palette. The Select tab shows a table as a bare outline, and enables you to make cell or nested table selections without the risk of resizing the selection or selecting content inside the cell.

Selected cells are outlined in bold in the document window and in the Table palette, and highlighted in source code views. In the Layout editor or Table palette, a black rectangle in the upper left corner of the selected cells can be dragged to a new location in the table or to create a new table. (Blue lines indicate the selection and sorting region.)

–From the Adobe GoLive CS online Help.

Formatting a table

You can format a table by specifying options in the Table Inspector, by applying a predefined table style using the Table palette, or by doing both. You need to use the Table Inspector to specify options for the table's basic appearance, such as its number of rows and columns. Predefined table styles let you quickly format specific table features, such as the color of individual table cells.

Now you'll use the Table Inspector to specify the number of rows and columns for the table. Because the third column doesn't contain data, you'll remove it from the table.

1 If necessary select the table in the appraise.html document.

2 In the Table Inspector, for Columns, enter **2**. Press Enter or Return.

You can determine the number of rows and columns in the table before you add the table to your page. In the Basic set of the Objects palette, Ctrl-click (Windows) or Command-click (Mac OS) on the Table icon. The Table icon appears as one cell. While still in the Objects palette, Ctrl-drag (Windows) or Command-drag (Mac OS) vertically and then horizontally until the table contains the desired number of rows and columns. When you release the cursor, the table is added to your document.

Now you'll add headings to each column of the table. You'll begin by adding an empty row at the beginning of the table.

3 Click the bottom or right edge of the first cell in the left column of the table to select it. (Make sure that you select the cell, not the text.)

The Cell tab is automatically selected in the Table Inspector.

4 In the Table Inspector, click the Add Row Above button to add a row above the current selection.

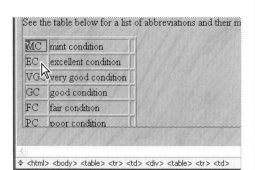

Clicking bottom edge of table cell to select it   *Add Row Above button*

5 Click inside the new first cell in the left column of the table to insert a cursor.

6 Type **Abbreviation**, press Tab to move the cursor to the first cell in the right column, and type **Meaning**.

Now you'll format the table using a predefined table style included with GoLive. First you'll preview the style in the Table palette.

7 Choose Window > Table to display the Table palette.

8 In the Table palette, click the Style tab. Then choose Green from the pop-up menu in the upper left corner of the Style tab.

9 Click Apply to apply the chosen style to the table.

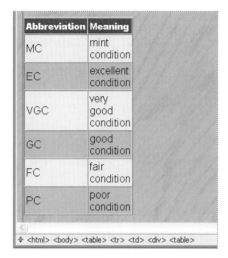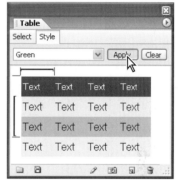

You can easily remove a predefined table style once you've applied it.

10 Click Clear to remove the chosen style from the table.

If you don't find a predefined table style that meets your needs, you can create your own style using the Table Inspector and a variety of palettes included with GoLive.

Now you'll specify options for the table's appearance using the Table Inspector.

11 In the document window of the appraise.html file, select the table.

12 In the Table Inspector, choose Auto from the Width pop-up menu.

13 For Border, enter **6** to increase the width of the table's border. For Cell Pad, enter **4** to increase the horizontal and vertical spacing of each table cell. For Cell Space, enter **4** to increase the space between table cells. Press Enter or Return.

Now you'll add a caption above the table.

14 Select Caption, and make sure that Above Table is chosen from the pop-up menu.

15 Click directly above the table to insert a cursor, and type **Abbreviations**.

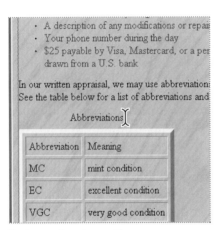

Typing caption above table   *Caption and Above Table options*

16 Click the Left Align button (☰) on the toolbar to align the caption to the left side of the table.

17 Select the "Abbreviations" text, and click the Bold button (**B**) on the toolbar.

💡 *Instead of selecting text by dragging, you can select a single word by double-clicking it or a line of text by triple-clicking it.*

Now you'll increase the font size of the "Abbreviations" text.

You can use the Font Size menu to apply custom font sizes that override the browser's preferences. Most browsers are set to display text at 12 points. The GoLive Font Size menu allows you to set relative font sizes that range from 1 to 7. The Font Size 3 is the baseline font size. It causes text to display in the font size set in the browser's preferences. A font size of 1 displays text at two font sizes smaller than the size set in the browser's preferences, a font size of 2 displays text at one font size smaller, a font size of 4 displays text at one font size larger, and so on.

18 Choose 4 from the Font Size menu on the toolbar, and click in the blank space outside the caption to deselect it.

Now you'll format the column headings.

19 Select the "Abbreviation" text in the first cell of the table, and choose Type > Style > Underline to underline it. Then select the "Meaning" text, and underline it.

Now you'll adjust the width of the columns in the table.

20 Click the bottom or right edge of any cell in the left column of the table to select it.

21 In the Cell tab of the Table Inspector, choose Pixel from the Width menu. For Width, enter **100**.

The selected cell and all other cells in its column increase in width.

22 Click the bottom or right edge of any cell in the right column of the table to select it. Choose Pixel from the Width menu. For Width, enter **140**.

 You can also adjust the width of a table column by positioning the pointer on the right edge of the column so that the pointer turns into a double-headed arrow, and dragging to the left or right.

23 Choose File > Save.

Changing the color of table cells

Now you'll change the color of the cells in the table to yellow.

1 Move the pointer to the left edge of the table, and click to select the table.

The Table tab is automatically selected in the Table Inspector.

2 In the Table Inspector, click the Color field to select the field and display the Color palette. (Be sure to click the Color field, not the checkbox.)

3 In the Color palette with the RGB slider selected, type **FFFFCC** in the Value text box, and press Enter or Return.

The selected color appears in the color preview box of the Color palette and the Color field in the Table Inspector. In addition, the color of the table cells changes to yellow.

Clicking left edge of table to select it

Clicking Color field in Table Inspector; choosing color in Color palette

You can also change the color of individual table cells. You'll change the color of the cells in the right column to green.

4 Move the cursor over the top edge of the right column until it changes to a down-facing arrow. Then click to select all of the cells in the column.

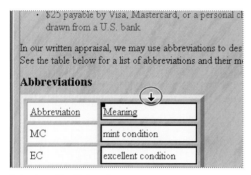

Selecting all cells in column

The Cell tab in the Table Inspector is automatically selected.

5 In the Table Inspector, click the Color field to select the field and display the Color palette.

6 In the Color palette with the RGB slider tab selected, type **99CC99** in the Hex Value text box, and press Enter or Return.

The selected color appears in the preview pane of the Color palette and the Color field in the Table Inspector. In addition, the color of the selected cells changes to green.

7 In the document window, click in the blank space outside the table to deselect all of its cells.

Sorting the contents of a table

GoLive makes it easy for you to sort the contents of a table, so that the contents of its rows or columns appear in alphabetical or numerical order. You can apply the sort to an entire table, specific rows, specific columns, or specific cells.

Now you'll use the Select tab of the Table palette to sort the contents of the table.

1 Move the pointer to the left edge of the table, and click to select the table.

2 In the Table palette, click the Select tab. (Choose Window > Table palette to open the Table palette if necessary.)

3 In the preview of the table that appears in the Select tab, drag to select all of the table cells except the cells in the first row, and click Sort.

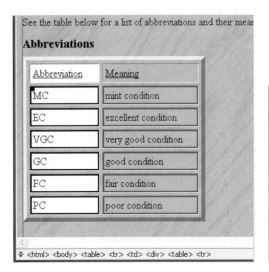
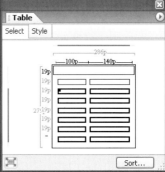

4 In the Sort Table dialog box, choose Rows from the Sort pop-up menu to indicate that you want to sort the order of the rows in the table. By sorting the order of the rows, you will make the contents of one or more columns appear in numerical or alphabetical order.

5 In the top leftmost Sort By pop-up menu, choose Column1 to specify the first column as the primary column to be used when sorting the table's contents. This means that sorting the contents of the first column will be the first priority for GoLive.

You'll specify for the first column to be sorted in ascending order.

6 Make sure that Ascending is selected from the pop-menu on the Sort By line.

Because the table only has two columns, you don't need to specify a secondary or tertiary column (Then By option) to be used when sorting the table's contents. Sorting the contents of the second column will automatically be the second priority for GoLive.

7 Click OK to sort the selected table cells using the criteria that you've specified.

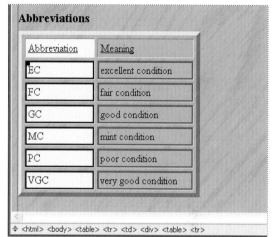

8 Click outside the table to deselect it, and choose File > Save.

Applying fonts

When you create text for a Web page in GoLive, you can choose whether to let the user's browser select the default font to be used when viewing your page or you can define a preferred font set.

The default in GoLive is to let the user's browser determine which font is used. You can check what fonts or font sets, if any, have been used on a page using the Type menu.

1 In the appraise.html document, choose Type > Font. Notice that None is selected because you haven't applied any particular font. This means that the user's Web browser will select the default font to use when viewing your Web page.

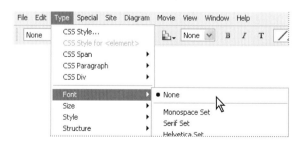

GoLive contains default sets of fonts that you can apply to text in your documents. One set contains the Times New Roman, Georgia, and Times fonts. If you use this set for your Web page, a visitor's browser will attempt to display text first in Times New Roman, second in Georgia, and third in Times. If none of the fonts in the set is installed on the viewer's system, the browser displays text using its default font.

Because all the other pages on the Gage Vintage Guitars Web site were created using the Helvetica font set as the preferred font set, you'll change the font of the entire page.

2 Click anywhere in the text on the appraise.html page to insert a cursor. Then choose Edit > Select All to select all of the text in the document.

3 Choose Type > Font > Helvetica to apply the Helvetica font set to the selected text.

4 Click inside the document to deselect the text.

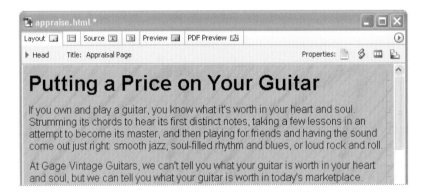

You can see the fonts included in the Helvetica font set in the Type menu.

5 Choose Type> Font > Edit Font Sets. If necessary, expand the Helvetica font set in the Font Set Editor.

6 When you have finished reviewing the font sets, click Cancel to close the Font Set Editor.

Most of the text in the appraise.html document changes to the Helvetica font. Notice, however, that the text in the table and the table caption continue to use the Times font. To change the fonts used by the text in the table, you need to select the table caption and cells individually.

7 Select the "Abbreviations" text in the table caption, and choose Type > Font > Helvetica. Then click outside the selected text to deselect it.

The text in the table caption changes to the Helvetica font.

8 Click the top edge of the left column to select all of the cells in the column. Click the top edge of the right column to add its cells to the selection. Then choose Type > Font > Helvetica, and click outside the selected table cells to deselect them.

The text in the table cells changes to the Helvetica font.

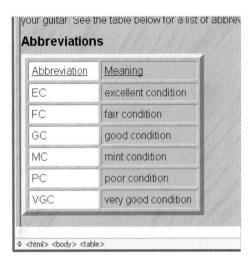

9 Choose File > Save to save your work.

⁇ *You can also use GoLive to create sets of fonts that you can apply to text in your documents. For more information, see "Creating and applying font sets" in the Adobe GoLive CS online Help.*

Capturing a table style

Now you'll capture the table style that you've created. When you capture a table style, the style is added to the Style tab of the Table palette, so that you can reuse the style and create a consistent look for tables throughout your Web site.

1 Click the top or left edge of the table to select it.

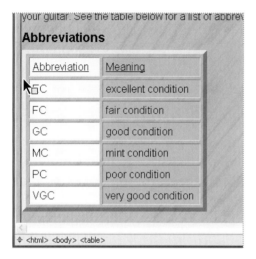

2 In the Table palette, click the Style tab.

3 Click the New Table Style button ( ) at the bottom of the palette to create a new table style.

4 In the New Table Style dialog box, type **Gage** as the name of the new table style.

5 Click OK to save the style of the selected table in the document window and save it as the new table style.

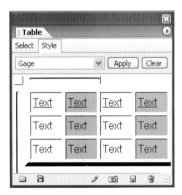

To apply the new style to another table, you can simply select the desired table in the document window, choose the name of the new table style from the pop-up menu in the upper left corner of the Style tab, and click Apply.

6 Close the Table palette.

Editing text

GoLive lets you edit text in your documents with the ease of a word-processing application:

• You can delete text by selecting it and pressing Delete, choosing Edit > Cut, or pressing Ctrl+X (Windows) or Command+X (Mac OS).

• You can find and correct spelling errors by choosing Edit > Check Spelling.

• You can find and replace text by choosing Edit > Find.

Finding and replacing text

Now you'll find the word "loud" and replace it with the word "powerful." You'll begin by setting preferences for finding text. You'll have GoLive keep the Find window in front of the document window when a match is found.

1 Choose Edit > Preferences (Win) or GoLive > Preferences (Mac).

2 In the left pane of the Preferences dialog box, click the Find icon to display preferences for finding text.

3 Choose Keep Find Window In Front from the When Match Is Found menu in the right pane, and click OK.

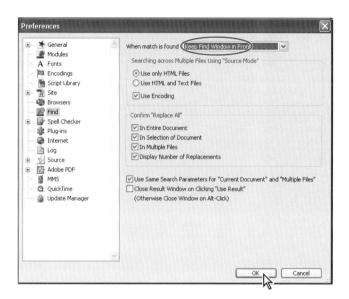

Now you'll search for the text to replace.

4 Scroll upward in the document window, so that you can view the beginning of the document. Then click before the main heading on the page to insert a cursor.

5 Choose Edit > Find.

6 In the Find window, select the Find & Replace tab. Then type **loud** in the Find text box.

7 Click the triangle (▷) next to Replace to open the Replace text box. In the Replace text box, type **powerful**, and click Find.

The word "loud" is highlighted in the document.

8 In the Find window, click Replace. In the document, "loud" is replaced with "powerful."

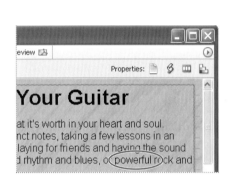
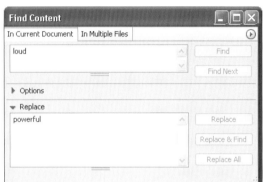

9 Close the Find window, and choose File > Save.

Checking spelling

No matter whether you type your own material or import material provided by others, it is a good idea to run Check Spelling whenever you finish constructing a page. You'll do that now.

1 Create an insertion point in the appraise.html document.

2 Choose Edit > Check Spelling.

3 In the Check Spelling dialog box, make sure that English (US) is selected from the Language pop-up menu and that the From Top option is selected.

4 You can click the icon next to More Options to see additional options that you can select for the spell checking operation.

5 Click the Start button to start spell checking.

The spell checker stops on "today's."

6 Click Ignore.

The spell checker stops on "stormey" and suggests "stormy" as an alternative.

7 Click Change to have GoLive correct the misspelled word.

8 The spell checker stops on "world's" and "Musician's" and a variety of correct but unusual words that are not in the dictionary. Click Ignore in each case.

9 The spell checker next stops on the abbreviations in the left column of the nested table. Click Ignore for each of the abbreviations since you don't want to add them to the dictionary.

The spell checker stops on e-mail because of the capitalization.

10 Because "e-mail" is your preferred capitalization, click Learn so that the word is added to the spell checker dictionary.

Be careful when adding words to the dictionary. The dictionary is used by the application, and therefore additions to the dictionary will apply to all documents rather than to a specific document.

11 Close the spell checking dialog box when you are finished.

12 Choose Files > Save.

Converting a layout grid to a table

For convenience, you used a layout grid to layout your Web page. While layout grids are easier to use than HTML tables, especially for novices, layout grids create more code than do HTML tables. Now that you are satisfied with the layout, you can easily convert the layout grid to an HTML table.

1 In the appraise.html page, click near to the edge of the page to select the layout grid. If you accidentally made your layout text box the same size as your layout grid, select the layout text box and resize it so that at least part of the layout grid is showing. (You can check whether you have selected the layout grid in the Inspector. If the Inspector is the Layout Grid Inspector, you have successfully selected the layout grid.)

2 Choose Special > Layout Grid to Table.

3 In the Convert dialog box, select the Strip Control Row and Column option and click OK. Your layout grid is converted to an HTML table.

The Strip Control Row and Column option removes the empty, one-pixel control row and column at the bottom and right side of the grid. For more information, see "Converting a layout grid to a table" in the Adobe GoLive CS online Help.

At this point you can delete any extra rows and columns if you wish.

4 Click outside the new HTML table, and choose File > Save to save your work.

Any time you need to update the layout of the page, you can convert the HTML table back to a layout grid by selecting the newly created layout table in the appraise.html document and clicking the Convert button for the Table to Layout Grid option in the Table tab of the Table Inspector. The table is immediately converted to a layout grid, and all the text within the page is contained in a layout text box.

You've completed the design of the Appraisal page for this lesson. Now you're ready to preview the page in GoLive.

Previewing in GoLive

1 In the document window, click the Preview tab to view the document in Layout Preview.

2 When you are finished, choose File > Close to close the appraise.html file.

Exploring on your own

Hypertext Markup Language (HTML) is used to publish information on the World Wide Web. In this lesson, you worked in GoLive's Layout Editor to design a Web page. When you work in the Layout Editor, GoLive writes HTML code for your page. Sometimes you may want to work directly with your page's HTML code. GoLive provides two different views of the HTML code, which you can use to design and edit your Web pages. The Source Code Editor lets you view the HTML code directly, and the Outline Editor lets you view the HTML code in a hierarchical, organized way.

Now that you've learned how to work in Layout Editor, try working in Source Code Editor and Outline Editor to edit the Appraisal page.

First you'll open the Appraisal page.

1 In GoLive, choose File > Open, and open the appraise.html file in Lessons/Lesson05/05End/.

2 In the appraise.html document window, select the main heading "Putting a Price on Your Guitar."

3 Click the Source tab ([T]) to display the document in the Source Code Editor.

4 Notice that the main heading is highlighted in the HTML source code. If necessary, scroll to the right in the document window, so that you can view the highlighted text.

```
14        <td height="1065" width="16"></td>
15        <td valign="top" height="1065" width="544">
16            <h1><font face="arial">Putting a Price on Your Guitar</font></h1
17            <p><font face="arial">If you own and play a guitar, you know wha
18            <div align="left">
19                <p><font face="arial">At Gage Vintage Guitars, we can't tell
20                <h2><font face="arial">Getting Your Guitar Appraised</font><
21                <p><font face="arial">To get a written appraisal of your gui
22            <ul>
```
```
16                                                      0%    ▼ ✦ 580 x 202 ▼
```

Now you'll use the Source Code Editor to change the paragraph format of the main heading from Header 1 to Header 2.

5 Select the text "<h1>" at the beginning of the line that contains the main heading. The text that you've selected is the start tag of an h1 element, which instructs the Web browser to display the main heading using the Header 1 format.

Now you'll change the h1 element to an h2 element by modifying its start and end tags.

6 Type **<h2>** to replace the selected text.

7 Select the text "</h1>" at the end of the line that contains the main heading. This is the end tag for the original h1 element.

8 Type **</h2>** to replace the selected text.

```
13 height="1065">
14 <td height="1065" width="16"></td>
15 <td valign="top" height="1065" width="544">
16     <h2><font face="arial">Putting a Price on Your Guitar</font></h2>
17     <p><font face="arial">If you own and play a guitar, you know what it's w
18     <div align="left">
19         <p><font face="arial">At Gage Vintage Guitars, we can't tell you wha
20         <h2><font face="arial">Getting Your Guitar Appraised</font></h2>
21         <p><font face="arial">To get a written appraisal of your guitar, brin
22     <ul>
```
```
16                                                      0%    ▼ ✦ 580 x 202 ▼
```

9 Click the Layout tab (▣) to return the document to Layout Editor. Notice that the paragraph format for the main heading now is Header 2.

Now you'll use the Outline Editor to return the paragraph format of the main heading to Header 1.

10 If needed, select the main heading.

11 Click the Outline Editor tab (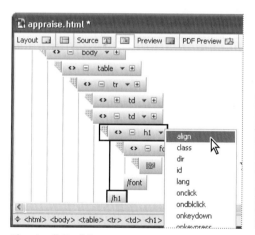) to display the document in the Outline Editor. Notice that the main heading has a black border around it in the outline.

12 Click to select the text "h2" text.

13 Type **h1** to replace the selected text, and click in the blank space outside the selected text to deselect it.

You'll also use the Outline Editor to center the main heading on the page.

14 Click the triangle to the right of the "h1" text to display a pop-up menu.

15 Choose "align" from the pop-up menu.

16 Click the triangle next to "align" to display another pop-up menu, and choose "center."

17 Click the triangle to the left of the "h1" text to expand the h1 element. Notice that GoLive has automatically changed the closing tag to match the opening tag.

Choosing "align" from pop-up menu

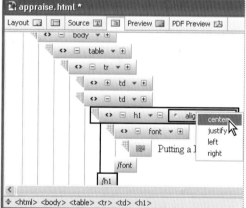

Choosing "center" from second pop-up menu

18 Click the Layout tab to return the document to the Layout Editor. Notice that the paragraph format of the main heading now is Header 1 and the main heading is centered on the page.

19 Choose File > Close to close the page. You don't need to save the changes that you've made.

Review questions

1 Name two ways of adding text to a document.

2 How do you apply a paragraph style to text? How do you apply a physical style to text?

3 How do you apply a predefined style to a table? How do you remove a predefined style from a table?

4 How do you add a caption to a table?

5 Which palette do you use to sort the contents of a table?

6 How do you learn more about the sets of fonts available for a document?

7 How can you find and replace text in a document?

Review answers

1 You can add text to a document by typing directly in the document window; importing text from another application into a table; using layout text boxes; using floating boxes; copying text from a document created in another application and pasting it into a GoLive document; and dragging a text clip, created from a SimpleText or Note Pad document, from the desktop to a GoLive document.

2 To apply a paragraph style, click anywhere in a paragraph and choose a paragraph style from the Paragraph Format menu on the toolbar or the Type > Header submenu. To apply a physical style, select the text, and click the Bold, Italic, or Teletype button on the toolbar, or choose a physical style from the Type > Style submenu.

3 To apply a predefined style to a table, choose a style from the pop-up menu in the upper left corner of the Style tab of the Table palette, and click Apply. To remove a predefined style from a table, make sure that the table is selected, and click Clear in the Style tab of the Table palette.

4 To add a caption to a table, select Caption in the Table Inspector, and choose Above Table or Below Table from the pop-up menu in the Table Inspector. Then click above or below the table to insert a cursor and type the text for the caption.

5 To sort the contents of a table, you use the Select tab of the Table palette.

6 To learn more about the sets of fonts available for a document, choose Type > Font > Edit Font Sets to display the Font Set Editor. In the Font Set Editor, select a set of fonts to display its contents.

7 You can choose Edit > Find to find and replace text in a document.

Lesson 6

6 Creating Navigational Links

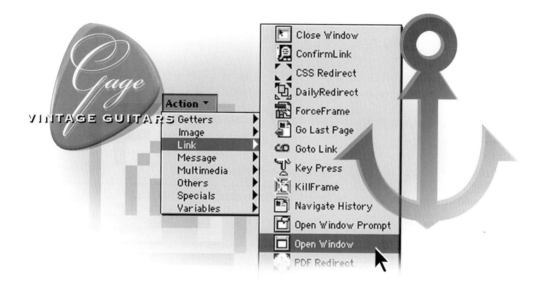

Once you've created content for your Web pages, you need to provide visitors with a way to get from one page to another. Navigational links let visitors jump from text or graphics on one page to areas on the same page or to other pages in the site or to other sites.

About this lesson

In this lesson, you'll learn how to do the following:

- Add navigational links to graphics on a Web page.

- Add hypertext links to a page.

- Add anchors that act as targets for links within a page.

- Add an action to a link.

- Change a link's color and highlight.

- Verify links.

- Create image maps and link them to a page.

- Add hotspots to an image map and change their shape.

- Edit links and anchors.

- Fix broken links and change link preferences.

This lesson takes approximately 45 minutes to complete.

If needed, copy the Lessons/Lesson06/ folder onto your hard drive. As you work on this lesson, you'll overwrite the start files. If you need to restore the start files, copy them from the *Adobe GoLive CS Classroom in a Book* CD.

Note: Windows users need to unlock the lesson files before using them. For more information, see "Copying the Classroom in a Book files" on page 2.

About links

As you have seen in earlier lessons, as you create your site and add all your resources to the site window, you can link or reference images or objects on the page to their source files using resource links. You can also create a navigational system between the pages in your site and add navigational links to other sites or external URLs. Adobe GoLive automatically updates the site with each new link you create and continually verifies the integrity of links as you build your site. If you move or rename a file in the site window, GoLive updates the links to the new paths.

Getting started

In this lesson, you'll explore linking from graphics and text, creating image maps, and adding an action to a link. You'll start the lesson by viewing the final lesson file in your browser to see what you'll accomplish.

1 Start your Web browser.

2 In your browser, open the *index.html* file in Lessons/Lesson06/06End/gage folder/gage/.

Final index.html file, viewed in Netscape browser

3 Click the links in the index.html file, and explore the site. (To save space on the Classroom in a Book CD-ROM, not all the links work. If necessary, use your brower's Back button to retrace your steps.)

4 When you've finished viewing the file, close your browser.

Opening a site

Follow these steps to open the site and begin this lesson.

1 Start Adobe GoLive.

By default, an introductory screen appears prompting you to create a new page, create a new site, or open an existing file.

Note: *You can set preferences for the introductory screen to not appear when you start GoLive. If the introductory screen doesn't appear, choose File > Open and go to step 3.*

2 Click Open to open an existing file.

3 Open the *gage* file in Lessons/Lesson06/06Start/gage folder/.

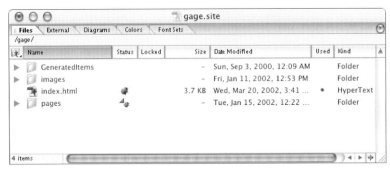

Gage site window

4 In the site window, double-click the index.html file to open it. This is the home page for the Gage Vintage Guitars Web site.

Because of font size differences between platforms, you may find that headline text runs to two lines as opposed to the single line in the illustrations used in this lesson. This is not a concern for this lesson.

Creating a navigational link from a graphic

Adding navigational links to a page lets viewers jump to other pages in the site, to locations on the same page as the link (called anchors), across the Web, and to non-Web resources such as FTP servers, newsgroups, and e-mail addresses.

In this part of the lesson you'll create a navigational link from the index.html file to the Stock page, so that viewers can jump from the home page to a list of items in stock for the company.

You'll start by seeing whether the index.html file contains any links and determining where and how to add a link to the file.

1 Click the Preview tab (▣) at the top of the index.html file document window, so that you can work for a moment in the Layout Preview.

2 Using the pointer, click various places in the document window. The file has two broken links—one to the repairs page and one to the appraisals page. You'll fix these broken links at the end of the lesson. The third link, to items in stock, is the link that you'll create now.

3 Click the Layout tab (▣) of the index.html file to return to the Layout Editor.

4 In the document window of the index.html file, click the Items In Stock image to try to select it. You won't be able to select the image because it's part of a component.

To review the construction of this component, see "Creating a component to be used as a navigation bar" on page 154.

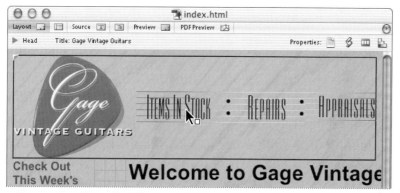

Trying to select unlinked graphic within component

To create the navigational link from the index.html file to the Stock page, you must open the component and add the link to that file. Adding the link to the component means that any changes you make later to the link will be applied automatically across the site.

5 Open the navbar.html file using any of these techniques:

• Double-click in the document window. (You are double-clicking the component.)

• Choose File > Open, and open the navbar.html file in Lessons/Lesson06/06Start/gage folder/web-data/Components/.

• Click the double arrow at the bottom right of the site window to display all of the site's contents. In the right pane of the site window, the Extras tab displays the site's web-data folder and its contents. The navbar.html file is located inside the Components folder.

Expanded site window

6 Close the file index.html.

When a component is embedded in your pages, you can easily edit the component by editing the source file (in this case, the HTML page containing the header) and then letting GoLive automatically update all pages on which the component is used.

7 Choose Window > Inspector to display the Inspector, or click the tab if the Inspector is collapsed.

8 In the navbar.html window, click the Items In Stock graphic to select it. The Image Inspector becomes active.

9 Click the Link tab of the Image Inspector. You use this tab to specify links.

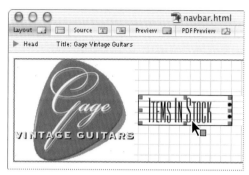

Selecting graphic within component

You can also create a new link by clicking the Create Link button on the toolbar, as you'll do later in this lesson.

You'll create your first link by using the Pick Whip button in the Image Inspector to link to a file in the site window.

10 If necessary, arrange and resize the document window, site window, and Image Inspector so that all three are visible on your desktop.

11 In the Link tab in the Image Inspector, click the Create Link button (⬜). Then drag from the Pick Whip button (⬜) to the stock.html file inside the pages folder in the site window. If the stock.html file isn't visible, position the pointer over the icon to the left of the pages folder until the folder opens, and then drag to the file.

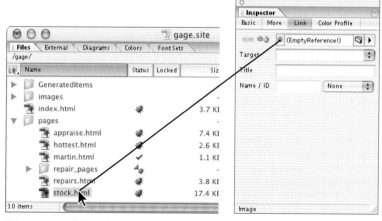

Using Point and Shoot button to link to stock.html file

The filename and directory path appear in the URL text box in the Image Inspector. If the link can't be made, the line snaps back to the Pick Whip button.

12 Click the Basic tab of the Image Inspector. In the Alt Text box, enter **Items In Stock** and press Enter or Return. Depending upon the browser that displays the page, the alternative text appears when users move their mouse over the image or in place of the image if the image fails to download.

13 Choose File > Save to save the navbar.html file. When prompted to update the files that use the component, click OK. Click OK again to close the Updating Component window. Close the navbar.html file.

Now you'll test the link to make sure that it works as you expect.

Testing a link

You can test your links using the Preview tab in the document window.

1 Open the home page by double-clicking the index.html page in the site window.

2 Click the Preview tab ( ), and then click the Items In Stock graphic. The stock.html file opens in its own document window.

Clicking linked graphic   *Takes you to the page*

Creating anchors

In this section, you'll create a link from a bulleted item to its corresponding topic later in the page. Anchors act as targets for links within the same page. Using an anchor lets viewers jump to the information without having to scroll. You can create a single link that connects to a single anchor. Or you can create several links that point to a single anchor point.

Now you'll work with the Stock page and add links to it. You'll start by creating a link from a bulleted list item to an anchor in a topic further down the page. You'll use the Point and Shoot feature, which will simultaneously create the anchor and the link to the anchor.

1 If necessary, click the stock.html document window to make it active. You opened the file when you tested the link that you just created. Click the Layout tab.

This file describes the Gage Vintage Guitars product line of acoustic and electric guitars, amps, pedals, and other equipment.

2 Click at the beginning of the second item in the bulleted list, "Electric Guitars," and drag to select the line. You'll create a link from this item to an anchor that you'll place in the corresponding topic (the "Electric Guitars" section) further down the page.

3 Hold down Alt (Windows) or Command (Mac OS), and drag from the selected text to a point directly to the left of the Electric Guitars heading. (Be careful not to release the mouse pointer over the graphic.) An elastic line extends from your start point and a cursor (short vertical line) follows the mouse pointer. To scroll down through the document, hold down the mouse button with the pointer located over the bottom border of the window.

After you release the mouse button, the document window springs back to the link point (the Electric Guitars item in the bulleted list). The URL field in the Text Inspector displays the unique name of the new anchor. Scroll back down to the Electric Guitars heading to see the anchor icon that was inserted next to it.

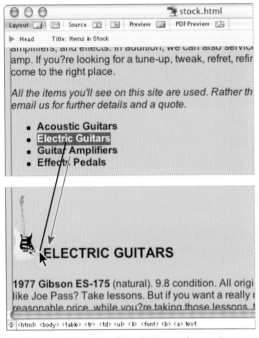

Alt/Command-dragging from bullet; anchor set in
Electric Guitars heading

The pick whip method is the easiest way to create an anchor. You can also use the Objects palette, which you'll do now.

4 In the stock.html file, scroll down until you see the "Guitar Amplifier" heading, about half way down the page.

5 Choose Window > Objects, or click the Objects tab if the palette is collapsed.

6 Click the Basic button (🔲) at the top of the Objects palette.

7 From the Basic set ( ) of the Objects palette, drag the Anchor icon to the "Guitar Amplifiers" section of the stock.html page. Place the anchor to the left of the heading.

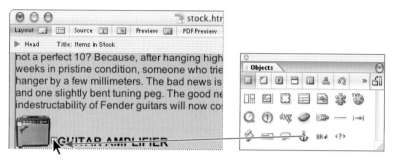

Dragging Anchor icon from Objects palette to text in document window

8 In the Anchor Inspector, enter a descriptive name for the anchor (we used "Amps"). Naming anchors lets you update them more easily, and helps you find and correct broken links when you're managing your site.

9 In the document window, scroll up to the bulleted list and drag to select the "Guitar Amplifiers" text.

10 In the Text Inspector, click the Create Link button ( ). Drag from the Pick Whip button to the Amps anchor that you just inserted. Hold the pointer over the bottom edge of the window to automatically scroll down the document as you drag from the Pick Whip button.

You've created a link between the list item and the topic later in the page. The anchor name (Amps) appears in the URL field of the Text Inspector (anchor names are always preceded by a "#" symbol).

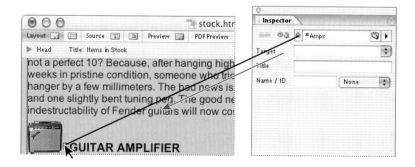

11 Choose File > Save to save your file.

Using anchors for links

An anchor is a specified location on a Web page that serves as the destination of a link.

Here are some guidelines to follow when creating anchors:

• You shouldn't place anchors directly on a layout grid. Instead, place anchors in the flow of HTML text, a layout text box, or a table cell. When you add an anchor to a layout text box or table cell, make sure that the box or cell has other contents, otherwise the anchor will not be recognized by Netscape Navigator. To work around this problem, you can add a nonbreaking space to the empty box or cell. To add a nonbreaking space, click inside the box or cell, and press Shift+spacebar (Windows) or Option+spacebar (Mac OS).

• You should place anchors near the left margin of the page, so that the anchors work more consistently across browsers.

• You won't be able to preview certain link and anchor combinations in Layout Preview.

• You should test links to anchors extensively in browsers before publishing your Web site. Anchors don't always work the same way in Netscape Navigator and Microsoft Internet Explorer.

Testing anchors

You've tried out previewing links using GoLive's Layout Preview. You can also see how links and anchors work in a Web browser by opening the file in a browser and testing the links. Now you'll preview the anchors that you just created.

1 Click the Preview in Browser button in the upper right corner of the toolbar. The document appears in the Web browser that you specified in the Preferences dialog box.

Preview in Browser button

2 Click the bulleted text to see how the links jump to the corresponding heads in the document. Use the Back button in your browser, or scroll up to return to the top of the page.

3 When you have finished previewing, exit or quit your browser. Then click the document window to return to the stock.html file.

4 Close all open files except stock.html and gage site file.

Creating hypertext links

Now you'll create some hypertext links. You'll select some text in the Stock page and link the text to another page. The technique is similar to creating a graphic link or a link to an anchor.

1 In the stock.html document window, scroll to the bottom of the page. You'll create hypertext links from the last line in the document: "Home | Stock | Appraisals | Repairs."

2 Double-click the word "Home" to select it. The Inspector changes to the Text Inspector.

3 Click the Create Link button (▭) in the Text Inspector.

You'll create your first hypertext link using the Pick Whip button in the Text Inspector to link to a file in the site window.

4 Drag from the Pick Whip button (▣) in the Text Inspector to index.html in the site window.

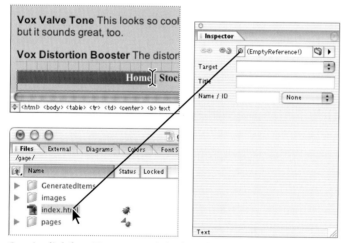

Creating link from Home text to index.html file using point and shoot method

5 If you make a mistake, select the Home text in the document window, and click the Remove Link button (▭) on the toolbar. Then repeat steps 3 and 4 to create the correct link.

You can also use the Remove Link button to unlink graphics.

Now you'll create a hypertext link to another file within the site by using the Inspector's Browse button to locate a file.

6 Select the text "Appraisals." Then click the Create Link button (🔗) on the toolbar.

7 In the Text Inspector, click the Browse button (🔗), select appraise.html in Lessons/Lesson06/06Start/gage folder/gage/pages/, and click Open.

Another way to specify a link in the Inspector is to enter the file's pathname in the URL text box.

Now you'll create the final hypertext link.

8 Select the "Repairs" text in the document window. Click the Create Link button (🔗) on the toolbar. In the Text Inspector, enter the file's relative pathname in the URL text box: **repairs.html.** (In this case no path is necessary, as repairs.html is in the same directory as stock.html.)

When you browse for the link destination or enter the URL, you can enter just the relative path (with the site folder name implied). Absolute URLs include the complete pathname of a file, including the site folder name. Relative URLs don't include the full pathname and can refer to a file in a subdirectory from which the file is linked. By default, GoLive is aware of the site folder, so that you don't need to enter it in the URL text box.

9 Choose File > Save to save the stock.html file.

10 To preview the links that you just created, click the Preview in Browser button on the toolbar, and then click a link to test it. (If you've connected each link correctly, the information it's linked to appears in the document window. If not, the browser will display an error message.) Use the Back button in your browser to return to the stock.html page. When you are finished testing the links, exit or quit your browser.

11 Close all open files except stock.html and the gage site file.

About absolute link paths

Site pages contain paths to a variety of linked files: other pages in the site, images displayed on the page, media items embedded in the page, and so on. GoLive automatically uses relative paths for the destinations of links. In most cases, relative paths are appropriate to use in paths. But, if necessary for special cases, you can selectively change the paths to make them absolute, or set a preference to have GoLive make all new paths you create absolute by default. When you make a path absolute, the entire path from the root folder to the linked file is provided. Otherwise only a relative path is provided.

Example: A page /root/pages/info/page.html (where root is the name of the root folder) contains the image /root/images/image.gif. The absolute path to the image file is /images/ image.gif. The relative path is ../../images/image.gif.

Absolute paths are useful in the following cases:

• If a form references a CGI script at the root level of the site directory (or any other subdirectory), any references to that file are usually written as absolute.

• If a common navigation bar is used on many pages that reside in folders at various hierarchical levels, you can use an absolute path specification throughout to reference its image files, allowing you to copy and paste the same code snippet onto all the pages.

However, absolute paths work only at sites where there is a Web server providing information about the location of the site's root folder. For the same reason, using absolute paths prevents you from previewing pages in a Web browser on your local computer—that is, a previewing browser has no way of locating this root folder.

Note: *An absolute path in GoLive is not a full path from the file system root or a fully qualified URL.*

Setting up absolute link paths

You can specify absolute paths for all new links or for specific links.

To make the path of a link absolute:

1. *Select the link.*

2. *Do one of the following:*

• Choose Relative from the URL pop-up menu in the Inspector, if it is checked. (Unchecked indicates the link is absolute.)

• Choose Edit from the URL pop-up menu in the Inspector. In the Edit URL dialog box, click Make Absolute, and then click OK.

You can also use the Edit URL dialog box to add URL parameters to the URL, and make the values for URL parameters come from dynamic content data sources.

To set a preference that makes all new links absolute:

1. Choose Edit > Preferences.

2. Expand General preferences and select URL Handling.

3. In the right pane, select Make New Links Absolute and click OK.

To specify a site setting that makes all new links absolute in the active site only:

1. Open a site.

2. Click the Site Settings button on the toolbar or choose Site > Settings.

3. In the left pane, select URL Handling.

4. In the right pane, select Make New Links Absolute and click OK.

–From the Adobe GoLive CS User Guide.

Creating external links

Until now, the links that you've created have been within pages (using anchors), and between pages in your site. You can also create links from your site to other sites on the Web. To do this, you'll create a link to an external URL.

First you need to store the URL that you want to use in the External tab of the site window. The External tab is useful for storing information that you may want to use in more than one place on your site. If you later need to update an item in the External tab, it is automatically updated wherever it appears in the site.

1 Click the External tab in the site window.

2 Drag the URL icon from the Site set (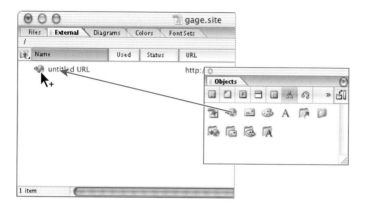) of the Objects palette to the External tab of the site window. This tab contains elements for sites, such as pages, URLs, and e-mail addresses.

A new, untitled URL entry is added to the External tab. Select the untitled URL, and the Inspector changes to the Reference Inspector (in Mac OS, click on the Inspector to change it). For this exercise, you'll create an external link to the Adobe home page.

3 With the URL you added in the External tab of the site window selected, rename the URL using either the Name field in the External tab or the Name field in the Reference Inspector. We used the name "Adobe URL." (This name is for reference only, to help you keep track of stored URLs.)

4 Press Enter or Return.

5 In the URL field of the Reference Inspector, change the URL text to the correct text for the URL to which you want to link. To link to the Adobe home page, for example, change "http://www.untitled.1/" to "http://www.adobe.com". Make sure that you leave "http://" at the beginning of the URL.

6 Press Enter or Return. The URL is updated in the External tab.

You can also add URLs to the External tab by dragging them from an open Web browser. For more information, see "Using site URLs and e-mail addresses" in the Adobe GoLive CS User Guide.

Now that the URL is added to the External tab, you'll create a link to it from text in the appraise.html page.

7 Click the Files tab in the site window. Then double-click the appraise.html page in the site window to open the page.

8 Click the External tab of the site window.

9 In the appraise.html document window, locate the text "Classic Guitar" at the end of the second paragraph of text, and drag to select it.

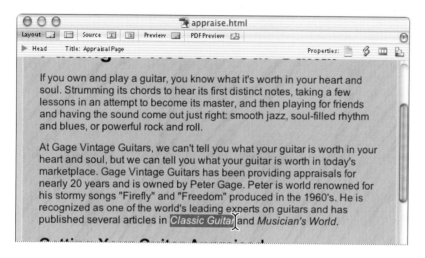

10 Click the Create Link button () in the Text Inspector.

11 Drag from the Pick Whip button in the Text Inspector to the Adobe URL in the External tab of the site window.

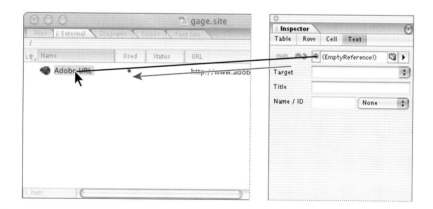

12 Choose File > Save to save the appraise.html file.

13 To preview the link that you just created, click the Preview in Browser button. Click the Classic Guitar link. The external Web site (www.adobe.com, in our example) replaces the appraise.html page in the browser window. Exit or quit your browser when you are finished.

Creating e-mail links

Now you'll add a link to the appraise.html page that brings up an e-mail window with an e-mail address in it. Like URLs, e-mail addresses can be stored in the External tab.

1 From the Site set ( ) of the Objects palette, drag the Address icon to the External tab of the site window.

Always store your URLs and e-mail addresses in the External tab of the site window. If you need to change the value of a site URL or e-mail address that you've used on several pages, you can change it in the site window and GoLive will update all the pages at once.

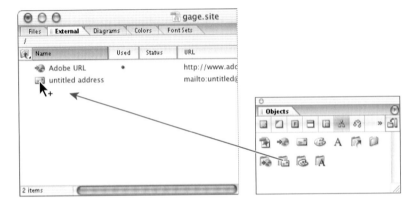

2 Double-click the Address icon in the site window to change the Inspector to the Reference Inspector.

3 In the Name field of the Reference Inspector, enter a name for the address, and press Enter or Return. For example, change "untitled address" to "Anne's Address." Although it's not required, entering names helps you manage addresses in a site.

4 In the URL text box, change the text after "mailto:" to a real e-mail address, and press Enter or Return. For example, change "mailto:untitled@1/" to "mailto:AnneSmith@mycompany.com". Make sure that you leave "mailto:" in the text box and that there are no spaces between it and the e-mail address.

5 In the appraise.html page, drag to select the text "e-mail us" at the bottom of the page.

6 Click the Create Link button ( ) in the Text Inspector.

The link is highlighted and underlined. Now you can attach the text as a link to the e-mail address you just created.

7 Drag from the Pick Whip button ( ) in the Text Inspector to the Address icon in the External tab of the site window.

8 Choose File > Save.

9 Click the Preview in Browser button ( ) on the toolbar to view your page. Scroll to the bottom of the page and click the e-mail link to display an e-mail editor.

10 Close your browser and the appraise.html page when you are finished.

Changing a link's color and highlight

Now that you've created some links, you'll see how easy it is to change their color. You'll use the Page Inspector to change a link's color and highlight.

1 With the Layout tab selected, click the Page icon (▤) in the upper right corner of the stock.html document window. The Inspector changes to the Page Inspector.

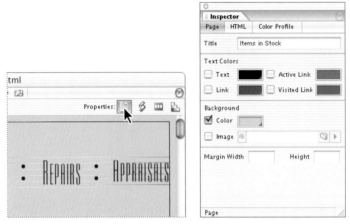

Clicking Page icon to display Page Inspector

2 Choose Window > Color to display the Color palette, or click the Color tab if the palette is collapsed.

3 Click the checkbox and then click the Link color field in the Inspector.

4 In the Color palette, select another color by entering a value in the hex value field (we used 006600). Press Enter or Return. You can also select another color by selecting the Swatch palette and clicking on a color of your choice.

The color that you choose should provide enough contrast between the page's background and text color so that it stands out, but not so much that it's distracting to the viewer. As you try different colors, you can view the effect on the links at the bottom of the stock.html page.

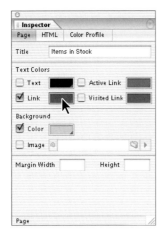

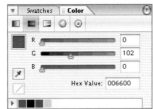

Clicking Link color field   *Selecting color from Color palette*

5 Repeat steps 3 and 4 for the Active Link and Visited Link color fields, selecting each field in turn. (We used 6600FF for Active Link and FF3300 for Visited Link.)

When selecting a color for visited links, it's helpful to viewers to pick a color that's opposite the link color on the color wheel. So, for example, if the link color is red, you could use green for the visited link color.

6 Choose File > Save to save your work.

7 To preview the link color and how it changes when the link is clicked, click the Preview in Browser button in the toolbar. The document appears in your Web browser.

8 In the browser, scroll to the end of the document, and click the Appraisals link to test it. Notice how the color changes when you click the link (the active link color) and after you've clicked it (the visited link color).

Note: *Depending on how they've set browser preferences, some visitors may not see the link colors that you've set.*

9 When you've finished testing the links, exit or quit your browser, and return to GoLive.

Creating an action

You can add actions to links to increase their interactivity. For example, you can use actions that open a second window when a link is clicked. Or you can add an action that displays or hides information when the mouse pointer is over a link. As you saw earlier in this lesson, you can also add an e-mail action to a link that lets viewers send comments to an address you set up. For more information on actions, see Lesson 10, "Using Actions and JavaScript."

Now you'll link the Custom Acoustic Guitar text on the Stock page to a page that contains a guitar image. Then you'll add an action to the link that opens the page in a separate window at a preset size.

1 In the stock.html page, select the text "1927 Martin 0-28K" in the first paragraph of the Acoustic Guitar section.

Keep in mind that text used as a link should be short and descriptive. Try to keep the text to no more than five words, so that it captures attention without requiring too much effort. If you inadvertently select too much text for a link, you can unlink the extraneous text using the Remove Link button.

2 Click the Create Link button (🔗) in the toolbar. If you don't click the Create Link button, the actions won't appear in the Actions palette.

3 Choose Window > Rollovers & Actions to open the Actions palette.

4 In the Events field of the Actions pane, select Mouse Click. Then click the Action button (▣) at the bottom of the Actions pane to activate the Action pop-up menu.

5 From the Action pop-up menu, choose Link > Open Window.

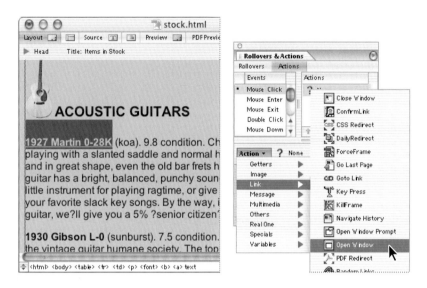

6 Click the Browse button (next to the Link text box in the Actions palette) and locate the martin.html file in the gage/pages/ folder. Click Open.

7 In the Actions palette, for size, enter **170** in the first text box and **325** in the second text box. Deselect Resize, Scroll, Menu, and Dir. You don't want the second window to resize, be scrollable, have a menu, or show a directory toolbar in some browsers.

💡 *Enter _blank in the Target box if you always want to display the linked page in a new untitled window.*

8 Choose File > Save to save the file.

9 Click the Preview in Browser button to view the stock.html file, then click the "1927 Martin 0-28K" text to test the action. Close your browser.

Previewing Open Window action

10 Close any open HTML files.

Using image maps

Image maps are images with hotspots. You can link image maps to other resources and connect the hotspots in the map to other scripted actions such as forms or mailing addresses.

Now you're ready to work on the final page of your site. You'll add an image map to an image of a guitar, and link the hotspots in the map to other pages. You'll start by opening the page in which you'll create the image map.

1 In the site window, click the Files tab and double-click repairs.html in the gage/pages/ folder to open the file.

2 Drag the Image icon from the Basic set (▣) of the Objects palette to the document window, so that the placeholder is centered beneath the Navbar component (at the top of the page). It's unnecessary to resize the placeholder, because it will resize automatically when you insert the image.

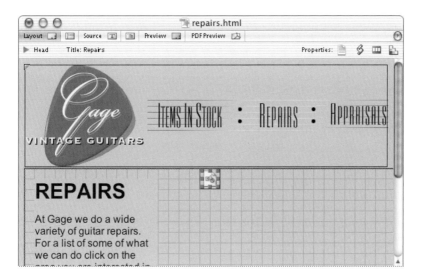

3 Click the Basic tab of the Image Inspector.

4 Link or reference the map.gif image, located in the gage/images/ folder, using either of these techniques:

• Drag from the Pick Whip button (▣) to map.gif located in the gage/images/ folder in the site window.

• Click Browse, navigate to the map.gif file inside the gage/images/ folder, and click Open.

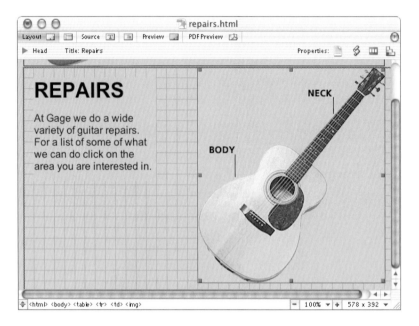

5 If necessary, drag the image to reposition it under the component.

Creating hotspots on an image map

You'll use the Guitar image to show specific repairs that guitars might need. First you'll create hotspots for the types of repairs on the guitar. Then you'll create links from the hotspots to information on repair stores.

1 In the Basic tab of the Image Inspector, type **Repair map** in the Alt Text box. This is the alternative text that appears if a browser can't display the image.

2 Click the More tab of the Image Inspector. Then select the Use Map option. This option lets you add an image map to an image, and activates the map tools on the toolbar.

You use the map tools to create an image map. The map tools include drawing tools for creating the hotspots of an image map.

3 In the Map Name text box, enter a name for the map, with the suffix **.map**. (We named the map guitar.map.)

Selecting Use Map option

4 Click the Create Polygon tool () on the toolbar.

A. Select Region button B. Region creation tools
C. Frame Regions button D. Select Color button

You'll use the Create Polygon tool to define an area that encompasses the neck of the guitar.

5 Click several times in sequence to draw a shape that encloses the guitar neck—this irregular shape will serve as the hotspot. Clicks after the second click define the shape. When you have defined the hotspot, click the Select Region tool ( ) to deselect the Create Polygon tool.

You can move the area you have defined. Click in the area you have defined to select it, and drag to the desired position. You can resize or change the shape of the area by selecting any of the points that define the area and dragging. If you don't like the area you have defined, simply select it, choose Edit > Delete or Clear, and start over.

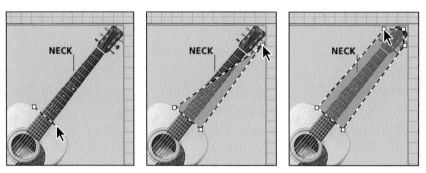

Select the polygon tool and click around the guitar neck to define a shape.

6 Click the Create Circle tool (⊙) on the toolbar. In the document window, drag a circular hot spot over the guitar body that overlaps the first hotspot that you created.

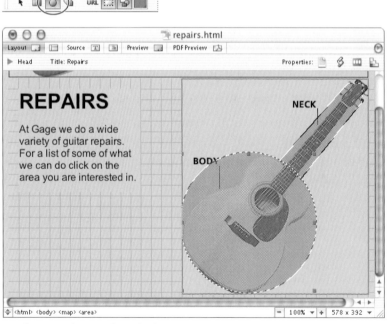

Overlapping polygon and circular hotspots

Editing hotspots

You can edit an image map's hotspots to change their shape, color, or border, as well as reposition hot spots and change how they overlap. Now you'll change the color and positioning.

1 Click the Select Color button (▣) (the eighth button from the left) on the toolbar. In the Color palette, enter a number in the hex value field or, in the Swatch palette, choose a color to change the fill color for the hotspot, and press Enter or Return. We used FF99CC. (Blue is the default.)

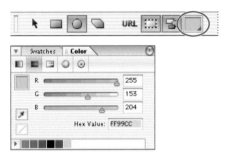

Select Color button and
Selecting color in Color palette

2 Click the Frame Regions button (▦) (the sixth button from the left) on the toolbar to activate the border around the hotspot. Because you added the circle last, the circular hotspot is selected.

When two hotspots overlap, you can change which is on top by selecting one of the hotspots and clicking either the Bring Region to Front or Send Region to Back button (▤).

Instead, you'll reposition the hotspots so that they don't overlap.

3 Click the Select Region tool (▸) (the leftmost button on the toolbar). In the document window, click the polygon hotspot to select it. Handles appear around it.

4 Drag the handles of the polygon hotspot to adjust it so that it no longer overlaps the circular one.

If necessary, you can use the same procedure to move the circular hotspot.

Dragging handles to adjust hotspot

Linking an image map with a Web page

To link an image map with a Web page, you use a technique similar to creating a hypertext link.

1 Select the polygon hotspot.

2 In the Map Area Inspector, link the polygon hotspot to the neck.html file using any of these techniques:

• Drag from the Pick Whip button (⊙) to the neck.html file, located in the gage/pages/repair_pages/ folder in the site window.

• Click Browse, navigate to the neck.html file, in the gage/pages/repair_pages/ folder, and click Open.

- In the URL text box, type the URL **repair_pages/neck.html**, and press Enter or Return. (It's OK to use a relative pathname.)

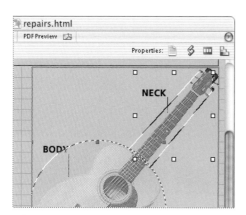

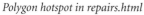

Polygon hotspot in repairs.html

Link to neck.html in Map Area Inspector

3 Repeat steps 1 and 2 to link the circular hotspot to the body.html file in the gage/repair_pages/ folder.

4 Choose File > Save to save the repairs.html file.

5 To test the hotspots, click the Preview tab in the document window, and click each hotspot. When you have finished previewing them, close the neck.html and body.html files.

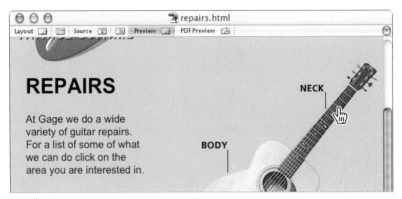

Clicking hotspot

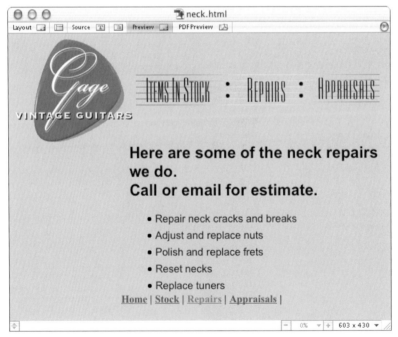

Result

6 Click the Layout tab in the repairs.html document window to return to Layout Editor.

Setting preferences for link warnings

GoLive signals broken links on pages within your site with link warnings. You can control the appearance of link warnings. The default color for broken links is red.

1 Choose Window > Highlight to open the Highlight palette where the link warning color is set. Select the Colors tab.

2 To select a different color for link warnings, click the Link Warning color field to open the Color palette.

3 Select a color.

4 Click the Show Border Only button () to toggle between outlining and highlighting broken links. The default is to highlight broken links.

5 Save and close the repairs.html file.

Finding and fixing broken links

In this final exercise, you'll fix the two broken links in the navbar.html file, the component that is used in the index.html page. By default, broken links appear outlined in red in the document window and in the Inspector URL text box.

1 Double-click the navbar.html file in the Extras tab of the site window.

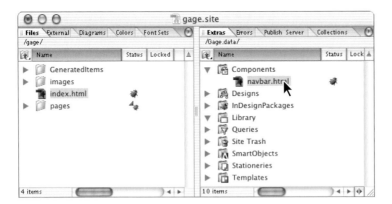

2 Click the Layout tab (⬛) of the navbar.html file to display it in Layout Editor.

3 To activate the display of link warnings, click the Link Warnings button (⬛) on the toolbar, or choose View > Link Warnings.

Images with broken links appear with a border in the color that you set in the previous section for the link warnings.

4 Select the Repairs image in the navbar.html document window.

5 Click the Link tab of the Inspector. Notice that the link appears broken, as indicated by the (empty reference!) text.

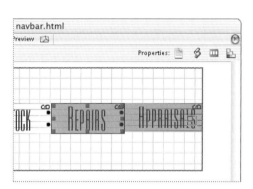

Broken link   *Link tab of Image Inspector*

6 In the Link tab of the Inspector, fix the link by dragging from the Point and Shoot button to the correct file, repairs.html, inside the pages folder in the site window. The Link Warning border will disappear after you deselect the Repairs image.

Repeat steps 4 through 6 to link the Appraisals image to the appraise.html file.

7 Choose File > Save to save the navbar.html file. When prompted to update the file, click OK and OK again.

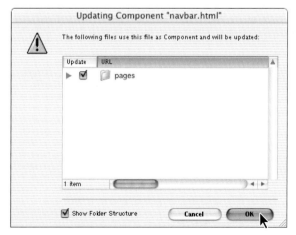

Updating component

8 Close the navbar.html file.

Previewing links

As a final step, you should make sure all your links work as expected by previewing them in your Web browser.

1 Start your browser.

2 From your browser, locate and open your completed index.html file located in Lessons/Lesson06/06Start/gage folder.

3 Click the links in the index.html file, and explore the site.

4 When you have finished viewing the file, close it.

5 Exit or quit your browser.

For additional practice in fixing broken links, see Lesson 13, "Managing Web Sites."

Review questions

1 What is a navigational link?

2 What is an anchor?

3 What is the best location for an anchor?

4 How do you add an action to a link?

5 How do you create a link in a component?

6 What is the difference between relative and absolute pathnames? Why is this difference significant for links?

7 What is an image map? How do you create one?

8 What is the purpose of a link warning?

Review answers

1 A navigational link is a jump from one location in a Web page to another location on the same page (to an anchor), locally within a site, across the Web, or to non-Web resources such as FTP servers, newsgroups, and e-mail addresses.

2 Anchors act as targets for links within the same page. You can create a single link that connects to a single anchor. Or you can create several links that point to a single anchor.

3 It's best to place anchors in the flow of HTML text, inside a layout text box, or inside a table. (You can add a small layout text box to the layout grid to hold the anchor.) You'll get more consistent results if you put the anchor near the left margin of the page. You cannot anchor directly to a graphic because HTML does not yet support this feature; instead, place the anchor near the top left of the graphic.

4 To add an action to a link, you first make a selection and create a link using the New Link button on the toolbar or in the Link tab of the Text Inspector. Then you use the Actions palette to add an action to the link.

5 To add a link to a component, you use the same technique as when adding other links, but you must first open the component file. When a component is updated, all the files that refer to it are also updated to pick up the change.

6 Absolute URLs include the complete pathname of a file, including the site folder name. Relative URLs don't include the full pathname and can refer to a file in a subdirectory from which the file is linked. When you browse for the link destination or enter the URL, you can enter just the relative path (with the site folder name implied). By default, GoLive is aware of the site folder, so you don't need to enter it in the URL.

7 Image maps are images with hotspots. You can link image maps to other resources and connect the hotspots in the map to other scripted actions such as forms or mailing addresses. To create an image map, you insert an image in your document, specify the image as an image map using the More tab in the Image Inspector, and add hotspots using the map tools on the toolbar. You then add links to the hotspots as you would any other links.

8 Link warnings appear as (empty reference!) in the text box in the Link tab of the Inspector (or as bug icons in the site window). Link warnings alert you to files with broken links that require fixing before uploading the files to a Web server.

Lesson 7

7 | Using Smart Objects

You can place non-optimized source files, including Adobe Photoshop, Adobe Illustrator, and Adobe LiveMotion files, directly on your Adobe GoLive Web pages. GoLive converts the files into Web-formatted graphics and uses the original source file to automatically generate a new Web-formatted version whenever you edit the graphic on your page. Smart Object technology revolutionizes the traditional workflow for creating Web graphics, making it more efficient and flexible.

About this lesson

In this lesson, you'll do the following:

• Learn about Smart Object technology and see it in action.

• Learn how to place, resize, and edit a Smart Photoshop object.

• Learn how to place and edit Illustrator files.

• Learn how to place and edit LiveMotion files.

• Learn how to edit a Smart Photoshop object that contains a variable and update your Web page automatically.

Note: To complete this lesson fully, you'll need Photoshop 5.5 or later, Illustrator 9.0 or later, and LiveMotion 1.0 or later installed on your hard disk. With the exception of the LiveMotion section, you can complete the lesson without these applications being installed, but the icons in the palettes and some dialog boxes may be different from those pictured.

This lesson takes approximately 45 minutes to complete.

If needed, copy the Lessons/Lesson07/ folder onto your hard drive. As you work on this lesson, you'll overwrite the start files. If you need to restore the start files, copy them from the *Adobe GoLive CS Classroom in a Book* CD.

Note: Windows users need to unlock the lesson files before using them. For more information, see "Copying the Classroom in a Book files" on page 2.

Getting started

You'll begin this lesson by using your Web browser to view a copy of the finished Web page.

1 Start your Web browser.

2 In your browser, open the *end.html* file in Lessons/Lesson07/07End/farm folder/farm/.

3 Scroll through the page, examining the placement of the images, especially the three at the top of the page. Those are the ones that you'll be placing. Be sure to wait for the animation to play.

4 If you wish, print the finished page to use as a reference as you go through the lesson. (The animation in the center of the page may not print.)

5 When you have finished viewing the page, close your browser.

About Smart Objects

Smart Objects provide an easy way to incorporate native Photoshop, Illustrator, and LiveMotion images, as well as PDF and EPS files, on your Web pages. The general procedures for adding any kind of Smart Object are similar: drag a Smart Object icon from the Smart set of the Objects palette to your Web page, and set the Smart Object's source file. Once placed, you can open any Smart Object in its authoring application by double-clicking the Smart Object on the page.

GoLive can automatically convert a source file from any of these programs to one of the formats supported by current Web browsers, optimize the image, and maintain smart links between the Web-safe copy and the source file for easy editing and automatic updating. Smart Objects provide an easier, better way to enliven your Web pages with graphics.

Note: *The generic Smart Object icon in the Smart set of the Objects palette supports non-Adobe source file graphics, such as .png and .bmp.*

When you use Smart Objects on your pages, resizing a Web image doesn't affect the source image's file size or resolution—so you can have multiple images of various sizes on your page all referring to the same source image. (You can resize images without leaving GoLive.) You can also use variables with the source image so you can change a single aspect of the image (such as text color) for each Web image on the page without actually changing the source image. If you want to modify a source image, you simply double-click the Smart Object and GoLive opens the image in the application it was created in.

In this lesson, you'll be creating a highly graphical home page for a bed and breakfast inn in the countryside. The starting page is partially done for you, but you'll add several graphics, and work on them using Smart Objects technology and GoLive.

🔢 For more complete information on using Smart Objects on your Web Page, see "Adding Images and Media" in the *Adobe GoLive CS Online Help*.

For information on placing images that are already in a Web-safe format, see "Adding an image using the Pick Whip button" on page 158.

Adding images to a Web page using Smart Objects

Smart Objects offer a more efficient and powerful way to add images to Web pages than the traditional work-flow of simply adding a Web-safe image. When you add Photoshop (PSD, BMP, PICT for Mac OS only, PCX, Pixar, Amiga IFF, TIFF, and TARGA), Illustrator (including AI and SVG), or LiveMotion (LIV), PDF or EPS source files to your layout, GoLive automatically places a Smart Object placeholder in the Layout Editor and prompts you to optimize the image in a Web-safe format. GoLive then creates a copy of the source file in a Web-safe format and maintains a link to the source file. The Web-formatted copy is referred to as the target file. The target file (not the source file) is eventually uploaded to the Web server since it is the actual referenced Web asset.

When the target file is generated, the source file remains unaltered and the optimization settings are saved in the target file. Because of this feature, you have the ability to generate multiple copies or variations of the source file throughout your Web site. Generated target files can be optimized as bitmap (for Photoshop, Illustrator, EPS, or PDF), SVG (for Illustrator) or SWF (for Illustrator or LiveMotion).

If you decide later that you don't want the Smart Object functionality for an image, GoLive can convert a Smart Object to a regular object. The Convert to Regular Image/Plug-in/Table command breaks the live con-nection between the target and source files. It also removes all GoLive specific HTML code from the object and removes the settings data from the target file.

–From the Adobe GoLive CS User Guide.

Using Smart Photoshop objects

In this first section of the lesson, you'll place two Smart Photoshop objects, resize one of them, and edit the color table in the other to achieve a special effect—all without leaving GoLive. Photoshop files can be in any of several supported formats: PSD, BMP, PICT (Mac OS only), PCX, Pixar, Amiga IFF, TIFF, and TARGA.

Placing a Smart Photoshop object

The first step involves placing a Smart Photoshop object on the page. The graphic is a Photoshop file that has been sliced in ImageReady.

1 Start GoLive.

2 Open the *farm.site* file in Lessons/Lesson07/07Start/farm folder/.

3 Right-click (Windows) or Control-click (Mac OS) in the site window, and choose New > New Folder from the context menu. Name the folder **images**. You'll be placing all your images here to keep the site window better organized.

💡 *When working with images and media files, be sure to have all files in your site window, including your source files. You can store source files in the folder named "SmartObjects" that is in the Site Data folder by default. Just drag source files into the SmartObjects folder in the Extras tab of the site window. This makes managing image files much easier and prevents broken links (images and media not appearing on your Web page). If you don't see the files in your site window after adding them to a folder (such as the folder named "images"), click the Refresh View button in the toolbar. For more information on managing your image files and folders, see Lesson 13, "Managing Web Sites."*

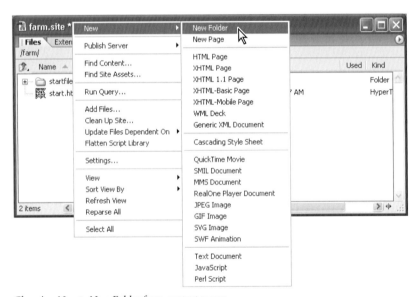

Choosing New > New Folder from context menu

4 Double-click the start.html file in the site window to open the page. Notice that the page consists of a seven-cell table with three images already in the bottom three cells.

5 Choose Window > Objects to open the Objects palette, or click the Objects tab if the palette is collapsed.

6 Click the Smart button (■) at the top of the Objects palette.

7 From the Smart set of the Objects palette, drag a Smart Photoshop object to the top left cell of the table.

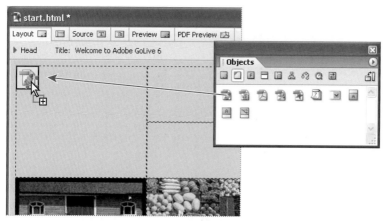

Dragging Smart Photoshop object icon to table cell

8 Choose Window > Inspector to open the Inspector, or click the Inspector tab if the palette is collapsed.

9 In the Basic tab of the Smart Photoshop Image Inspector, for Source, click the Browse button (⬜) and locate cow.psd in Lessons/Lesson07/07Start/farm folder/farm/startfiles/. Click Open.

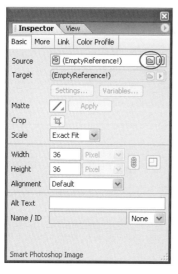
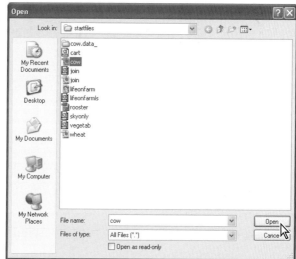

The image opens in the Save for Web dialog box. This image has been sliced in ImageReady (there are four slices: the cow itself, and three sky slices to the left, right, and below the cow). The GoLive Save for Web feature takes care of image optimization, creating a Web-formatted copy that may even include HTML as in the case of a sliced PSD or SVG file. This Web-formatted copy, called a *target file*, is what appears on your live Web page.

10 In the Save for Web dialog box, click the Optimized tab.

11 Select the Slice Select tool (✄), and click the cow slice in the optimized image.

12 Select JPEG High from the Settings pop-up menu. Unnamed is the default value.

13 Click one of the three slices containing the sky, and shift-click the other two sky slices to add them to the selection. They are located on the left, the right, and just below the cow slice.

14 Select GIF 32 No Dither from the Settings pop-up menu.

15 Click Save.

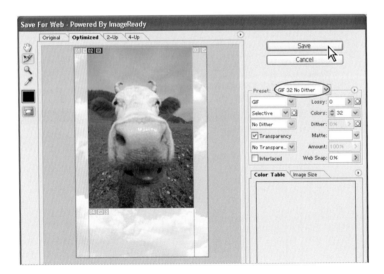

You are prompted to select a location for the cow.data folder that will be created automatically to store all the slices in a Web-safe format.

16 In the Specify Target File dialog box (Windows) or Save dialog box (Mac OS), open the images folder you created, and click Save.

GoLive converts the sliced Photoshop image into several Web-safe images, adding the appropriate extension to each image. In this example, there will be at least three GIF images and one JPEG image. All remain linked to the original Photoshop file. Note that when you import sliced images as you did here, you can set different conversion settings for each slice.

17 Select the image you just added to the page, and in the Alt Text box of the User Slice Inspector, enter **Cow image**.

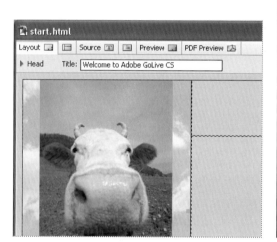

18 Choose File > Save As, and save the start.html document as **working.html** in Lessons/Lesson07/07Start/farm folder/farm/.

Resizing a Smart Photoshop object

Now you'll need to resize the image that you just placed. Resizing GIF or JPEG images themselves often provides less than satisfactory results. Smart Objects technology lets you return to the source image (in this case, a sliced Photoshop file), and create new, resized Web-safe images from the original file. The new file uses the settings that you already applied in the Save for Web dialog box when you first placed the Smart Photoshop object. The original Photoshop file remains unchanged.

Note: Since SWF and SVG formats are vector-based and scalable, their Smart Objects— Smart LiveMotion or Smart Illustrator—are not reoptimized when they are resized.

1 With the image selected, Shift-drag the bottom right handle until the cow image is approximately the same width as the milk wagon image in the cell below.

To select the entire sliced image and not just a slice, move the pointer over the top right corner. When the cursor changes to this ( ), click to select the entire sliced image. If you click when the cursor looks like this ( ), you will select a slice rather than an entire image, and the Settings button will be disabled.

If you resize a Smart Object image and wish to return it to its original size, click the Set to Original Size button ( ) in the Inspector.

2 Choose File > Save to save the document as working.html in Lessons/Lesson07/07Start/farm folder/farm/.

You can also resize an image by going back to the Save for Web dialog box. We want the cow image to have exactly the same width as the wagon image in the cell below it.

3 Select the wagon image and note its width in the Image Inspector. (The width was 204 pixels in our document.)

4 Select the entire cow image (not just a slice), and click Settings in the Smart Photoshop Table Inspector.

Selecting the cow image

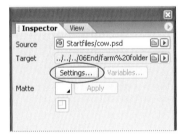

Clicking Settings

5 In the Optimized panel of the Save for Web dialog box, click the Image Size tab. Make sure the Constrain Proportions option is checked, and enter **204** as the width. Note the image size (our image was 204 by 309 pixels). You'll need these dimensions later when you resize the image that you'll place in the top right cell. Click Apply.

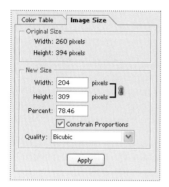

6 Click Save in the Save for Web dialog box.

Note: You can return to the Save for Web dialog box at any time and experiment with different settings.

Editing a Smart Photoshop object

Next you'll add another Smart Photoshop object to the page, and edit the image's color table to achieve a special effect—again, without ever leaving GoLive.

 1 From the Smart set of the Objects palette, drag a Smart Photoshop object icon to the top right cell of the table.

2 In the Basic tab of the Smart Photoshop Image Inspector, for Source, click the Browse button (⬚), and locate wheat.psd in Lessons/Lesson07/07Start/farm folder/farm/startfiles/. Click Open.

This time you'll create a customized set of values in the Optimized panel of the Save for Web dialog box.

3 In the Optimized panel of the Save for Web dialog box, select GIF and No Dither from the two pop-up menus in the Settings section.

4 Change the value of Colors to 20. (The Settings pop-up menu is set to Unnamed because this is not a predefined optimization setting.)

5 In the Color Table tab, double-click the darkest brown color.

Double-clicking the darkest brown color

6 In the Color dialog box (Windows) or Color Picker (Mac OS), choose a color, and click OK. (We used red.) All of the areas of the image with the dark brown color are changed to the new color.

Notice that the color table reminds you of the color change that you have made. Replacing colors using this technique is an easy way to achieve some eye-catching special effects.

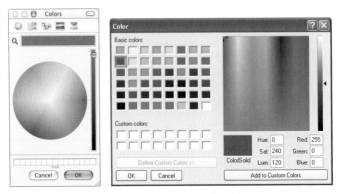

Color Picker dialog   *Color dialog box (Windows)*
box (Mac OS)

7 Click Save in the Save for Web dialog box.

8 In the Specify Target File dialog box (Windows) or the Save dialog box (Mac OS), select the images folder you created, and click Save to save the converted image (wheat.gif) in your images folder.

Now you'll make the wheat image the same size as the cow image (our cow image was 204 by 309 pixels).

9 Select the wheat.gif Smart Photoshop object in the top right cell of your Web page.

10 In the Basic tab of the Smart Photoshop Image Inspector, enter the Height and Width dimensions that you noted for the cow image earlier. Press Enter or Return.

The cow and wheat images should be the same size now.

11 In the Alt Text box, enter **Wheat image**.

12 Choose File > Save to save your work.

Creating multiple versions of an image using variables

Variables provide an important feature for building a Web site in GoLive. Variables let you create different versions from one Smart Object image by controlling variables established in LiveMotion, Illustrator, or Photoshop. You can specify all the settings within GoLive; you don't have to open the source application to define the variables. For example, you might have an image with text containing the price of an item. If you want to quickly modify the price, there's no need to create separate image files. It's easy just to modify the text variable in the image. Depending on whether the image file is an Illustrator, LiveMotion, or Photoshop file, you can set variables that affect such elements as the text content, image visibility, or object color, style, and texture.

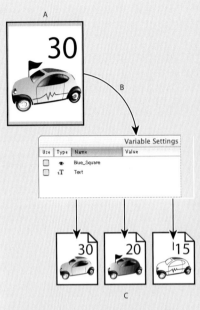

GoLive uses the Smart Objects feature when working with variables. When you add a Smart Object to the page, GoLive detects whether the file has variables. If variables are present, GoLive opens the Variable Settings dialog box. The Variable Settings dialog box offers different settings depending on the type of Smart Object being added to the page (LiveMotion, Illustrator, or Photoshop).

When you have set the variables, click OK. GoLive either uses Save for Web (for Illustrator or Photoshop files) or launches LiveMotion to generate the target file with the modified variable settings. As with all Smart Objects, only the target file is affected by the modified settings; the source file remains unaltered. The power of variables is that you can create more than one target file, each with different images and text created by assigning different variable settings. And since you're working with Smart Objects, if you update or modify the source file, all versions on pages open in a Layout Editor are automatically updated.

Creating different versions of an image using variables
A. Source file with variables
B. User sets the variables and a target file is generated
C. Different versions of an image can be created, each with different variable settings

For information about assigning variables in a file, consult the Adobe LiveMotion 2.0 and Adobe Illustrator CS User Guides. For information about adding a text layer in Photoshop, see the Adobe Photoshop CS User Guide.

Note: GoLive will only recognize variables in an Illustrator file that has been saved in SVG format.

–From the Adobe GoLive CS User Guide.

Using Smart Illustrator objects

You can place Smart Illustrator objects on a Web page just as easily as Photoshop images.

Sources files for Smart Illustrator objects can be in Illustrator AI or Illustrator SVG format. Target files created from an AI source file can be in bitmap (GIF, JPEG, PNG, or WBMP), SVG, SVGZ, and SWF formats. Target files created from an SVG source file can be GIF, JPEG, PNG, and WBMP formats.

Placing a Smart Illustrator object

You'll now add a Smart Illustrator object to the page and resize it.

 1 From the Smart set of the Objects palette, drag a Smart Illustrator object icon to the top middle cell of the table.

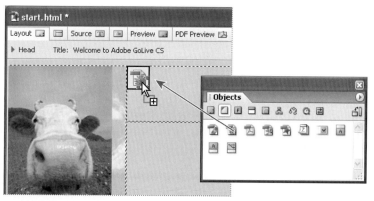

Dragging Smart Illustrator object icon to table cell

2 In the Smart Illustrator Image Inspector, click the Browse button ( ) for Source, and locate lifeonfarm.ai in Lessons/Lesson07/07Start/farm folder/farm/startfiles/. Click Open.

3 If the Conversion Settings dialog box appears, choose Bitmap formats, and click OK.

Note: *The Conversion Settings dialog box appears only with AI files, not with SVG files.*

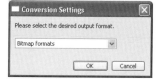

4 In the Optimized panel of the Save for Web dialog box, select the image. Select GIF and No Dither from the two pop-up menus in the Settings section, and reduce the value of Colors to 20.

5 Click Save in the dialog box, and save the file to your images folder.

Resizing a Smart Illustrator object

Now you'll resize the image that you just placed.

1 Resize the placed Illustrator file to the same size (232 by 174 pixels) as the Vegetables image in the bottom center cell using the Smart Illustrator Image Inspector.

2 In the Smart Illustrator Image Inspector, enter **Life on the Farm** in the Alt Text box.

3 Choose File > Save to save your work.

4 Double-click the Smart Illustrator object on your page. Illustrator starts, and the original lifeonfarm.ai source file appears. If the Convert Color Mode dialog box appears, click OK to accept the default values. Make some changes to the file (for example, change the color of the white rectangle to yellow as we did), and then save the file and close Illustrator.

Note: If the Smart Object's application does not open, choose Edit > Preferences, expand General icon in the left pane, select User Interface, and make sure that the Launch Other Applications to Edit Media Files option is checked.

5 Return to GoLive. When you do, GoLive automatically updates the Smart Illustrator object on your page to reflect the changes you just made to the source file in Illustrator.

Using Smart LiveMotion objects

You can add LiveMotion files to your Web pages in the SWF format. This lets you add lively animated images to your site that remain linked to LiveMotion native source files. Any changes you make in GoLive or in LiveMotion are updated for you when you open the html page in the Layout Editor.

Note: You must have LiveMotion installed on your hard disk to complete this section of the lesson.

Configuring LiveMotion

Prior to using Smart LiveMotion objects in GoLive, you must make the following export settings in LiveMotion itself.

1 Start LiveMotion, if it is not already running.

2 Choose Window > Export. (You need to have a file open to access the Window menu, so open a new file if necessary.)

3 Select SWF in the top pop-up menu of the Export palette.

4 Close LiveMotion.

Placing a Smart LiveMotion object

1 From the Smart set of the Objects palette, drag a Smart LiveMotion object icon to the top middle cell of the table just below the Smart Illustrator object.

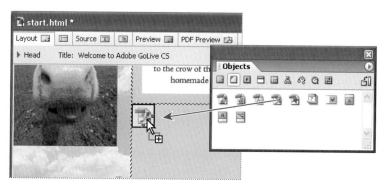

Dragging Smart Live Motion object icon to table cell

2 In the Basic tab of the Smart LiveMotion Image Inspector, click the Browse button (▣), and locate rooster.liv in Lessons/Lesson07/07Start/farm folder/farm/startfiles/. Click Open.

3 LiveMotion opens in the background, and the Updating from Source File progress bar tells you that the file is being converted. You'll also see Generating a SWF File and Generating a Report progress bars. A Save dialog box appears.

4 Save the image to your images folder. Note the .swf extension. This tells you the file is in the SWF format.

5 Preview the working.html page in your browser to see the animation by clicking the Show in Browser button in the upper right corner of the toolbar. The document appears in the Web browser that you specified in the GoLive Preferences dialog box. When you're done, close your browser and return to GoLive.

6 Double-click the Smart LiveMotion object on your page. LiveMotion starts, if it's not open, and the original rooster.liv source file appears. Make some changes to the file (for example, change the color of the black rectangle), and save the file.

Note: If the Smart Object's application does not open, choose Edit > Preferences, expand General preferences icon in the left pane, select User Interface, and make sure the Launch Other Applications to Edit Media Files option displayed in the right pane is enabled.

7 Go back to GoLive. When you do, GoLive automatically updates the Smart LiveMotion object on your page to reflect the changes that you just made to the source file in LiveMotion.

Note: Since Smart LiveMotion objects are always placed as SWF—a vector-based format that scales well—LiveMotion does not have to be open in the background when you resize a Smart LiveMotion object on your Web page.

8 Save your document, and preview it again in your browser.

Editing a variable in a Smart Photoshop image

In this section of the lesson, you'll edit a variable in the Photoshop file that contains the text for the Bed and Breakfast Inn. The text, which begins, "Join us in July ...", was created as a text layer in the Photoshop file. Knowing that this text may need to be updated periodically, it was created as the top text layer in the Photoshop file. Anytime a layered Photoshop file is placed as a Smart Photoshop Image, GoLive automatically treats the topmost text layer as a variable. You'll see how easy it is to edit the variable from the Variable Settings dialog box. You don't even need to open Photoshop.

For information about adding a text layer in Photoshop, see the *Adobe Photoshop CS Online Help*. Select the image in the bottom right of the Web page—the image of sky with the text that begins, "Join us in July ...".

1 In the Smart Photoshop Image Inspector, make sure that the source file is join.psd, and click the Variables button.

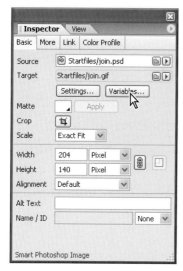
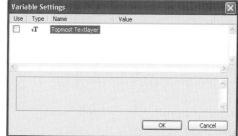

2 In the Variable Settings dialog box, click the Use option in the Use column, and click in the text box to enter new text. To reflect a change in season, we entered, "**Join us in October and enjoy fresh autumn vegetables, dairy products, and fruits straight from the fields, dairy barns, and orchards that encircle the Inn.**"

Note: If you select the Use option for a text variable and don't enter any text, the original text is deleted. GoLive treats the empty text box as the new value of the text variable.

3 Click OK.

GoLive automatically updates the text on your Web page.

4 Choose File > Save to save your document, and then close the file.

Review questions

1 How does an image placed with the Image icon differ from one placed as a Smart Object?

2 How do you place a Smart Object?

3 What happens to the source file when you resize a Smart Object on your page?

4 Which dialog box contains all the settings you can use when you place a Smart Photoshop object?

5 How do you open the source file for a Smart Object within GoLive?

Review answers

1 An image placed on a Web page with the Image icon has to be in a Web-safe format such as GIF, JPEG, or PNG. An image placed as a Smart Object can be in a variety of non-Web-safe bitmapped and vector-based formats created by Photoshop, Illustrator, and LiveMotion. GoLive converts the image to a Web-safe format and retains a live link to the underlying source file. If you change the source file in its native application, your Web page will be updated automatically the next time you open the page in GoLive. If you resize the image on the Web page, GoLive goes back to the source file and creates new Web-safe images for optimal appearance of the resized files without changing the source image.

2 To place a Smart Object of any kind (Photoshop, Illustrator, or LiveMotion), you simply drag the corresponding Smart Object icon from the Smart set of the Objects palette to your Web page. Then you set the source file for the Smart Object in the Inspector. A series of prompts leads you the rest of the way.

3 Nothing! The great thing about Smart Objects is that your source files remain unchanged. GoLive recreates only the Web-safe versions that appear on your Web page, leaving the source files untouched.

4 The GoLive Save for Web dialog box appears whenever you place a Smart Photoshop object. It appears for Smart Illustrator objects, if you choose a bitmapped format in the initial Conversion Settings dialog box. It never appears for Smart LiveMotion objects since they are always in the vector-based SWF format.

5 You can open the source file (in its native application) of any Smart Object by double-clicking the Smart Object on your Web page. If this doesn't work, Choose Edit > Preferences (Win) or GoLive > Preferences (Mac), expand General icon in the left pane, and choose User Interface. Select the Launch Other Applications to Edit Media Files option in the right pane.

8 | Working with Frames

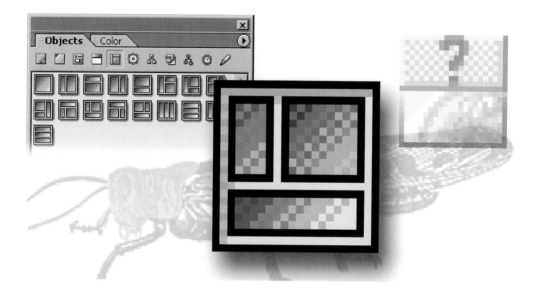

Frames are very useful for controlling the layout and structure of your Web site. They can be used both as a navigation tool and to show more than one type of information at the same time. In this lesson, you'll create a frame set with three frames and add content to the frames.

About this lesson

In this lesson you'll learn how to do the following:

- Create a frame set.

- Change frame set options using the Frame Set Inspector.

- Configure individual frames using the Frame Inspector.

- Add content to frames.

- Create targeted links within the frame set.

- Link the frame set to your home page.

This lesson takes approximately 45 minutes to complete.

If needed, copy the Lessons/Lesson08/ folder onto your hard drive. As you work on this lesson you'll overwrite the start files. If you need to restore the start files, copy them from the *GoLive CS Classroom in a Book* CD.

Note: *Windows users need to unlock the lesson files before using them. For more information, see "Copying the Classroom in a Book files" on page 2.*

About frame sets

A frame set is an HTML page that holds several frames, each of which contains a separate document. Using a frame structure, you can display several HTML documents at once, each in its own pane within the Web browser window. Each pane works independently and can be scrollable or static, depending on its purpose. For example, you can use frames to create an onscreen navigation aid or a table of contents that remains visible in one frame while the viewer scrolls through a page in another frame.

A frame set doesn't contain the individual HTML pages that are displayed—it simply provides them with a structure. If you look at the source code for a page containing a frame set, it just has basic HTML meta-information and a few lines of code defining the frame set—nothing else.

The simplest frame set contains two frames, one for navigation purposes and one to display content. The frame set you will create in this lesson will have three frames: a navigation frame, a main page frame, and a banner image frame.

In general, creating a page layout using frames involves the following steps:

• Creating the pages of content that will be displayed in the frames, and then creating a blank page to use for the frame set.

• Setting up the frame set and naming the frames.

Note: *At least one frame in the frame set must be resizeable.*

• Linking each frame to a content page. If the frame will display multiple pages, link it to the first page you want to appear by default.

• Opening the content page that you plan to use as a navigational aid or table of contents, and specifying the destination pages and target frame for every link on the page.

If you are using a Netscape CSS Fix action, add the action in the head section of the pages that appear within the frames and not in the head section of the frame set.

Structure of a frame set

In this lesson, you'll create a frame set titled frameset.html and then display various content pages in it, as shown in the following illustration.

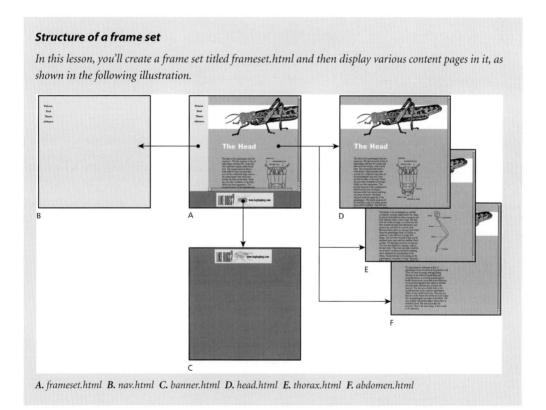

A. frameset.html B. nav.html C. banner.html D. head.html E. thorax.html F. abdomen.html

Getting started

In this lesson, you'll create a frame set for a Web site called bugbody and then add the content to the frames. First you'll view the finished site in your Web browser.

1 Use your browser to open the Web page *index.html* in Lessons/Lesson08/08End/bugbody folder/bugbody/.

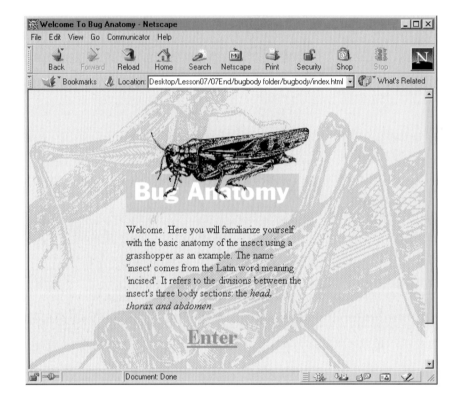

This is the bugbody site's home page. As it is not part of the frame set, it appears as one page across the whole browser.

Note: Frames don't work well with Web search engines because frame sets have no content. For this reason, it's a good idea to not use a frame set for your index (or home) page. Also, you can't set bookmarks in the browser for frame-based Web pages because the URLs map to the frame set rather than the desired pages.

2 Click the text "Enter." This link is to an HTML page called frameset.html.

Although you can see content in this page, frameset.html only contains code for the site's frame set. The content pages are separate HTML pages that open up inside the frame set.

Notice that the page has three frames: the information about the grasshopper's head is the main frame, the list of contents is another frame, and the animated image at the bottom of the page is another.

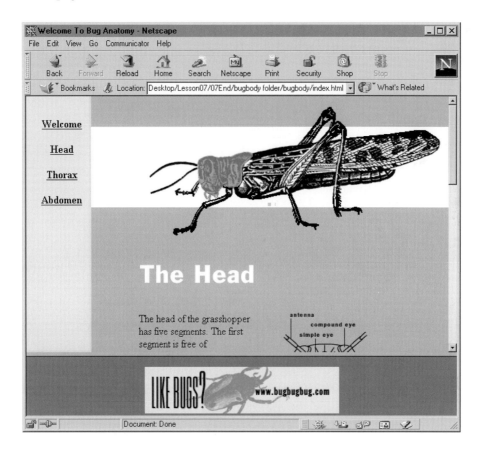

3 Click the links in the list of contents to explore the site.

4 When you have finished viewing the site, exit or quit your browser.

Creating a frame set

When you create a new Web site using frames, you need to set up the page containing your frame set first, and then carefully consider how you want the frames to look. Only then should you start adding and formatting your content pages.

You'll begin this lesson by opening the bugbody Web site and creating a new HTML page containing a frame set.

1 Start Adobe GoLive.

By default, an introductory screen appears prompting you to create a new page, create a new site, or open an existing file.

Note: You can set preferences for the introductory screen to not appear when you start GoLive. If the introductory screen doesn't appear, choose File > Open and go to step 3.

2 Click Open to open an existing file.

3 Open the *bugbody* site file in Lessons/Lesson08/08Start/bugbody folder/.

This site contains a home page (index.html) and several content pages. These pages are not currently set out in frames. You'll create a frame set for the site's content pages.

4 Choose File > New Page to create a new page.

5 Select the page title, "Untitled Page"

6 Type **Bug Parts** as the new title, and press Enter or Return.

Now that you've created a new page, you can add a frame set to it. When you work with frames, you start by selecting a frame set from the Objects palette, and then configuring it in the Frame Editor of the document window.

7 Click the Frame Editor tab (▦) of the document window to display the Frame Editor. It currently says No Frames.

8 Click the Frames button (▤) at the top of the Objects palette.

Frames set of Objects palette

The Frames set contains a variety of frame set templates, with up to three frames in them. Each template shows you how the frames will appear on the page.

Note: *The first icon on the top row, Frame, shows just one frame. You can use this to add another frame to a frame set.*

 9 In the Frames set of the Objects palette, select the icon shown at the left of this step (Frame Set: fixed bottom, variable top right) and drag it from the Frames set to the Frame Editor. A frame set appears in the document window.

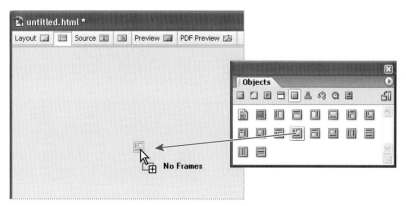

Dragging frame set to Frame Editor

Notice that each frame contains the words "No Name" and the words "Empty Reference!". You'll name each frame and fill it with content later in this lesson. But now is a good time to take a look at the source code for the new frame set.

10 Click the Source tab (▣) of the document window to display the Source Code Editor. The source code for this page consists of the frame tags and some meta-information.

11 Click the Frame Editor tab to return to the Frame Editor.

12 Choose File > Save, and save the page as **frameset.html** in Lessons/Lesson08/08Start/bugbody folder/bugbody/pages/.

💡 *You can copy a frame set to other documents or save a reusable copy of a frame set by dragging the frame set to the Library tab in the site window or the Library set in the Objects palette.*

Making changes to the frame set

You can make several changes to a frame set, such as changing its orientation or borders, by using the Frame Set Inspector.

1 If the Inspector is not already open, choose Window > Inspector to open it, or click the tab if the Inspector is collapsed.

2 Click the internal border above the bottom frame to change the Inspector to the Frame Set Inspector.

You can select any internal border of the frame set to change the Inspector to the Frame Set Inspector. Click inside any frame to change the Inspector to the Frame Inspector.

A. Size B. Orientation C. Border properties

3 Select the Horizontal Orientation option and notice how this changes the appearance of the frames on both sides of the selected border. Then reselect the Vertical Orientation option.

Note: These options do not change the orientation of the entire frame set, but only of the frames adjacent to the selected border.

4 Select the BorderSize option, enter **10** in the text box, and press Enter or Return. Notice how the change applies only to the border that you selected in the Frame Set Inspector.

5 Select the BorderColor option, and click the gray color field to open the Color palette. (If your Color palette is collapsed into a side tab, you may need to click the tab to open the Color palette.)

6 Click the triangle in the right upper corner of the Color palette and select Only Web Colors. Then select a color by either clicking in the color grid of the Swatches palette or by typing a value in the Color palette's Hex Value box and pressing Enter or Return. (We entered 99CC99 in the Value field.) Notice how this changes the color of *all* the internal borders.

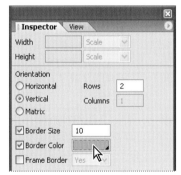

Selecting BorderColor field in Frame Set Inspector

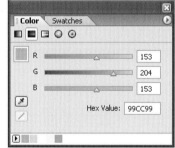

Choosing color in Color palette

7 Select the internal border between the top two frames.

8 Notice in the Inspector that this frame is set to a horizontal orientation. Select the Vertical Orientation option to see how this affects the orientation of the frames and then reselect the Horizontal Orientation option.

9 Select the BorderSize option and enter **0** in the text box. Then select the BorderFrame option, and choose No from the pop-up menu. The border will not appear in a browser, although you can still see a black line in the Frame Editor.

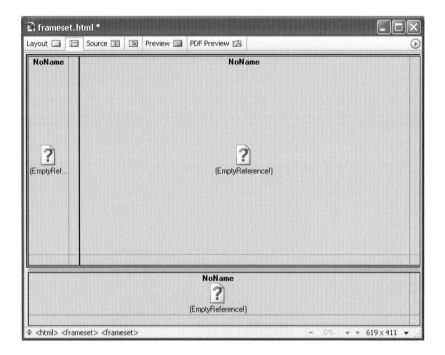

Note: Many Web designers use borderless frames and use the same background color for the content pages displayed in the frame set to give the impression of a frameless Web site.

10 Choose File > Save to save your work.

Setting up the content frames

Now you'll use the Frame Inspector to name the content frames in your frame set, resize them, and specify their scrolling behavior.

1 Click anywhere in the top left frame to select it. This opens the Frame Inspector.

The Frame Inspector lets you specify options for a selected frame. You can resize and name a frame, link it to a content page, and set its scrolling and resizing properties. You can also turn content viewing on or off.

A. Size B. Name C. URL entry
D. Pick Whip button to URL link
E. Scrolling F. Resize Frame G. Browse button

2 In the Name text box of the Frame Inspector, enter **navigation** as the name of the frame.

Now you'll set the size of the frame. You can do this in several ways:

• Enter a precise pixel size for each pane.

• Enter a percentage of the browser window for each pane.

• Scale a frame to fit the browser window.

You'll set the size of the navigation frame to a precise pixel size. Because this frame will contain a navigation bar, it should be the same width in all browsers and at all screen resolutions to ensure that the wording for the links can be seen at all times.

3 Make sure that Pixel is chosen in the Width pop-up menu, enter **110** in the text box, and press Enter or Return to resize the frame. Notice that the left-hand frame is now slightly larger than it was.

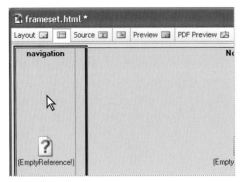

Selecting navigation frame *Specifying pixel size*

4 Leave Resize Frame deselected. This prevents viewers from changing the layout of your frames.

5 Choose No from the Scrolling pop-up menu to make the pane nonscrolling.

A navigation pane is more useful if it's nonscrolling. Rather than force site viewers to scroll through links, you should reduce the pane's content. If your site has too many pages to show on the navigation pane, consider reorganizing the site into areas and using the navigation pane to take a viewer to those areas, rather than straight to individual pages. Each area can have its own contents list, showing its pages.

Now you'll format the main content frame.

6 Select the top right frame. In the Frame Inspector, verify that Scale is selected from the Width pop-up menu.

If a viewer resizes the browser window, the Scale option allows this frame to resize automatically, expanding or contracting to fill all of the browser window to the right of the navigation frame.

Note: *If you specify an absolute size in pixels for one frame, you must set at least one more frame of the same orientation to Scale, or the frame set will scale all frames in that direction.*

7 In the Name text box, enter **main**.

8 Choose Yes from the Scrolling pop-up menu. This will add vertical and horizontal scrollbars to the frame.

Now you'll format the bottom frame.

9 Select the bottom frame, and name it **banner**.

10 Set its Height to 90 pixels. This is slightly larger than the image that will fill this frame, to allow for shifting in different browsers.

11 Choose No from the Scrolling option pop-up menu. Press Enter or Return.

Main and banner frame settings

12 Choose File > Save to save your work.

Adding content to frames

It's time to add content to each of your three frames by linking them to content pages. You'll do this in several ways:

- By using the Browse button (⬛) in the Frame Inspector.
- By using the Pick Whip button (⬛) in the Frame Inspector.
- By dragging a content file directly to a frame.

You're going to use each method as you add content to the three frames.

First you'll browse for a file. This technique is particularly useful if the content file does not reside in the same folder as the rest of your Web site.

1 Select the navigation frame on the left of the page. In the Frame Inspector, click the Browse button (⊠), navigate to nav.html in 08Start/bugbody folder/bugbody/pages/, and click Open. An icon representing the file appears in the frame.

In Mac OS, click the Preview Frame button (▶) in the Frame Inspector. The contents list in nav.html appears in the frame. (You can click the button again to turn off the display, but leave it on for now.) This feature is not available in Windows; however, you can preview using the Preview tab.

Now you'll try another technique for adding a content file. If the file resides in your Web site, you can use the Pick Whip button in the Frame Inspector to add content to a frame.

2 If necessary, drag the document window to a place on your screen where you can see both the main frame of your frame set and the files in your site window.

3 In the site window, open the pages folder.

4 In the document window, select the main frame.

5 In the Frame Inspector, drag from the Pick Whip button (⊚) to the head.html file in the site window to create a link.

The final method for adding content to a frame—by dragging—is perhaps the easiest.

6 If necessary, drag the document window to a place on your screen where you can see both the bottom frame of your frame set and the files in your site window. (You may need to resize frameset.html to do this.)

7 Drag banner.html from your site window to the bottom frame. The banner.html file is now linked to the frame, as indicated in the Inspector.

8 Click the Preview tab (Windows) or the Frame Preview tab (Mac OS) in the document window to display the contents of all three frames.

Note: When you want to add an image as the content of a frame, you must first put the image into an HTML page. A frame will not show a plain image file.

Preview tab (Windows)

Frame Preview tab (Mac OS)

9 Choose File > Save to save your frame set.

When working with frames, keep in mind the following browser limitations:

• *Single-frame pages do not display in Netscape browsers earlier than Netscape 6.*

• *Browsers tend to offset the content of a page from the edge of their main display area and from the inner edges of frames by a few pixels. This behavior can cause sizing problems. To help solve this problem, you can set the margins of the frame set document to zero.*

• *Nesting frame set documents within the frames of other frame sets is possible but can cause serious navigation problems.*

–From the Adobe GoLive CS online Help.

Creating targeted links

Although your frames can be used simply to display these three Web pages, they are much more powerful when used to navigate and view your entire site. You'll enable a viewer to change the content of the main frame by using targeted links from the navigation (contents) pane to other pages.

1 In the site window, double-click the nav.html file to open it.

2 Select the word "Thorax" in the nav.html file.

3 In the Text Inspector, click the Create Link button ( ), and then use the Pick Whip button to create a link to thorax.html in the site window.

This creates a link between the two pages. But which frame will it appear in? You want it to appear in the main frame, so you must select that frame as the target.

4 In the Table Inspector, under the Text tab, type the word main into the Target box.

Now when a visitor clicks on this link in the Contents, thorax.html will replace head.html in the main frame.

5 Choose File > Save to save your work.

6 Click the Preview tab and click the Thorax link to test your link. The thorax.html file should open. Close the thorax.html file when you are finished, and return to the Layout view of the nav.html file.

Creating a return link to the home page

You are going to target the Welcome link on this page to the home page. This will allow viewers to return to the home page at any time, and from anywhere in your site.

1 Select the Welcome link in nav.html.

2 In the site window, make sure that index.html is visible.

3 In the Text Inspector, click the Create Link button, and then use the Pick Whip button to create a link to index.html.

4 This time in the Text tab of the Table Inspector, choose _parent from the Target pop-up menu.

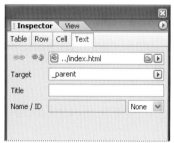

The _parent option specifies the browser window as the target and causes the browser to change the content of the entire window. The browser will replace the frame set with one pane that shows the home page; it will no longer display the navigation bar or banner.

The other two links have already been done for you.

5 Save and close the nav.html file.

6 In the file frameset.html, click the Frame Editor tab to return to the Frame Editor, and make sure the frame set is selected and not one of the frames inside of it. (Select the frame set by clicking any of its horizontal or vertical dividers.) Then click the Preview in Browser button in the upper right corner of the toolbar. The file frameset.html appears in the Web browser that you specified in the GoLive Preferences dialog box.

7 Click each of the links in the Contents pane (select the Welcome link last). The linked pages appear in the main pane.

Note: *Some pages open in separate windows rather than in the frameset. Later in the lesson, in the section "Adding an action to always load the frame set" on page 327, you'll fix this so that all pages open in the required frameset.*

Notice that when you click the Welcome link, the site's home page fills the entire browser window. This shows the effect of setting the link's target to _parent. However, you will also notice that nothing happens when you click Enter. You'll fix this link next.

8 Close your browser.

Linking the frame set to your home page

Now you need to create a link from your home page to the new frame set. This link usually says something like Enter. When a viewer clicks it, the frame set opens, displaying your site's opening content pages.

Note that you don't create a link to a content page. Instead you create a link to frameset.html, which will open showing the three content pages in its frames.

1 In the site window, double-click the index.html file to open it. Make sure that the site window is visible, and that the pages folder is open.

2 In index.html, select the text Enter.

3 In the Text tab of the Table Inspector, click the Create Link button (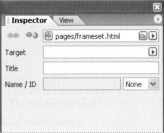), and then use the Pick Whip button to create a link to frameset.html.

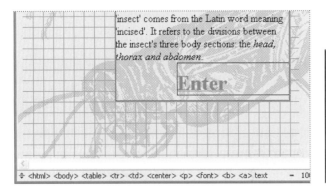

4 Choose File > Save to save both index.html and frameset.html.

You can test the Enter/Welcome link using the Preview in Browser button if you wish. Close your browser when you are finished.

Adding an action to always load the frame set

As the bugbody site is set up now, it's still possible to browse an individual page (such as abdomen.html) without the frame set, so that it fills the entire browser window. This could produce unwanted consequences if the site were actually on the Web. For example, a search engine might locate content in the abdomen.html page and return the URL for that page to a viewer. Clicking on that URL would open abdomen.html in the entire browser window, with no access to the navigation bar or any other page in the site.

To prevent this from happening, you can add a ForceFrame action to the individual content pages in your site. The ForceFrame action identifies the frame set associated with the page and instructs the browser to load the page in the frame set, thus preserving the site structure.

1 In the site window, double-click the abdomen.html file in the pages folder to open it.

2 Click the triangle at the top left of the page to open the head section pane of the document window.

3 Click the Smart Objects button () at the top of the Objects palette.

4 Drag the Head Action icon from the Smart set of the Objects palette to the head section pane.

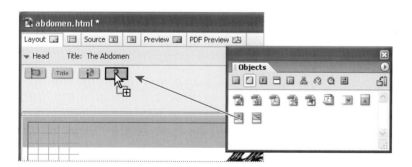

5 In the Head Action Inspector click Show Action Palette. Select OnLoad is from the Events menu. Then click on the Action button. From the Action pop-up menu, choose Link > ForceFrame.

6 Now you need to select the frame set. Either use the Pick Whip button and create a link to frameset.html in the site window, or use the Browse button to select frameset.html.

7 Close the head section pane of the document window.

8 Save and close all open HTML files.

Previewing in a Web browser

Now that you've created a frame set and content frames for your Web site, you can preview the finished site in a browser.

1 In your browser, locate and open the completed index.html file in Lessons/Lesson08/08Start/bugbody folder/bugbody/.

2 Click the Enter link in the index.html file, and explore the site.

3 When you've finished viewing the pages in the site, close your browser.

Review questions

1 Where will you find a set of ready-made frame layouts?

2 How do you set a frame size to a specific number of pixels?

3 How do you add color to a frame border?

4 How do you add a scrollbar to a frame?

5 What are the three ways to fill a frame with content?

6 How can you preview the content in your frame set without launching a browser?

7 Why would you add a ForceFrame action to a Web page?

Review answers

1 You will find a set of ready-made frame layouts in the Frames set of the Objects palette.

2 Select the frame. In the Frame Inspector, choose Pixel from the Width or Height pop-up menu, and enter the number of pixels in the text box.

3 Select the frame border. In the Frame Set Inspector, select the BorderColor option, and then click on the color field to open the Color palette. Use the sliders in the color palette to choose a color, type in a hex value or choose from the recent colors list in the Color palette.

4 Select a frame. In the Frame Inspector, choose Yes from the Scrolling pop-up menu.

5 Select a frame. You can fill it with content:

• By browsing for a file in the Frame Inspector.

• By using the Pick Whip button on the Frame Inspector to link to a file.

• By dragging a file from the site window to the frame.

6 Click the Preview tab (Windows) or Frame Preview tab (Mac OS) of the document window, or double-click on the page icon in a frame to open its content file in another window.

7 You add a ForceFrame action to the head section of a page to make sure that the page is always viewed as part of a frame set, rather than as an individual page filling the browser window.

Lesson 9

9 | Creating Rollovers

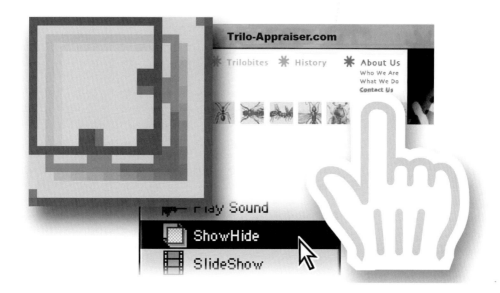

In this lesson, you'll design a navigation bar for the home page of a Web site. First you'll create rollover buttons that change in appearance when your mouse moves over them. Next you'll create a drop-down menu effect, assigning actions to the rollover buttons so that drop-down menus appear when your mouse moves over the buttons.

About this lesson

In this lesson, you'll learn how to do the following:

- Add Layers to a page, so that you can overlap objects.

- Create rollover buttons inside layers on a page.

- Add images inside layers on a page.

- Add actions to rollover buttons for showing and hiding layers.

- Add actions to a rollover button to create a drop-down menu effect.

- Link a rollover button to a page on the Web.

- Preview a page in a Web browser.

This lesson takes approximately 45 minutes to complete.

If needed, copy the Lessons/Lesson09/ folder onto your hard drive. As you work on this lesson you'll overwrite the start files. If you need to restore the start files, copy them from the *Adobe GoLive CS Classroom in a Book* CD.

Note: *Windows users need to unlock the lesson files before using them. For more information, see "Copying the Classroom in a Book files" on page 2.*

Getting started

In this lesson, you'll work on the design of the home page of a Web site for a company called Trilo-Appraiser.com, which specializes in selling and appraising trilobites.

You'll work on the design of a navigation bar for the page by adding rollover buttons to the page and then assigning actions to these buttons.

Rollover buttons are buttons that change in appearance when your mouse moves over them or clicks them (referred to as the Over and Down state in Adobe GoLive, respectively). You can assign actions to rollover buttons that are triggered by mouse events. Examples of actions that you can assign to a rollover button are showing and hiding a layer or jumping to another destination. For more complete information on using actions, see Lesson 10, "Using Actions and JavaScript."

First you'll view the finished home page in your Web browser.

1 Start your browser.

2 Open the *index.html* file, the home page for the site, in
Lessons/Lesson09/09End/trilobite folder/trilobite/.

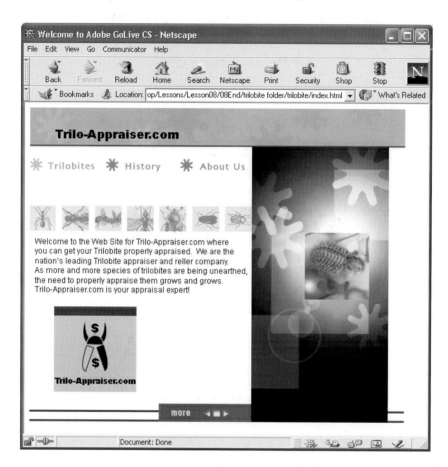

The home page welcomes viewers to Trilo-Appraiser.com and shows a short trilobite GIF
animation as the page is opened. The page contains a number of different rollover effects.

3 Move your mouse over the green, aqua, and orange rollover buttons to see the rollover
animations. Notice how the star changes in appearance if you pause over it. Move your
mouse over the text labeled Trilobites, History, and About Us. Notice that pausing on any
of these rollover buttons causes a drop-down menu to appear. Drag your mouse over the
items in the drop-down menu and notice that each item in the drop-down menu is a
separate rollover whose appearance changes when you move the mouse over it. And lastly
notice the show and hide effects as you move from one drop-down menu to another. In
this lesson, you'll learn how to create all these effects.

In a finished site, these drop-down menu items would be a second level of navigation. Because this site isn't finished—it contains only this home page—only one of these second levels of navigation is active.

4 In the About Us drop-down menu, click Contact Us. For this lesson, we linked the Contact Us button to the Adobe Web site, so that you can see how a button can be linked to another page on the Web.

5 Click the Back button in your browser to return to the home page for the Trilo-Appraiser.com Web site.

6 When you have finished viewing the home page, close it and exit or quit your browser.

Opening the home page

You'll begin this lesson by opening the home page for the Trilo-Appraiser.com Web site in Adobe GoLive. To make this lesson manageable, we have already created two of the navigation bar elements—Trilobites and History—for you, together with their drop-down menus. As you work through this lesson, note the naming convention used for the image files. Using a consistent naming and numbering style makes it easier to manage the large number of images used in a project like this one.

1 Start Adobe GoLive.

By default, an introductory screen appears prompting you to create a new page, create a new site, or open an existing file.

Note: You can set preferences for the introductory screen to not appear when you start GoLive. If the introductory screen doesn't appear, choose File > Open and go to step 3.

2 Click Open to open an existing file.

3 Open the *trilobite* site file in Lessons/Lesson08/08Start/trilobite folder/.

The site window for the Trilobite Web site appears with the Files tab selected.

Now you'll open the home page for the Trilobite Web site.

4 Double-click the index.html file in the Files tab of the site window.

The home page appears with the Layout tab selected. The page contains a single, large image and several layers. One layer contains an animated GIF image. Two additional layers contain rollovers and images—Trilobites and History. Two hidden layers contain drop-down menus that were created in advance for you. These are the rollovers and drop-down menus that you previewed in "Getting started" on page 334.

5 Choose Window > Inspector to display the Inspector, or click the tab if the Inspector is collapsed.

6 Click anywhere on the home page except on the layer that contains the trilobite image. Notice how most of the content of the page is selected. This is because this page consists of one large image on which are placed a number of layers. The Inspector changes to the Image Inspector, confirming that you have selected an image. (As a reminder, the word "Image" appears at the bottom of the Inspector to indicate that it has changed to the Image Inspector.)

7 Now click on the border of the monochrome trilobite image on the right of the page. The layer is selected when the hand points to the left. Notice that the Inspector becomes the Layer Inspector. If you click on the image placeholder inside the layer, the Inspector becomes the Image Inspector.

8 Scroll down to the bottom of the page, where you'll see a stack of yellow layer markers in the left corner.

9 Notice that the first or top marker is selected. Notice that the name in the Layer Inspector is animation. This is the layer that contains the trilobite animation.

10 Select the second layer marker. The name in the Layer Inspector is Button01. This is the layer that contains the green star and the text, Trilobites.

11 Select the fourth layer marker. The name in the Layer Inspector is Navigation01. Note also that the Visible option is deselected.

If possible, enlarge the document window so you can see both the layer icon and the top of the document. You can reduce the size of the document window when you finish this section.

12 If necessary, scroll to the top of the page so you can see the layer containing the Trilobites text. In the Layer Inspector, select the Visible option. A layer that contains the drop-down menu appears.

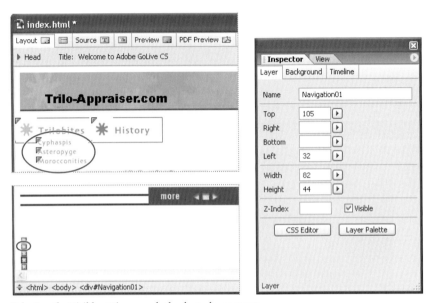

Selecting the Visible option reveals the drop-down menu.

You'll leave this drop-down menu visible as you continue with the lesson. There is a similar hidden layer for the History drop-down menu. You'll leave it hidden.

Adding a layer to hold a rollover button

Now you're ready to finish the navigation bar by adding the About Us portion. When finished, the navigation bar will contain six rollovers at the top level—three stars each with a rollover effect, and three text images that trigger the appearance of a drop-down menu. Each star and text pair is placed inside a layer on the page. Layers are useful because they allow you to overlap objects on a page. Using layers, you can position the rollover buttons on top of the single, large image that makes up the background of this page. *Understand, however, that you don't need to place rollover buttons in layers—you can place rollover buttons directly on a page, on a layout grid, or inside a table cell.*

First you'll add a layer to the page. Then you'll place the rollover button inside the layer.

1 Scroll downward in the document window until you reach the series of yellow markers for the layers that contain the animated trilobite GIF image and the Trilobite- and History-related layers.

Even if you change the position of a layer, its marker remains at the original point of insertion.

2 Click in the blank space to the right of the last layer marker, so that a cursor appears.

3 Choose Window > Objects to display the Objects palette, or click the Objects tab if the palette is collapsed.

 4 Drag a Layer icon from the Basic set (▣) of the Objects palette to the cursor in the document window. You can also double-click the Layer icon to automatically place a marker and a layer at your cursor location.

An empty layer is added to the document window, and the Inspector changes to the Layer Inspector.

5 Scroll downward in the document window, so that you can view the layer that you've added to the page.

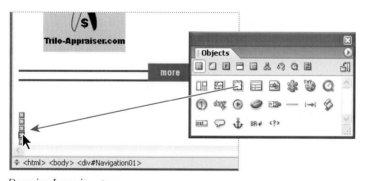
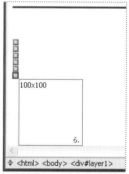

Dragging Layer icon to cursor   *Result*

Now you'll use the Layer Inspector to set attributes for the layer. First you'll name the layer, so that you can differentiate it from other layer that you'll add to the page. Then you'll specify its position on the page and its size.

6 Make sure that the layer is selected. To select a layer, move the pointer over an edge of the layer, so that the pointer turns into a hand pointing left. Then click an edge of the layer to select it.

7 Because the layers for the Trilobites and History elements are named Button01 and Button02, enter **Button03** for Name in the Layer Inspector. Enter **234** for Left, enter **76** for Top, and enter **115** for Width and **38** for Height. Select Pixels from the pop-up menus for Width and Height. Press Enter or Return. Remember these settings are approximate and you may need to manually move the layer.

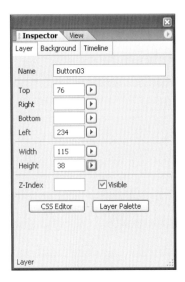

8 Scroll upward in the document window, so that you can see the new position and size of the layer.

This is the layer that will hold your orange star rollover and the rollover, About Us, that you'll associate with the drop-down menu.

9 Choose File > Save.

Note: To display properly, layers require Web browser versions 4.0 or later. To see what a layer would look like in a Web browser that does not support cascading style sheets, turn off CSS support in the browser's preferences.

About naming rollovers

Rollovers require two or three similar images, which appear in the same spot on the page. The first image (named Normal in the Rollovers tab of the Rollovers & Actions palette.) is the normal appearance of the rollover—the way it appears when the mouse pointer is somewhere else on the page in a browser. The second image (named Over in the Rollovers tab of the Rollovers & Actions palette) is a different version of the image (for example, a highlighted appearance), which appears when the user's mouse pointer is on top of the rollover. The third image (named Down in the Rollovers tab of the Rollovers & Actions palette) appears when the user clicks on the rollover.

In GoLive you can add rollovers by adding an image placeholder from the Basic set of the Objects palette and set rollover properties in the in the Rollovers tab of the Rollovers & Actions palette. You can use the Detect Rollover Images feature to automatically assign images to rollovers, which saves time and ensures consistency. (This feature is on by default.)

The Detect Rollover Images feature automatically assigns Over and Down rollover images in one step. You just specify the filename of the normal image (the one that displays when the page is first opened), and GoLive automatically finds the respective over and down state images if you used the appropriate naming convention. For example, if you specify your normal image as *filename*, GoLive automatically looks for and references *filename_over* and *filename_down*. Your rollover image names must also have the proper file extensions, such as .gif, .jpg, or .png, and be in the same folder.

Note: You can view the three sets of naming conventions used by the Detect Rollover Image feature, and you can edit the settings if you have your own naming convention for rollover images.

Creating a rollover button

Now you'll add a placeholder for the rollover button you're going to place in the layer.

1 Click the Basic set button at the top of the Objects palette, and drag the Image icon from the Basic set of the Objects palette to the empty layer in the document window.

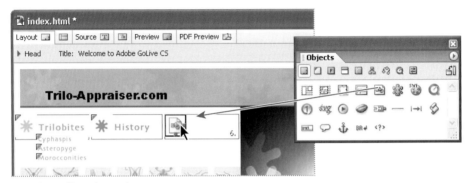

Dragging Rollover icon to layer

Choose Window>Rollovers and Actions to open the Rollovers and Actions palette. The Rollovers tab lets you specify three different images for three different states of a rollover button: how the button appears by default (Normal), how the button appears when your mouse moves over it (Over), and how the button appears when held down (Down). There are 3 others - Click, Up and Down.

First you'll specify an image for how the button appears by default.

2 In the Files tab of the site window, open the images folder and locate the 03_star.gif file.

3 Make sure the Image placeholder is selected in the index.html document.

4 In the Rollovers tab in the Rollovers and Actions palette, make sure that the Normal icon is selected. Then drag the 03_star.gif file in the Files tab of the site window to the selected image holder.

Notice that the Detect Rollover Images feature in GoLive automatically references the Over image, 03_star_over.gif in the Rollovers & Actions palette.

 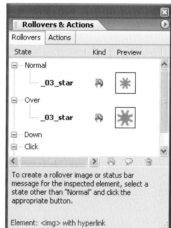

Referencing the Normal image automatically references the Over image if the files are named correctly

The path to the file appears in the text box of the Image Inspector, and the button image appears in the document window.

If you are creating your rollover images in ImageReady 3.0 or earlier, set the HTML output options to Include GoLive Code so your rollovers are fully editable in GoLive.

5 In the Rollover tab of the Rollovers & Actions palette, click the Over icon to select it. Verify that the correct path and file name appear in the text box.

If you were adding a third action, associated with clicking the mouse button, for example, you would name the third source file for the button image *filename*_down.gif, and GoLive would automatically find and link to the correct image for the Down state of the button.

If you change the name or location of any file referenced by a rollover object, GoLive automatically asks you whether to update the links for the rollover. You don't have to keep track of rollover links yourself. You can test this by changing the name (in the site window) of one of the image rollover files you just linked, and pressing Enter or Return. GoLive will ask you if you want to update the necessary files. Click OK, and verify in the Inspector that the rollover image file name has been changed. If you do this, don't forget to change the filename back to the correct file name when you're finished.

6 Choose File > Save to save the index.html file.

Rollover images normally display with the same dimensions as the base image. If any of your rollover images have different dimensions, you can resize them in a graphic editor, or simply change the base image's Width and Height values in GoLive from Pixel to Image in the Image Inspector.

Adding an image to a layer

Now you'll complete the navigational button by adding an image that contains the text "About Us."

 1 From the Basic set (▣) of the Objects palette, drag an image icon into the layer that you added earlier and drop it to the right of the orange star.

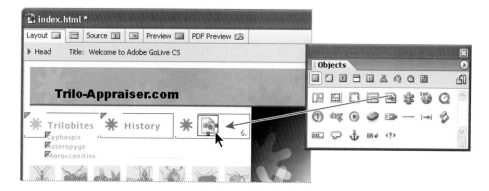

2 Be sure the image placeholder is selected, and in the Basic tab of the Inspector, drag from the Pick Whip button to the 03_about.gif in the image folder in the Files tab of the site window.

3 In the Alt Text text box of the Image Inspector, enter **About Us**. Alternative text is displayed in browsers that are configured not to display images; it is also used by voice-recognition software. In Windows, alternative text also appears in a browser window when a user's pointer hovers over the image.

4 Choose File > Save to save your work.

Creating a drop-down menu

The drop-down menu you'll create in this lesson involves three steps. First you'll create the content of the drop-down menu, then you'll add actions to show and hide the menu, and finally you'll specify that the drop-down menu is hidden when the page loads.

Adding the drop-down menu content

Now you'll add the secondary level of navigation that will become the drop-down menu. You'll add one more layer below the "About Us" rollover, and you'll place three rollover object boxes in it that could be linked to other parts of the Trilobite.com Web site or to another Web site. Later in this lesson, you'll add an action to the "About Us" rollover to show and hide this secondary level of navigation.

First you'll add another layer to the page.

1 Scroll downward in the document window until you reach its end.

2 Click in the blank space to the right of the last layer marker, so that a cursor appears.

 3 Double-click the Layer icon in the Basic set (▪) of the Objects palette to add a layer in the document window.

As you did earlier in the lesson, you'll use the Layer Inspector to name the layer, specify its position, and specify its size.

4 Select the newly added layer (you may need to scroll down the index.html document page to see it).

5 In the Layers Inspector, enter **Navigation03** for Name. (The layers for the drop-down menus associated with Trilobites and History are named Navigation01 and Navigation02.) Enter **267** for Left, enter **105** for Top, enter **82** for Width, and enter **44** for Height. Make sure that Pixels is selected from the pop-up menus for Width and Height. Press Enter or Return.

6 Scroll upward in the document window, so that you can see the new position and size of the Navigation03 layer. Remember, you may have to make some manual adjustment to get the layer where you want it.

Now you'll add three rollover images to this layer.

 7 Drag the Image icon from the Basic set of the Objects palette to the layer you just added in the document window.

The Inspector changes to the Image Inspector. Now you'll link the image placeholder to an image file.

8 With the Image placeholder selected, drag from the top Pick Whip button in the Image Inspector to the 03_who.gif file inside the images folder in the Files tab of the site window. Select Window>Rollovers and Actions to display the Rollovers palette. Notice that the Over Image is automatically linked to the 03_who_over.gif.

The path to the file appears in the Source text box in the Image Inspector and the image appears in the document window.

9 Enter **Who we are** in the Alt Text text box.

Now you'll add two more rollovers to this same layer, using the same method.

10 Drag a second Image icon from the Basic set of the Objects palette to the same layer. The Image placeholder will position itself below the placeholder you just added.

11 With the Image placeholder selected, drag from the top Pick Whip button in the Image Inspector to the 03_what.gif file inside the images folder in the Files tab of the site window. Notice again that the Over Image is automatically linked to the 03_what_over.gif in the Rollovers tab of the Rollovers & Actions palette. In the Image Inspector, enter **What we do** in the Alt Text text box.

12 Drag a third Image icon from the Basic set of the Objects palette to the same layer. Again, the Image placeholder will position itself below the placeholder you just added.

13 With the Image placeholder selected, drag from the top Pick Whip button in the Image Inspector to the 03_contact.gif file inside the images folder in the Files tab of the site window. Notice that the Over Image is automatically linked to the 03_contact_over.gif in the Rollovers tab of the Rollovers and Actions palette. In the Image Inspector enter **Contact us** in the Alt Text text box.

14 Choose File > Save to save your work.

Adding a link to a rollover button

Before you add actions to hide and show the secondary navigation menus, you'll add a link from one of the rollover buttons to the Adobe Web site.

1 Select the placeholder in the index.html document that contains the Contact Us text.

2 In the Link tab of the Image Inspector, enter http://www.adobe.com in the URL text box.

3 Choose File > Save.

For more information on adding links to pages, see Lesson 5, "Creating Navigational Links."

Showing and hiding the drop-down menu

Now your navigation bar is almost complete. In this section of the lesson, you'll add actions to the About Us rollover button to create a drop-down menu effect. You'll specify that the About Us layer (Button03) will be visible when the page is loaded, and you'll add actions to this layer to show and hide the secondary navigation menu so that its associated image appears when you move your mouse over the button and disappears when you move your mouse away from the button.

First you'll add actions to the About Us navigation button. Notice that you add the actions to the About Us image, not to the layer that contains the image.

1 Select the 03_about.gif in the Button03 layer. Be sure to select the image and not the layer. If you have correctly selected the image, the Inspector will be the Image Inspector.

2 In the Image Inspector, click the Link tab, and enter # as a placeholder. The Actions tab of the Rollovers & Actions palette is not available unless you do this.

3 Choose Window > Rollovers and Actions and select the Actions tab.

4 In the Actions tab, under Events, select Mouse Enter to specify an action to occur when the mouse moves on top of the button. Then click the Create new item button (🖳) to add an action to the Actions list box.

💡 *You may want to expand the top half of the Actions palette so that you don't have to use the scroll bar to show the registered actions. Place your cursor on the line dividing the upper and lower portions of the palette, and when the cursor turns into a two headed vertical arrow, drag down.*

5 From the Action pop-up menu, choose Multimedia > ShowHide. From the Layer pop-up menu, choose Navigation03 (remember this is the layer that contains the secondary navigation menu for the About Us rollover). From the Mode pop-up menu, choose Show. This action shows the secondary navigation menu when the mouse enters the About Us rollover image.

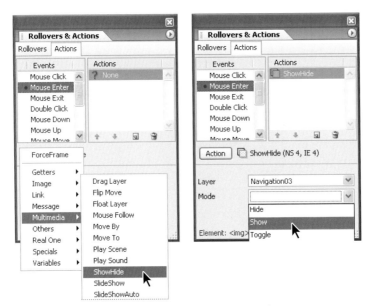

Choosing ShowHide action   *Choosing Show mode*

Now you'll add two more actions to the same image to hide the other two drop-down menus—Trilobites and History.

6 In the Rollovers & Actions palette with the Actions tab selected, under Events, select Mouse Enter to specify an action to occur when the mouse moves over the button. Then click the Create new item button (▣) to add a second action to the Actions list box.

7 From the Action pop-up menu, choose Multimedia > ShowHide. From the Layer pop-up menu, choose Navigation01. From the Mode pop-up menu, choose Hide.

8 Repeat steps 6 and 7, hiding the Navigation02 layer.

Although we added the first two pairs of rollover buttons and drop-down menus for you, you'll have to add a Hide action to each in order to hide the About Us drop-down menu. (The Hide action can't be added until the layer containing the drop-down menu exists.)

9 In the index.html document, select the Trilobites image in the layer Button01.

10 In the Actions tab, click Mouse Enter in the Events column, and click the Create new item button.

11 From the Action pop-up menu, choose Multimedia > ShowHide. From the Layer pop-up menu, choose Navigation03. From the Mode pop-up menu, choose Hide. This action will cause the About Us drop-down menu to disappear when the mouse moves over the text Trilobites.

12 Repeat steps 9 - 11 for the History image in the layer Button02, adding an action to hide Navigation03 again.

13 Choose File > Save.

Hiding the drop-down menu when the page loads

In this final step, you'll hide the secondary levels of navigation—the drop-down menus—when the page loads and until a Mouse Enter event occurs.

1 In the index.html document, select the Navigation03 layer—the layer that holds the Who We Are, What We Do, and Contact Us text.

2 In the Layer Inspector, deselect the Visible option. This makes the layer invisible until the mouse moves over it.

Earlier in this lesson, you made the Navigation01 layer—the layer that holds the Cyphaspis, Asteropyge, and Morocconities text—visible so you could see the format of the drop-down menu that you were creating. You'll hide that layer again.

3 Select the Navigation01 layer. In the Layer Inspector, deselect the Visible option. This makes the layer invisible until the mouse moves over it.

4 Now all three secondary drop-down menus are invisible until the mouse rolls over the text Trilobites, History, or About Us.

5 Choose File > Save to save your work.

Managing layers

You can use the Layers palette to temporarily lock, hide or show a layer as you work. Settings in the Layers palette do not affect the display of the layers in the browser. You can also use the Layers palette to quickly select multiple layers for alignment and grouping.

Note: Some settings in the Layers palette are only temporary and will be overridden when you switch document views or click the Play button in the DHTML Timeline Editor for an animated layer.

Temporary settings help you work with multiple layers regardless of their status in the Layers Inspector.

Previewing in a Web browser

Now that you've finished modifying the home page of the Trilobite.com Web site, you'll preview the page in a browser.

1 Click the Preview in Browser button on the toolbar to preview the page in the Web browser that you selected in the GoLive preferences.

2 When you have finished viewing the home page, close it and exit or quit your browser.

Review questions

1 Can you add a rollover button directly on a page?

2 Name two reasons why you would add a rollover button inside a floating box.

3 What is the purpose of the small marker that appears when you add a floating box to a page?

4 What is the purpose of the Rollovers tab in the Rollovers & Actions palette?

5 Which palette do you use to add an action to a rollover button?

6 Which objects on a page can you show or hide using the ShowHide action?

Review answers

1 Yes, you can add a rollover button directly on a page, on a layout grid, inside a table cell, or inside a floating box.

2 You would add a rollover button inside a floating box if you want the rollover button to overlap another object on the page, such as a large image. You would also add a rollover button inside a floating box if you want to show or hide the button using actions assigned to other buttons on the page.

3 The small marker marks the original position of the floating box on the page. You can select this marker to show its properties in the Floating Box Inspector.

4 You can use the Rollovers tab in the Rollovers & Actions palette to specify three different images for three different states of a rollover button: how the button appears by default, how the button appears when your mouse moves over it, and how the button appears when clicked. You can also use the Rollover Inspector to link a rollover button to a Web page.

5 You use the Actions palette to add an action to a rollover button.

6 You can show or hide layers using the ShowHide action.

10 | Using Actions and JavaScript

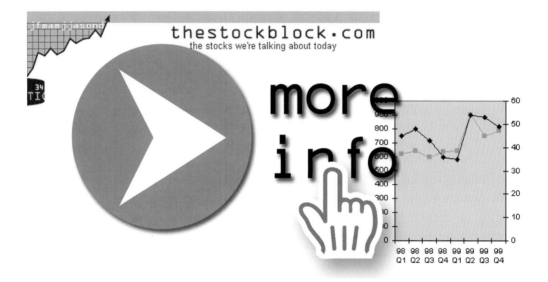

Adobe GoLive lets you attach premade scripts called actions to links, images, and floating boxes. Actions can trigger events such as playing animations, switching a viewer with an older Web browser to a special version of your Web site, and changing the contents of images. You can add your own JavaScript scripts to Adobe GoLive's repertoire for even greater flexibility.

About this lesson

In this lesson, you'll learn how to do the following:

- Create head actions that run automatically when a page is loaded in a Web browser.

- Create a browser switch action.

- Create an action that automatically resizes the browser window.

- Apply actions to layer, images, and links.

- Add JavaScript scripts to page elements.

This lesson takes approximately 45 minutes to complete.

If needed, copy the Lessons/Lesson10/ folder onto your hard drive. As you work on this lesson, you'll overwrite the start files. If you need to restore the start files, copy them from the *Adobe GoLive CS Classroom in a Book* CD.

Note: Windows users need to unlock the lesson files before using them. For more information, see "Copying the Classroom in a Book files" on page 2.

Getting started

You'll begin this lesson by using your Web browser to view a copy of the finished Web page.

1 Start your Web browser.

2 In your browser, open the *index.html* file in Lessons/Lesson10/10End/stockblock folder/stockblock/.

3 Scroll through the page, and experiment with its buttons and interface. Notice the automatic resizing of the window when the page opens, the pop-up ticker box, the appearance of info boxes, live update of stock transactions, and the dynamic browser status bar that notifies you when you buy, sell, or dump stocks.

4 When you have finished viewing the page, close your browser.

Creating head actions

Head actions are special premade scripts inserted into the header of a Web page. Some run automatically just before or after the viewer opens the page in a Web browser. Others are "on call" and run only in response to something the viewer has done—for example, clicking a link or image. You'll insert several head actions into the page for this lesson. The first three actions are among the most common Web designers find necessary to implement in a site.

Creating a browser switch action

Visitors using older Web browsers may not see a Web page correctly if it contains features and technology such as JavaScript, frames, and layer. It's important to provide a way for those viewers to see an alternative page when they view your Web site. You can also use a browser-switch script to direct visitors using Netscape and Internet Explorer browsers to separate pages if your page contains elements that are not supported equally by both browsers.

A browser switch action automatically takes viewers to any page you designate, even if it's only a page saying that your site doesn't support their browser. (Note that the browser-switch script isn't recognized by version 2.0 browsers and Microsoft Internet Explorer 3.01 for Mac OS.)

The page you're building in this lesson uses functions specific to version 4.0 browsers, so adding a browser switch action to the page is a good idea if you think your users are likely to have browsers prior to version 4.

1 Start Adobe GoLive.

By default, an introductory screen appears prompting you to create a new page, create a new site, or open an existing file.

Note: You can set preferences for the introductory screen to not appear when you start GoLive. If the introductory screen doesn't appear, choose File > Open and go to step 3.

2 Click Open to open an existing file.

3 Open the *stockblock* site file in Lessons/Lesson10/10Start/stockblock folder/.

4 Open the index.html file in the Files tab of the site window.

5 Click the triangle next to the page title at the top of the document window to open the head section of the page. Notice that there are several JavaScript objects already in the header. You'll use them later in this lesson to calculate stock transaction information.

Clicking triangle to open head section

6 Choose Window > Objects to open the Objects palette, or click the Objects tab if the palette is collapsed.

7 Click the Smart button () at the top of the Objects palette.

8 From the Smart set of the Objects palette, drag the Browser Switch icon to the head section of the document window.

Dragging Browser Switch icon to head section

9 If the Inspector is not open, double-click the icon that you just placed in the head section of the page to bring up its attributes in the Inspector, or click the tab of the Inspector if the palette is collapsed.

In the Browser Switch Inspector, you can select the browsers that support the features on your page. In this lesson, you'll use the default Auto to have GoLive determine browser compatibility.

The other default attributes are correct and don't need to be changed. If you already had an alternate page designed, you could enter the page's name in the Alternate Link text box. This is the page that viewers with older browsers would see instead of the current page. For this lesson, replace (Empty Reference!) with # so that the site doesn't display a broken link in the site window.

10 In the head section of the document window, drag the Browser Switch icon so that it is as far to the left as possible but follows the encoding information (you'll drop the Browser Switch icon to the right of the Encode icon). You want this browser switch action to run before any others, so that visitors with older browsers will be switched to the alternate page right away before the rest of the page loads.

Dragging Browser Switch icon to left to follow the encoding information

11 Choose File > Save.

Adding a Netscape CSS Fix action

Some versions of Netscape Navigator contain programming that causes Web pages with layers to have trouble displaying properly when viewers resize the browser window (layers are built with cascading style sheets). Now you'll add a head action that prevents this problem. It's a good idea to add this action to any page containing animated layers and to always test your animations or actions in a variety of browsers and versions.

1 From the Smart set (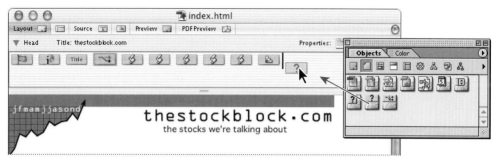) of the Objects palette, drag the Head Action icon to the head section of the document window.

Dragging Head Action icon to head section

You want this action to run when the page is loading, so you'll leave the Exec. pop-up box set to OnLoad in the Head Action Inspector.

2 From the Action pop-up menu in the Head Action Inspector, choose Others > Netscape CSS Fix.

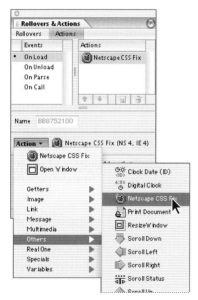

Choosing Others > Netscape CSS Fix from Action pop-up menu

3 Choose File > Save.

Resizing a browser window automatically

Now you'll insert a head action that automatically resizes the browser window to fit the design of your Web page, so that viewers see the page exactly as you intended.

1 From the Smart set ( ) of the Objects palette, drag the Head Action icon to the head section of the document window.

2 In the Head Action Inspector, leave the Exec. pop-up menu set to OnLoad in the Inspector because you want this action to run when the page is loading.

3 From the Action pop-up menu, choose Others > Resize Window.

4 Set both the Width and Height resize value to 550. This ensures that the browser window will be 550 pixels tall and wide—just big enough to display the More Info copy.

5 Choose File > Save.

6 Click the Preview in Browser button in the upper right corner of the toolbar to view the file in the Web browser that you specified in the GoLive Preferences dialog box. Notice how the resize window head action that you just created works.

Note: *The Resize Window action is not always reliable in Netscape browsers.*

7 Close your browser.

Using actions to manipulate layers

In this part of the lesson, you'll start applying actions to elements on the page. You can apply actions to various elements, including layers, images, and links.

You'll be using actions in this section to make the stock ticker already at the top of the page (a layer called Quotes) retractable, so that it won't take up space when it's not needed. You'll do this by creating another layer containing an image that will extend or collapse the ticker when clicked.

1 In GoLive, scroll to the bottom of the index.html page.

2 Create an insertion point to the right of the last of the four yellow layer anchors at the bottom of the page.

 3 In the Basic set ( ) of the Objects palette, double-click the Layer icon to add a layer at the bottom of the index.html page.

You'll set the exact position of the new layer using the Layer Inspector.

4 Select the layer. (Remember, the pointer changes to a left facing hand when you're ready to select a layer.) You may have to scroll down to see it.

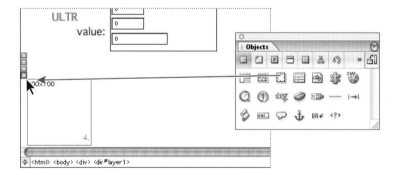

5 In the Layer Inspector, rename the box **QuoteTrigger**, and set the Left value to **451** and the Top value to **94**, and press Enter or Return. The layer jumps to the right of the stock ticker at the top of the page. You may have to scroll up to see it.

 6 From the Basic set of the Objects palette, drag the Image icon into the layer that you just created and renamed.

7 With the Image icon still selected in the layer, use the Browse button in the Image Inspector to set Source to the tab.gif image file located in Lessons/Lesson10/10Start/stockblock folder/stockblock/images/.

8 Select the QuoteTrigger layer. Resize it using the Layer Inspector to set its dimensions to 26 by 40 pixels (the same size as the tab.gif image), and press Enter or Return. This image will be the trigger for the stock ticker's motion.

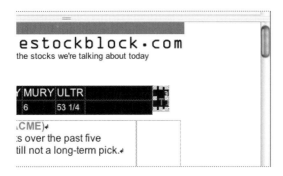

9 Select the tab.gif image. (Click inside the layer to select the image rather than the layer.) In the More tab of the Image Inspector, make sure that the Border option is selected and that Border is set to 0 so that the image does not have a border.

10 Click the Link tab in the Image Inspector, and click the Create Link button (⬚).

11 Enter # in the empty field. Linking an object to # simply links the object to an empty anchor on the current page—in others words, to nowhere. You can only apply actions to an image that is assigned a link. This technique lets you apply an action to an image and remain on the current page. For additional information on creating links, see Lesson 6, "Creating Navigational Links."

12 Choose File > Save to save your work.

Now that you have the layer created and positioned and the image set up to serve as a trigger, you can begin applying actions.

13 Choose Window > Rollovers and Actions to open the Actions palette. Listed on the left are several events. You want the ticker to be displayed when a viewer clicks the image, so select the Mouse Click event and click the Create new item button (⬚). This button is called the Create New Item button or the New Action button, depending on the platform you're working on. For simplicity, in this lesson it is simply called the New button.

Clicking New button

14 Make sure that the new action, None (opposite Mouse Click event), is selected. The Action pop-up menu for None is now enabled. Choose Multimedia > Flip Move from the Action pop-up menu. The Flip Move action toggles a layer between two positions each time the action is triggered.

Choosing Multimedia > Flip Move from Action pop-up menu

15 Choose QuoteTrigger from the Layers palette. Position1 refers to the first position to which you want the layer to jump. In this case, that's the current position of the box, so click the Get button. The values for the current position of the QuoteTrigger box are added.

16 Set the Position2 values to **1** and **94**—almost flush left with the left side of the window. This will place the layer all the way to the edge.

17 Make sure the Animation option is selected, and enter **3** in the Ticks box. This will animate the movement so that the box moves out and in, in a series of three steps, and doesn't simply pop into place.

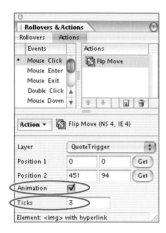

18 In the Actions tab of the Rollovers & Actions palette, click the New button (▣) again to add another action to the Mouse Click event. Again, select the newly added action, and choose Multimedia > Flip Move from the Action pop-up menu.

19 Choose Quotes from the Layers palette, and again click the Get button next to Position1.

20 Set the Position2 values to **-450** and **95**. This positions the Quote layer outside the browser window until it moves in when triggered.

21 Make sure that the Animation option is selected, and set the Ticks value to **3**.

22 Choose File > Save to save your work.

You'll now want to move the Quotes and QuoteTrigger floating boxes to their starting positions.

23 Choose Window > Layers to open the Layers palette. Select the Quotes layer in the Layers palette. In the Layers Inspector, set its Left value to **-450** and make sure that the Top value is **95**.

24 Select QuoteTrigger in the Layers palette. In the Inspector, set its Left value to **1** and make sure that the Top value is **94**.

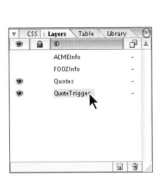

Selecting floating box

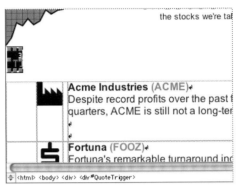

Repositioned floating box

25 Choose File > Save.

26 Click the Preview in Browser button in the upper right corner of the toolbar. The document appears in the Web browser that you specified in the GoLive Preferences dialog box. Notice that when you click on the tab, the bar opens to show stock ticker information, and when you click on the tab again, it closes. When you are finished, close your browser.

Creating actions on call

You've already seen in the first section of this lesson how head actions can be created that automatically load when the viewer first opens the page. In this section, you'll create some more head actions that rely on an OnCall trigger; that is, the action happens only when it is explicitly called in response to a viewer clicking a button or doing something on the page. You'll add an image to existing layer, create some "on call" head actions, and then assign the actions to the image in order to display a More Info box with information on the selected company.

Prepping images for actions

To the right of the main body of the page are two overlapping layers (not currently visible) containing more information on two companies featured on the site. These More Info boxes are designed to appear when the viewer clicks a More Info button next to a company in the main table. You'll take a quick look at these boxes and then add an image to act as a trigger to display a More Info box when clicked.

1 In the Layers palette, click in the eye column opposite ACMEInfo (an eye should appear in the column). The ACMEInfo layer appears in the document window to the right of the main table. You may have to scroll to the right in the document window to see it. Click in the eye column in the Layers palette again to make the box disappear (the eye should disappear).

Notice that an equivalent Info layer is available for Fortuna (FOOZ).

Now you'll create a trigger so that a visitor can see the appropriate More Info box when the trigger is clicked.

2 In the index.html document window, scroll so that the table entry for ACME Industries is visible.

3 From the Basic set (▣) of the Objects palette, drag an Image icon to the right-most cell of the table containing company information, in the row for ACME Industries.

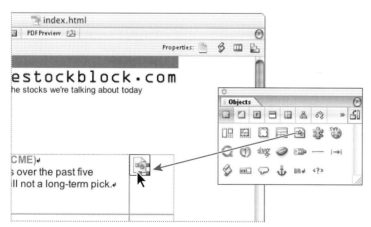

Dragging Image icon to table cell

4 With the Image icon that you just placed selected, set its Source, using the Browse button in the Basic tab of the Image Inspector. Set its Source to the image more.gif located in Lessons/Lesson10/10Start/stockblock folder/stockblock/images/. Be sure you set the link in the Basic tab of the Inspector and not the Link tab.

5 With the more.gif image in index.html selected, in the Basic tab of the Image Inspector, make sure that the Border option is selected and that Border is set to 0 so that the image does not have a border. (Be sure you're working in the Basic tab and not the Link tab for this step.)

6 Click the Link tab in the Image Inspector, and click the Create Link button.

7 Enter # in the empty field, just as you did with the tab.gif file earlier.

8 Choose File > Save to save your work.

Adding "on call" actions to images

Now that the image has been prepped, you can create the "on call" head actions that will make the More Info boxes work properly when the image is clicked. Since you want to display only one More Info box at a time, you'll create a group of head actions that will close all of the boxes in case any are showing when the visitor clicks a More Info button.

 1 From the Smart set ( ) of the Objects palette, drag the Head Action icon to the head section of the document window.

Dragging a Head Action icon to the document window automatically opens the head section of the document.

2 In the Head Action Inspector, choose OnCall from the Event pop-up menu.

3 In the Name field, enter **closeInfo**.

4 From the Action pop-up menu, choose Specials > Action Group. An action group can contain more than one action.

5 Click the New button () to add an action to the group, and select the newly added action (? None).

Clicking New button

6 Choose Multimedia > ShowHide from the lower Action pop-up menu.

7 Set the action's attributes using the Layers pop-up menu so that this ShowHide targets the ACMEInfo layer, and set the mode to Hide using the Mode pop-up menu.

Choosing Hide from Mode pop-up menu

8 Click the New button (⬛) again, and select the new action.

9 Again choose Multimedia > ShowHide from the lower Action pop-up menu, and set the target to the FOOZInfo layer and the mode to Hide, using the Layers and Mode pop-up menus.

10 Close the head section of the page.

11 Choose File > Save to save your work.

Now that you have the necessary "on call" actions defined, you can assign the actions to the More Info image that you inserted earlier.

12 If necessary, select the more.gif image in the document window.

13 In the Actions palette, select the Mouse Click event, and add three new actions by clicking the New button (⬛) three times. Since the actions are not yet defined, each appears with the name None.

Note: *If no events are present in the Actions palette, make sure you entered # in the Link tab of the Inspector.*

14 Select the first action, and choose Others > Scroll Right from the lower Action pop-up menu.

15 Set Scroll Pixels to **300** and Scroll Speed to **50**.

16 Select the next action, and choose Specials > Call Action from the lower Action pop-up menu. This lets you call an action already defined—in this case, closeInfo.

17 Choose closeInfo from the Action pop-up menu.

Choosing closeInfo

So far the assigned actions scroll the window to the right and close any info boxes that might be open. Now it's time to define the final action, so that it opens the correct More Info layer.

18 Select the final action, and choose Multimedia > ShowHide from the Action pop-up menu. Since the image is in the ACME row, set the layer to be ACMEInfo and the mode to Show.

If you don't see the third action you created, scroll down in the palette window or increase the size of the top portion of the Actions palette. Place your cursor over the dividing line between the upper and lower half of the palette. When the cursor turns into a double-headed vertical arrow, drag down to enlarge the Actions area.

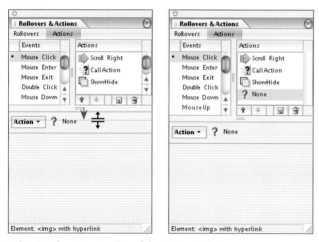

Enlarging the upper portion of the Actions palette

19 Choose File > Save.

Copying graphics with actions attached

Instead of doing all these steps for each company, you can easily duplicate the
More Info button that you just created for ACME for use elsewhere and change
attributes as necessary. Here you'll copy the More Info button and modify it for
the next company listed.

1 Ctrl-drag (Windows) or Option-drag (Mac OS) to drag a copy of the More Info
image to the last cell in the FOOZ row.

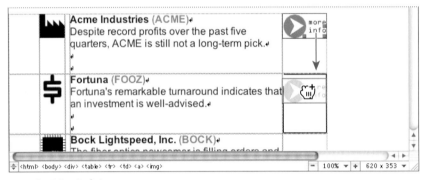

Dragging More Info image

2 Make sure that the copy of the image you just created is selected. In the Actions tab of
the Rollovers & Actions palette, all the actions will remain the same, except the final
ShowHide.

3 Select the ShowHide action.

4 Change the Layers palette that reads ACMEInfo to FOOZInfo. Remember that ACMEInfo and FOOZInfo are the names of the two More Info layer. This will now display the proper information for the row.

Choosing FOOZInfo from pop-up menu

5 Choose File > Save.

6 Click the Preview in Browser button in the upper right of the toolbar. The document appears in the Web browser that you specified in the GoLive Preferences dialog box. At this point in the lesson you can open the More Info box to reveal stock information, but you can't close it. You'll add that action in the next section.

7 Close your browser.

Adding actions to text links

As you saw in your browser, once a More Info box is opened, there is no way to close it. You can fix this by adding mouse events to the "close this" text link already set up in the two More Info layers, ACMEInfo and FOOZInfo. If you look at the text link in the Inspector, you'll notice that it's set as a link to #—the same technique that you used earlier with images so that you could assign actions to them.

1 In the Layers palette, select ACMEInfo in the ID column to show the ACMEInfo layer. Make the layer visible and editable by clicking in the eye column.

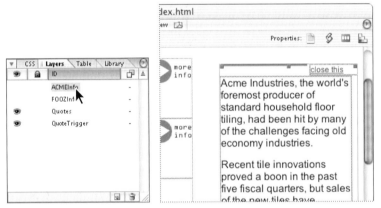

Selecting the layer   *Selected layer*

2 In the document window, drag to select the "close this" text. (Be sure that you have the ACMEInfo ID selected in the Layers palette before you try to select the "close this" text in the document window.)

3 In the Actions tab of the Rollovers & Actions palette, select the Mouse Click event, and add two actions by clicking the New button (🖲) twice.

4 Select the first newly added None action, and choose Others > Scroll Left from the Action pop-up menu, setting Scroll Pixels to **300** and Scroll Speed to **50**.

5 Select the second None action, and choose Multimedia > ShowHide from the Action pop-up menu.

6 Set Mode to be the ACMEInfo layer and Mode to Hide.

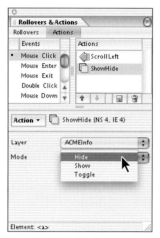

Choosing Hide from Mode pop-up menu

7 Hide the ACMEInfo layer by clicking in the eye column in the Layer palette.

8 Repeat steps 1–7 for the FOOZInfo layer.

9 Choose File > Save.

10 Click the Preview in Browser button in the upper right corner of the toolbar to preview the document in the Web browser that you specified in the GoLive Preferences dialog box. You should now be able to close the stock information box.

11 Close your browser.

Assigning JavaScript scripts to page elements

In this section, you'll see how to assign JavaScript scripts to various page elements. We've already inserted several scripts in the head section of the document. You could also write your own custom scripts and use them in your own projects.

The included JavaScript scripts serve as functions that let viewers increase, decrease, or dump an amount of stock at the Web site, and then show an update in the lower part of the page for the current number of stocks in the visitor's portfolio. You'll first add some buttons that will call these scripts when triggered.

1 Drag the Image icon from the Basic set () of the Objects palette to the row immediately below the text about ACME Industries (to the left of the first return arrow) and add a space by pressing the Spacebar once. If you have difficulty dragging the Image icon, you can place your cursor at the required point in the table and double-click the icon in the Basic set of the Objects palette. The icon will be placed at the location of the cursor.

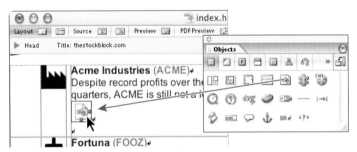

Dragging Image icon to row below text

2 Repeat step 1 twice so that you have three images, each separated from the previous one by a space.

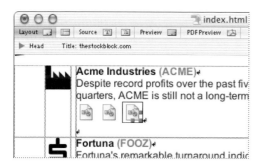

💡 *Create an insertion point on the first empty line below the text. Double-click the Image icon in the Objects palette to add an image placeholder, and then press the spacebar on your keyboard. Repeat this sequence twice to add a total of three image placeholders, each separated by a space.*

3 Using the Browse button (🔲) in the Image Inspector's Basic tab, set the Source of the first image to buy.gif, the second to sell.gif, and the third to dump.gif. All are located in Lessons/Lesson10/10Start/stockblock folder/stockblock/images/. (Be sure you set the links in the Basic tab of the Inspector and not in the Links tab.)

4 Make sure that the Border option is selected for each image and that the Border is set to 0.

5 In the Image Inspector's Link tab, set each image as a link using the Create link button and entering # as the link.

You'll want to let the visitor know that something has changed when a transaction has been made by notifying them in the browser's status bar.

6 Click the triangle next to the page title at the top of the document window to open the head section of the page.

7 Drag a Head Action icon from the Smart set (📦) of the Objects palette into the head section of the document. Make sure that it's selected.

8 In the Inspector, set Event to OnCall, and choose Message > Set Status from the Action pop-up menu.

9 Enter **statusMessage** as the action name in the Name text box.

10 Enter **Your portfolio has been updated. See below.** in the text box.

11 Choose File > Save to save your work.

Now you'll assign actions and scripts to the Mouse Click event for the first graphic.

12 Select the buy.gif image in the document window, select Mouse Click in the Actions palette, and add two actions to this event by clicking the New button (▣) twice.

13 Select the first None action, and choose Specials > Call Function from the Action pop-up menu. The Call Function action lets you access a ready-made JavaScript script.

14 Choose increment—the prewritten JavaScript in the document head pane—from the Function pop-up menu.

15 Enter **0** as the Argument. The Argument in this function simply identifies the company. ACME will be 0, FOOZ will be 1, and so on. Entering 0 tells the action to increment ACME's information.

16 Select the second None action, and choose Specials > Call Action from the Action pop-up menu.

17 Choose statusMessage from the Action pop-up menu.

18 Choose File > Save.

19 Click the Preview in Browser button on the toolbar to preview your page and try out the Buy button. Clicking the buy.gif image adds one of ACME's stocks to your portfolio and notifies you of the transaction in the browser status bar (bottom left of the browser window). You may need to scroll down the page to see this.

20 Repeat steps 12–18 for the sell.gif and dump.gif images, choosing the decrement function for sell.gif and the dump function for dump.gif, and leaving the Argument in each instance as 0, since all relate to ACME.

21 Select, and then copy and paste the three buttons into the appropriate cell for the Fortuna company. Be sure to increment the Argument of each button for each subsequent company by 1, so that all FOOZ buttons are 1, and so on.

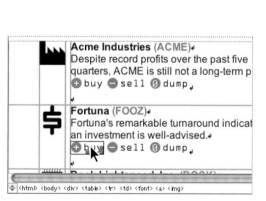

22 Choose File > Save.

23 Click the Preview in Browser button in the upper right corner of the toolbar to preview the document in the Web browser that you specified in the GoLive Preferences dialog box.

24 When you are finished, close your browser and exit or quit GoLive.

Review questions

1 How do you create a head action?

2 Why is including a browser switch action a useful feature for a home page of a Web site?

3 How do you set an image as a link that allows you to assign an action to the image and lets the visitor remain on the current page?

4 How do you assign an action to a link?

5 What is the difference between OnCall and OnLoad actions?

6 How is a JavaScript script different from an action in the Actions palette?

Review answers

1 You create a head action by dragging a Head Action icon from the Smart set of the Objects palette to the head section of a document.

2 Including a browser switch action on the home page of your Web site lets you direct visitors using older browsers to an alternate version of your site. This lets you use the latest Web technologies without worrying whether the site will appear as-designed on older browsers that cannot display frames or cope with JavaScript scripts or floating boxes.

3 You select the image, click the New Link button in the Inspector, and set the link to #. After you have done this, you can assign actions to the image so that it can respond to mouse clicks or other events.

4 You select the desired link and assign actions to it using the Actions palette.

5 An OnCall action runs only when some event, such as a mouse click by a viewer, triggers the action. An OnLoad action automatically runs when a viewer first opens the page in a browser.

6 The actions available in the Action palette are premade actions that come with GoLive. A JavaScript script is a function called by the Call Function action. Writing your own scripts, if you're familiar with JavaScript, provides a way to augment the GoLive built-in actions with your own custom scripting code.

11 | Creating Forms

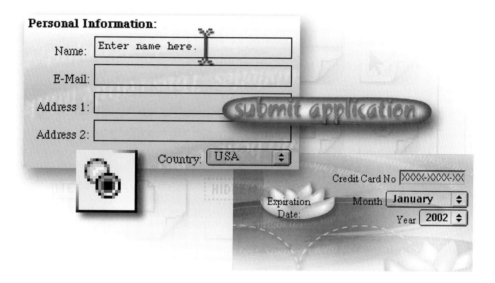

Forms are interactive elements that allow you to collect data from your visitors. They enable visitors to request information or products and to submit personal information, such as their name, address, and credit card number.

About this lesson

In this lesson, you'll learn how to do the following:

• Use a table to place form fields precisely on a page.

• Add a variety of form fields to a table, including text fields and a pop-up menu.

• Store frequently used objects in the Library set of the Objects palette, and add the objects to a page.

• Add radio buttons, a clickable image, and a Reset button to a form.

• Modify a list box in a form.

• Specify the order in which form fields are selected when viewers press the Tab key repeatedly.

This lesson will take about 45 minutes to complete.

If needed, copy the Lessons/Lesson11/ folder onto your hard drive. As you work on this lesson you'll overwrite the start files. If you need to restore the start files, copy them from the *Adobe GoLive CS Classroom in a Book* CD.

Note: Windows users need to unlock the lesson files before using them. For more information, see "Copying the Classroom in a Book files" on page 2.

Getting started

In this lesson, you'll complete the design of a membership application form for a Web site called poetrypond.com. You'll create one section of the form that visitors will use to enter their personal information and then add your section to the partially completed form. You'll also add a variety of form fields to the partially completed form, including radio buttons, a clickable image, and a Reset button.

First you'll view the finished membership application form in your Web browser.

1 Start your browser.

2 From your browser, open the *index.html* file in Lessons/Lesson11/11End/forms folder/forms/. The index.html file is the home page for the poetrypond.com Web site.

3 Click the frog on the page to go to the membership application form. (None of the other links on this page are live.)

The membership application form contains a variety of form elements, such as text fields for entering personal information, a list box for selecting poetry workshops, radio buttons for selecting a payment type, and a clickable image designed for submitting the application over the Web.

4 Try filling out the form by entering your personal information into the text fields and making selections from the list box, pop-up menus, and radio buttons.

Because the form has been designed for this lesson only, you won't actually be able to submit your application over the Web.

5 When you have finished viewing the form, close your browser.

To submit and collect information from a form over the Web, you often use a Common Gateway Interface (CGI) application on a Web server to collect and route the data to a database. The names of the form fields must match those set in the CGI application. Keep in mind that CGI scripts must be built outside of Adobe GoLive and require some knowledge of computer programming. CGI applications are usually set up by a Web server administrator. Your Internet Service Provider (ISP) may also offer CGI scripts for use by customers with hosted sites. Be sure to check with your ISP about the availability of CGI scripts for handling forms.

About designing forms

You design forms on an HTML page by dragging form elements from the Objects palette onto your page and using the Forms Inspector to set options for the elements. Follow these steps to design a form:

- *Plan your form on paper. A clear understanding of the purpose, kind of information you need from your viewers, and how the form will look are very important. Mock up several layouts, test the logic of the flow and the ease of use.*

- *Drag the Form icon onto a GoLive page. The form element tells the browser that the page is a form and specifies the location of the script that processes the viewer's data. The form element contains all the other elements of your design. Add a table to your page to provide the structural foundation of the form. Tables will help you arrange the form fields more easily. Also, placing form fields inside table cells will give you more predictable results across the different browsers and operating systems. You can control the table through the Table Inspector.*

- *Add form elements by dragging them into the table cells. These become the fields your viewers will use to enter and post information. The palettes and the Inspector let you customize the fields and manage the data they collect.*

• *Add a Submit button so your viewers can submit their data to the server.*

• *Create a tabbing chain to help your viewers navigate your form. You can specify the order in which the focus moves from one field to the next.*

• *Preview your form in a browser and test its functionality.*

–From the Adobe GoLive CS online Help.

About forms

The following illustration shows the finished layout of the membership application form in GoLive.

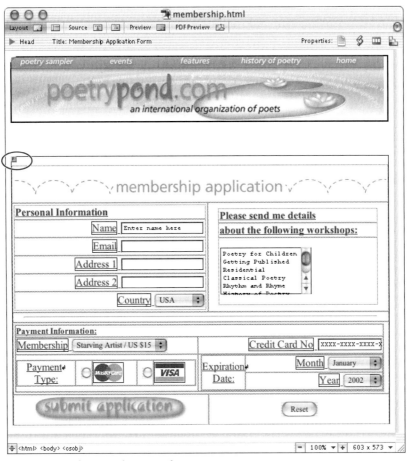

Form icon identifies area of page as a form.

If you want to examine how the form is structured, open the *membership.html* file in GoLive. You'll find the file in Lessons/Lesson11/forms folder/forms.

Notice that the form is laid out within a box enclosing the Form icon (⬛). (The box is added automatically by GoLive.) When you add this icon to a page, you are actually adding a Form element to the HTML source code for the page. The Form element identifies a Web page or section of a Web page as a form and instructs the browser where and how to return form information for processing. The presence of the Form icon is necessary for the form to display and function properly. Make sure that it precedes any form elements.

⬛ For information on how to add a Form icon to a page, see the *Adobe GoLive CS Online Help*.

Notice also that the form is actually laid out using a table with two columns and five rows. Notice also that some of the cells in the table contain nested tables (a nested table is a table contained inside other table). Tables are useful for precisely placing form fields on a page, and you're more likely to get predictable results if you place form elements in HTML tables, rather than on layout grids or directly on a page.

The contents of each row in the main table are as follows:

• The first row of the main table contains the membership application image, which spans both columns.

• The second row contains two cells, each containing a nested table. The nested table in the first cell contains text fields for entering personal information. (This is the part of the table you will create and add.) The nested table in the second cell contains text and a list box for selecting poetry workshops.

• The third row contains a line spanning both columns.

• The fourth row contains a nested table for entering payment information. This nested table actually contains two more nested tables, one for entering a membership type and payment type, and one for entering a credit card number and expiration date.

• The fifth row contains two cells, one with a clickable image designed for submitting the application over the Web and one with a Reset button.

If you opened the file membership.html in GoLive, close the file now.

Creating the Personal Information section of the form

To get you started with the design of the membership application form, we've already partially created the form for you. You'll create the section of the form that visitors will use to enter their personal information. To do this, you'll create a table on a new page, add form elements to the table, save the table as a library item, and then insert the table into the existing form.

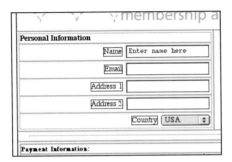

1 Start Adobe GoLive.

By default, an introductory screen appears prompting you to create a new page, create a new site, or open an existing file.

Note: You can set preferences for the introductory screen to not appear when you start GoLive. If the introductory screen doesn't appear, choose File > New Page, and go to step 3.

2 Click New Page to create a new page.

3 Choose File > Save As, rename the page **name_form.html**, and save it in Lessons/Lesson11/11Start/forms folder/forms/.

4 Select the page title, "Untitled page"

5 Type **Personal Information** as the new title.

Making selections within tables

As you design a table and add images and other content to it, selecting cells or nested tables can become difficult. GoLive provides you with a variety of ways to select cells, rows, columns, and nested tables to suit your needs. You can make selections directly in the document window, in the markup tree bar, or in an outline of the table in the Select tab of the Table palette. The Select tab shows a table as a bare outline, and enables you to make cell or nested table selections without the risk of resizing the selection or selecting content inside the cell.

Selected cells are outlined in bold in the document window and in the Table palette, and highlighted in source code views. In the Layout editor or Table palette, a black rectangle in the upper left corner of the selected cells can be dragged to a new location in the table or to create a new table. (Blue lines indicate the selection and sorting region.)

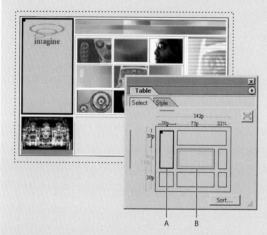

Selecting a table cell with the Select tab of the Table palette
A. Selected table cell B. Nested table

–From the Adobe GoLive CS online Help.

Adding a table for the form layout

Now you'll add a table to the page. You'll use the table to place form fields precisely on the page.

We recommend that you always lay out a form using one or more tables. Although you can place form fields on a layout grid on the page, we don't recommend this technique because the layout of a form created with a layout grid can vary depending on the visitor's browser and screen resolution.

1 Choose Window > Objects to display the Objects palette, or click the Objects tab if the palette is collapsed. Make sure that the Basic button (■) is selected in the Objects palette.

2 Drag a Table icon from the Basic set of the Objects palette to the page.

Important: Because you are creating a table that will be inserted into an existing form, you don't need to start by adding the Form icon from the Forms set of the Objects palette. If you were creating a form from scratch, you would have to add the Form icon to your page first.

3 Choose Window > Inspector to display the Inspector, or click the Inspector tab if the Inspector is collapsed.

4 Select the table in the document window by moving the pointer over the top or left edge of the table until the pointer changes to the table selection pointer (⬐), and then click.

If you place an insertion point in a table cell, select content in a cell, or select a table cell, you can press Ctrl+Enter (Windows) or Control+Return (Mac OS) to navigate outward from a cell to a table, to a parent table cell within a table, or to a nested table.

5 In the Table Inspector, enter **6** for Rows, enter **1** for Columns, make sure that Pixel is selected from the Width pop-up menu, and enter **300** for Width. Press Enter or Return.

You can also set the number of rows and columns in a table as you drag the Table icon from the Basic palette. As you select the Table icon in the Basic palette, press Ctrl (Windows) or Command (Mac OS). A one-cell table appears. Drag vertically or horizontally to increase the number of rows or columns, respectively. When the table is the correct size, release the Ctrl or Command key and drag the icon into the document window.

New table

Setting table properties in Table Inspector

Now you'll add a heading to the first cell of the table. This is the heading of the section of the form that you are creating.

6 In the document window, click in the first table cell to create an insertion point, and type **Personal Information:**.

7 Select the text that you just entered, and choose Type > Structure > Strong to make the text bold.

The Strong attribute is used for strongly emphasizing text. In most browsers, it makes the selected text bold.

8 Choose 2 from the Font Size menu (None ⬍) on the toolbar. By choosing a smaller relative font size, you can prevent the text from wrapping in the table cell when viewed in most browsers.

Remember that text generally appears larger in browsers for Windows. If you are designing your forms in Mac OS, you should keep your text small and leave extra space in your table cells. As a general rule, you should check your forms in browsers for both Windows and Mac OS before uploading them to a Web server.

9 Choose File > Save to save the page.

Adding a name field

Now you'll add a text field to the table so viewers can add their names. When adding a text field, you'll also want to add a label. The label tells viewers what information should be entered into the field.

1 Click the Forms button (▣) at the top of the Objects palette. The Forms set contains a variety of elements that you can add to a form, including the Form element icon itself.

All GoLive form elements fully support HTML 4.0 standards, including labels, tab order, and access keys, and are backward compatible with the HTML 3.2 specification.

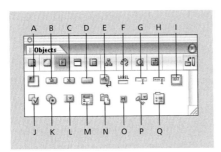

A. *Form* B. *Submit Button* C. *Reset Button*
D. *Button* E. *Form Input Image* F. *Label*
G. *Text Field* H. *Password* I. *Text Area*
J. *Check Box* K. *Radio Button* L. *Popup*
M. *List Box* N. *File Browser* O. *Hidden*
P. *Key Generator* Q. *Fieldset*

 2 Drag a Label icon from the Forms set of the Objects palette to the second cell of the table.

3 Select the word Label. Then type **Name** to change the label text.

💡 *To quickly select the label text, double-click it.*

4 Select the text that you just typed, and choose 2 from the Font Size menu (None ▼) on the toolbar.

Now you'll add the text field for the visitor's name.

5 Click after the label box to insert a cursor. (Be sure to click after the label box, not the label text.) Then press the spacebar to add a space.

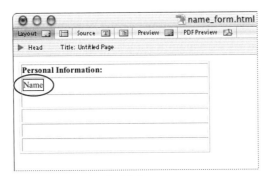

Adding a space after the label

6 Drag a Text Field icon from the Forms set of the Objects palette to the cursor in the document window. Be careful that you don't drag a Text Area icon by mistake.

💡 *If your cursor is positioned correctly in the document window, you can also place the text field by double-clicking the Text Field icon in the Objects palette.*

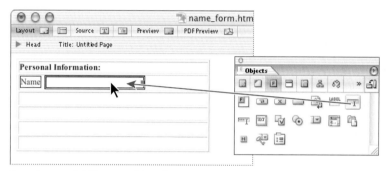

Dragging text field icon to table cell

The Inspector changes to the Form Text Field Inspector.

7 In the Form Text Field Inspector, enter **nameField** for Name. This names the text field.

8 For Value (Windows) or Content (Mac OS), type **Enter name here.**

The text that you just entered also appears in the text field in the document window. When filling out the text field, visitors can replace the text with their own information.

💡 *If you prefer to design your form without the use of labels, you can simply enter information for the text field in the Content (Mac OS) or Value (Windows) text box.*

9 Enter **20** for Visible, and press Enter or Return. This is the number of characters that can be displayed in the field.

10 Enter **40** for Max, and press Enter or Return. This is the maximum number of characters that can be entered into the field. The viewer would have to scroll to read more than the 20 characters initially visible.

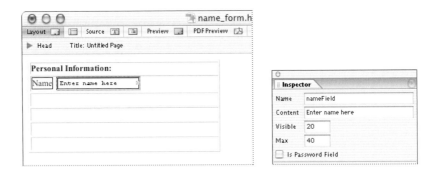

11 Choose File > Save to save your work.

Adding address fields

Now you'll add three text fields to the table that visitors will use to enter their e-mail address and postal information. To save time, you'll begin by copying and pasting the label and text field from the second cell of the table to the third, fourth, and fifth cells.

1 In the document window, select the contents of the second cell in the table. (The second cell contains the Name label and the text field that contains the text "Enter name here.") An easy way to select the contents is to place the insertion point in the cell, and then choose Edit > Select All.

2 Ctrl-drag (Windows) or Option-drag (Mac OS) from the second cell down to the third cell. The contents of the second and third cell should now match.

3 Ctrl-drag or Option-drag from the third cell down to the fourth cell. The contents of the third and fourth cells should now match.

4 Ctrl-drag or Option-drag from the fourth cell down to the fifth cell. The contents of the fourth and fifth cells should now match.

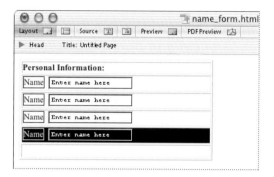

5 Change the label text in the third cell to **E-Mail**, change the label text in the fourth cell to **Address 1**, and change the label text in the fifth cell to **Address 2**.

6 In the third cell (with the "E-Mail" label), select the text field (not the text). In the Form Text Field Inspector, enter **emailField** for Name.

7 Delete the text in the Value (Windows) or Content (Mac OS) text box. Most viewers will understand what to enter in this text field by following the example set by the name text field. Alternatively you could edit the Value (Windows) or Content (Mac OS) text box by replacing the word "name" with "e-mail address." Leave the Visible and Max entries at 20 and 40, respectively.

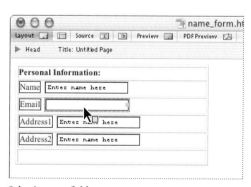

Selecting text field

Specifying its properties

8 Select the text field in the fourth cell with the "Address 1" label. In the Form Text Field Inspector, enter **address1Field** for Name. Delete or change the text in the Value (Windows) or Content (Mac OS) text box. Leave the Visible and Max entries as is.

9 Select the text field in the fifth cell with the "Address 2" label. In the Form Text Field Inspector, enter **address2Field** for Name. Delete or change the text in the Value (Windows) or Content (Mac OS) text box. Leave the Visible and Max entries at 20 and 40.

Notice that every text field has an Is Password Field option in the Form Text Field Inspector. You select this option if you want a viewer to enter a password into the field. For this lesson, you'll leave it blank.

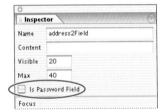

Aligning table cells

Now you'll use the Table Inspector to align the contents of the table cells that contain text fields.

1 Move the pointer over the right or bottom edge of the second table cell until the pointer changes to an arrow (▸). Click to select the cell.

The Inspector changes to the Table Inspector, with the Cell tab automatically selected.

2 Shift-click the third, fourth, and fifth table cells to add them to the selection. (Neither the top nor the bottom row is selected.) All table cells that contain text fields should now be selected.

3 In the Cell tab of the Table Inspector, choose Middle from the Vertical Alignment menu. Choose Right from the Horizontal Alignment menu.

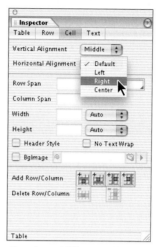

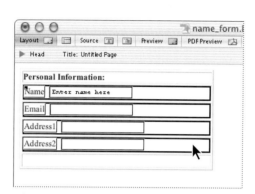

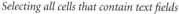

Selecting all cells that contain text fields

Choosing middle vertical and right horizontal alignment

4 Click in the blank space outside the table to deselect its table cells.

5 Choose File > Save to save the page.

Linking labels to text fields

Now you'll link each label to its corresponding text field on the page. By linking a label to a text field, viewers can activate the text field by clicking its label. For example, viewers can click the "Name" label to insert a cursor in the text field for entering their name.

First you'll link the "Name" label to its corresponding text field.

1 Move the pointer to an edge of the "Name" label, so that the pointer turns into this ( ). Then click the label to select it. The Inspector changes to the Form Label Inspector.

2 In the Form Label Inspector, drag from the Pick Whip button ( ) to the text field that corresponds to the "Name" label. The Reference text box in the Form Label Inspector displays a reference to the text field named ID_nameField. The automatically generated number appended in the reference helps GoLive associate the label and field.

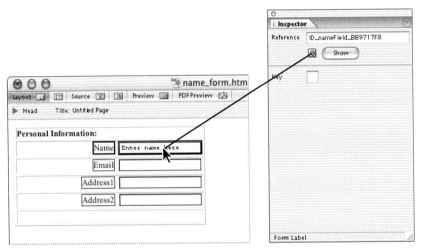

Linking label to text field

3 Select the "E-Mail" label, and link it to its corresponding text field using the Pick Whip button in the Form Label Inspector.

4 Link the "Address 1" and "Address 2" labels to their corresponding text fields.

Note: *If you copy and paste a label that has been linked to a form field, you need to relink the new label to the correct field. Otherwise both labels will refer to the same field.*

5 Choose File > Save to save the page.

Creating a pop-up menu

Pop-up menus provide viewers with multiple options from which they can choose. Now you'll add a pop-up menu that viewers will use to choose the country in which they live.

 1 Drag a Label icon from the Forms set ( ) of the Objects palette to the sixth cell of the table.

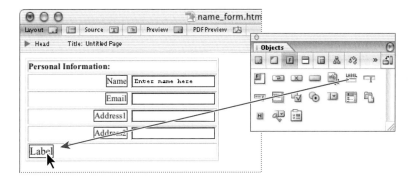

2 Double-click the word Label to select it. Then type **Country** to change the label text.

3 Select the text that you just typed, and choose 2 from the Font Size menu (None) on the toolbar.

4 Click after the label box to insert a cursor. (Be sure to click after the label, not in the label text.) Then press the spacebar to add a space.

 5 Drag a Popup icon from the Forms set of the Objects palette to the cursor in the document window. A placeholder for the pop-up menu appears in the document window.

6 Move the pointer over the right or bottom edge of the sixth table cell until the pointer changes to an arrow. Click to select the cell.

The Inspector changes to the Table Inspector, with the Cell tab automatically selected.

7 In the Table Inspector, choose Middle from the Vertical Alignment menu. Choose Right from the Horizontal Alignment menu.

8 Select the pop-up menu placeholder in the document window. The Inspector changes to the Form Popup Inspector.

9 In the Form Popup Inspector, enter **countryPopup** for Name. This names the pop-up menu.

You'll leave the Rows option set at 1. This means that one row (or item) will be visible in the pop-up menu.

Now you'll use the Form Popup Inspector to add items to the pop-up menu.

10 In the Label and Value columns, click the first row to select it. (The first item is currently labeled "first" with a value of "one.")

11 In the text box at the bottom of the Form Popup Inspector, select the text "first," and enter **Canada** to replace it. Press Tab. In the second text box, enter **Country_Canada** to replace the word "one," and press Enter or Return.

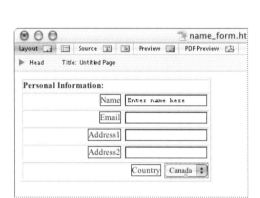 

The label "Canada" will appear as an item in the pop-up menu, and the value "Country_Canada" will be returned to the CGI script for the form when a visitor chooses this item.

12 Select the second item in the list box. (The second item is currently labeled "second" with a value of "two.") Use the text boxes at the bottom of the Form Popup Inspector to enter **France** as its label and **Country_France** as its value.

13 Select the third item in the list box, and enter **Germany** as its label and **Country_Germany** as its value.

Now you'll add a fourth item to the pop-up menu.

14 To create a fourth item, click the Create new item button () at the bottom of the Inspector. Then enter **USA** as the label and **Country_USA** as the value.

By default, the first item that you added to the pop-up menu (Canada) will appear in the browser. However, because most potential viewers for this particular Web site will be from the United States, you'll change the default to display USA.

15 In the Form Popup Inspector, select the country you want to appear by default in the pop-up menu (in this case USA), and click the check box next to the text box that contains the text "USA" at the bottom of the Form Popup Inspector.

Specifying menu item to appear by default

The pop-up menu in the document window now displays the text "USA."

16 Choose File > Save to save the page.

Setting table properties

You have finished adding the form fields to the table. Now you'll remove the border from the table and set other table properties. If you plan on removing the table's border in your forms, we recommend that you not do so until the table is finished. It's easier to select table cells when the border is set at its default value of 1.

1 Move the pointer over the left or top edge of the table, so that the pointer turns into this ( ). Then click to select the table. The Inspector changes to the Table Inspector, with the Table tab automatically selected.

You can use the Inspector to determine whether you have selected the table or a form field.

2 In the Table Inspector, enter **0** for Border, **2** for Cell Pad, **0** for Cell Space, and press Enter or Return.

3 Choose File > Save to save the page.

4 Click the Preview tab to see what your table will look like in a browser. You can open the pop-up menu to view your country choices. Click the Layout tab to return to the Layout Editor when you are finished previewing.

Storing frequently used objects

With GoLive, it's easy to copy and paste objects from one page to another. You can store frequently used objects in Library palette and then quickly add the objects to your pages. (Window>Library)

> ### Collecting and organizing site assets
>
> *Site assets include templates for pages and sites, and custom sets of files, text, objects, colors, fonts, and URLs that you can collect and use on any page in your site. These can be especially useful when several people are building a site. You collect and store site assets in the site window, in you site's data folder and as objects in the Library palette. The Library palette enables you to store application-wide or site-specific assets, and displays previews of site assets in its preview pane.*
>
> *GoLive includes many preset page templates, stationery files, and snippets for common Web design tasks. These presets are organized in the application-wide groups in the Templates, Stationery, and Snippets tabs of the Library palette.*

Now you'll store the table that you've just created in the Library palette, so that you can quickly add it to the membership application form.

1 Display the Library palette. Choose the snippets button. Click the left or top edge of the table in the document window to select it. (The Table Inspector will be active if you have selected the table correctly.)

2 Drag the selected table from the document window to the Library palette under Snippets>Application-wide>Tables. An icon for the table appears in the Library palette with the text "snippet" next to it. (You can rename this by selecting the text and entering a new name.)

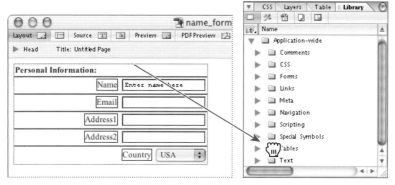

Dragging table to Library set of Objects palette

3 Click the text snippet to select it. Click the test snippet one more time and rename it to **Name and Address** and click OK. This names the table snippet.

You can delete an object from the Library palette by selecting it, and choosing Edit > Clear or pressing Delete.

Now you'll use the Library set of the Objects palette to add the table to the membership application form.

4 Choose File > Close to close the name_form.html file.

5 Choose File > Open, and open the membership.html file in Lessons/Lesson11/11Start/forms folder/forms/.

The membership application form opens.

6 Resize the membership.html window to view as much of the form as possible.

Notice that the form is missing a few images and form fields.

7 Drag the Name and Address table icon from the Snippets tab of the Library palette to the table cell in the form that is directly below the words "Membership Application."

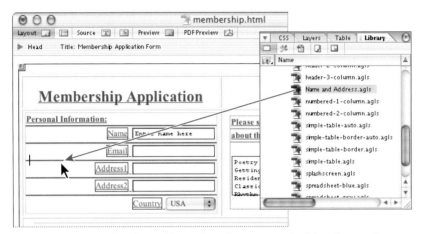

Dragging the name and address table icon from the Snippets tab of the Library palette to the main table in the membership application form

8 Choose File > Save to save the page.

The Personal Information table you created was sized to fit perfectly in the designated cell of the main table for the membership application. If you had not sized the Personal Information table correctly, you could adjust the size of the Personal Information table in the Table Inspector. Before you begin creating a form, however, it's a good idea to carefully plan its layout. You should always decide on the contents of the main table, paying special attention to whether or not you will add nested tables to it. Careful planning will save you from having to redesign your form's layout during the creation process.

Adding an image that spans two columns

Now you'll replace the words "Membership Application" by adding an image to the page. First you'll adjust the table columns so that the words "Membership Application" span two columns.

1 Move your pointer over the bottom edge of the cell that contains the words "Membership Application," so that the pointer changes to an arrow. Then click to select the cell.

The Inspector changes to the Table Inspector, with the Cell tab automatically selected.

2 In the Table Inspector, enter **2** for Column Span, and press Enter or Return.

Now you'll replace the text with an image.

3 Triple-click in the text to select the words "Membership Application," and press Delete.

You'll add the image to the form using a file in the site window.

4 Choose File > Open, and open the forms site file in Lessons/Lesson11/11Start/forms folder/.

The site file contains a media folder, the index.html file, and the membership.html file. It also contains the name_form.html file that you created earlier in this lesson; however, before this file displays in the site window, you need to update the contents of the window. If you had created the new page, name_form.html from the site window, the page would have been visible right away.

5 Choose Site > Refresh View to update the contents of the site window.

6 In the site window, expand the media folder. Then drag form_header.jpg from the media folder in the site window to the empty table cell that previously contained the words "Membership Application." The image is added to the cell.

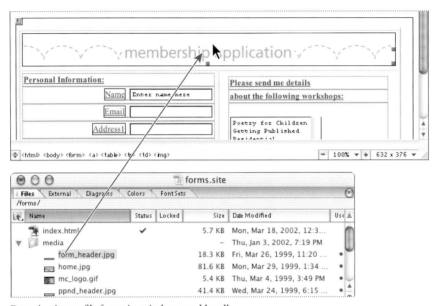

Dragging image file from site window to table cell

7 Click in the document window, and choose File > Save to save the page.

Adding radio buttons

The Payment Information section in the lower right corner of the form already contains a nested table with one row and five columns that has been inserted into the main table. You'll add a group of radio buttons to this section so that viewers can select a payment type.

If you created the Payment Type section from scratch, you would create it much in the same way as the Personal Information section. You would create a table with one row and five columns. Then you would type the text "Payment Type" in the first cell and insert images of a MasterCard and VISA card into the third and fifth cells. You would then add radio buttons to the second and fourth cells, as you are about to do now.

1 Click the Forms button (▣) at the top of the Objects palette. Then drag the Radio Button icon from the Forms set of the Objects palette to the empty table cell located to the left of the MasterCard image in the document window.

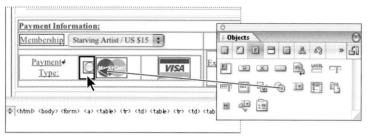

Dragging Radio Button icon from the Forms set of the Objects palette to table cell

The Inspector changes to the Form Radio Button Inspector.

2 Click the radio button that you added to the page to select it.

3 In the Form Radio Button Inspector, enter **paymentType** for Group. This names the group of radio buttons.

You'll use the same group name for the second radio button that you'll add to the page. Using the same group name for the two radio buttons ensures that visitors can only select one option from the group.

4 Enter **mastercard** for Value. This is the value that will be returned to the CGI script for the form when a viewer chooses this option.

5 Check the Selected option. This makes MasterCard the preselected option.

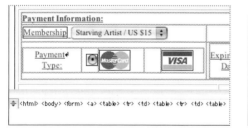 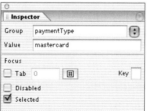

Note: *It's not required that you preselect any of the radio buttons.*

Now you will copy the radio button that you just created, paste it into the empty table cell and then edit the properties of the copied radio button in the Radio Button Inspector.

6 Ctrl-drag (Windows) or Option-drag (Mac OS) the radio button to the empty table cell next to the Visa image.

7 You'll use the same group name for the second radio button in the document window, so leave paymentType selected for Group in the Form Radio Button Inspector. Remember, using the same group name for the two radio buttons ensures that visitors can only select one option from the group.

8 Enter **visa** for Value, and uncheck the Selected option.

9 Choose File > Save to save the page.

Now you'll preview the page to test the form fields that you've added to the page so far.

10 Click the Preview in Browser button in the toolbar. The document appears in the Web browser that you specified in the GoLive Preferences dialog box.

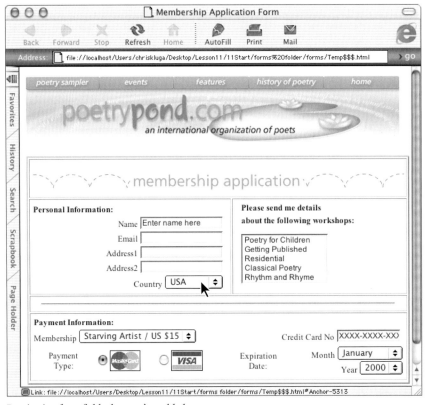

Previewing form fields that you've added to page

11 Test the form fields that you've created by entering your name and address, choosing a country, and selecting a payment type.

12 When you are finished previewing the form, close your browser and return to the membership.html file in the Layout Editor.

Modifying a list box

A list box in the upper right of the form provides viewers with a list of workshops from which they can choose. The list box was created much in the same way as the Country pop-up menu earlier in the lesson. You'll make several changes to the list box. First you'll specify that the list box display six items rather than five.

1 Click in the list box to select it. The Inspector changes to the Form List Box Inspector.

In the Form List Box Inspector, notice how the items for the list box have been entered in the same way as the Country pop-up menu. Each item has a label and value.

2 Enter **6** for Rows, and press Enter or Return. This will increase the number of rows (or items) visible in the list box to six.

You'll add more items in a minute, but first you'll make the list box into a multiselection form field, so that users can select more than one workshop.

3 Select the Multiple Selection option.

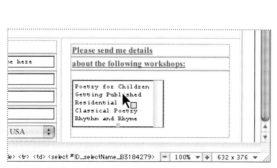

Selecting list box

Setting options in Form List Box Inspector

Now you'll add three more items to the list box.

4 Click the Create New Item button () at the bottom of the Form List Box Inspector to create a new item. In the left text box at the bottom of the Inspector, delete the text "item," enter **History of Poetry**, and press Tab. In the right text box, enter **Workshops_History**, and press Enter or Return.

5 If necessary, scroll down the list box in the Form List Box Inspector to view the item you just added. (You can also increase the size of the Inspector by dragging its lower right corner.)

6 Click the New Item button to create a second new item, and enter **European Poetry** as its label and **Workshops_European** as its value.

7 Click the Create New Item button to create a third new item, and enter **African Poetry** as its label and **Workshops_African** as its value.

8 Choose File > Save to save the page.

Now you'll preview the page in GoLive to verify that the list box works as it should. Notice that only six workshops are displayed in the pop-up menu and that the user must use the scroll bar to access the workshops that you added.

9 Click the Preview tab in the document window. To select more than one item in the list box in the Preview mode, click the first item and then Ctrl-click (Windows) or Command-click (Mac OS) to add additional items to your selection. You can also Shift-click to select a contiguous range of items in the list.

10 Click the Layout tab in the document window to return to the Layout Editor.

Adding a clickable image

Next you'll add a clickable image to the form for submitting the application over the Web. This feature is one of the ways you can enable viewers to submit a form. An alternative way is to add a Submit button, which is discussed in "Adding a Reset button" on page 421.

1 If necessary, scroll down the membership.html window to display the bottom of the form. The main table used to lay out the form has two empty cells in its last row.

2 Click below the MasterCard image to insert a cursor in the empty table cell on the left.

 3 Drag a Form Input Image icon from the Forms palette to the cursor in the document window. A Form Input Image placeholder is added to the table cell, and the Inspector changes to the Form Input Image Inspector.

4 If necessary, rearrange your desktop so that the Form Input Image placeholder is visible in the document window and the submit.jpg file is visible in the media folder in the site window. Then click the Form Input Image placeholder in the document window to reselect it.

5 Drag from the Pick Whip button (⊚) in the Form Input Image Inspector to submit.jpg in the media folder in the site window. The submit application image is added to the table cell.

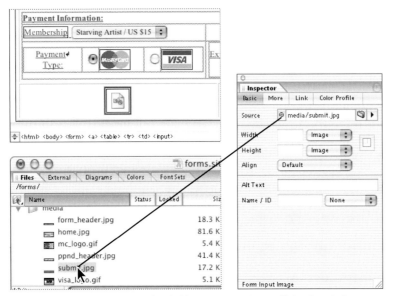

Connecting Form Input Image placeholder on page to image file in site window

6 In the Alt Text box, enter **Submit Image** as an alternative text message for the image.

7 Click the Basic tab of the Form Input Image Inspector. Enter **submitImage** for Name next to the Is Form option. This names the clickable image.

8 Click the More tab of the Form Input Image Inspector. Select the Border option so it's checked and enter a value of **0**, if necessary. This prevents a border from marring the appearance of the image.

9 Choose File > Save to save the page.

Adding a Reset button

You can add buttons to your form in at least two ways. The first method is to create an image of a button and link it to one or more actions. The second method is to use the Submit or Reset button in the Forms set of the Objects palette.

• The Submit button sends a visitor's information to your database and closes the form.

• The Reset button deletes all of the visitor's information and returns the form to its default settings.

Now you'll add a Reset button to the form.

 1 Drag a Reset Button icon from the Forms palette to the empty table cell to the right of the submit application image. The Inspector changes to the Input Button Inspector.

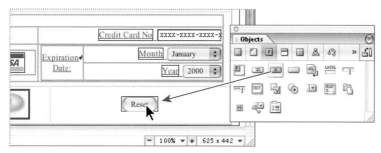

Dragging Reset Button icon from the Forms set of the Objects palette to table cell

The necessary options for the Reset button are preset; however, you can change the button name from Reset by checking the Label option in the Input Button Inspector and entering a new name in the Label text box.

For more information about creating a Normal button, see "Creating buttons and check boxes" in the *Adobe GoLive CS Online Help*.

2 Choose File > Save to save the page.

Changing the main table's border and cell spacing

Now that you have finished adding images and form fields to the form, you can remove the border of the main table and the cell space of its table cells. (Both the border and cell space are currently set at 2, which has made it easier for you to select the table and its cells while modifying the form.)

1 In the document window, click the left or top edge of the main table (above the Membership Application row) to select it. The Inspector changes to the Table Inspector, with the Table tab automatically selected.

2 In the Table Inspector, enter **0** for Border, **0** for Cell Space, and press Enter or Return.

3 Choose File > Save to save the page.

4 Click the Preview tab in the document window, and check how the page appears in Layout Preview.

5 Click the Layout tab in the document window to return to the Layout Editor.

Creating a tabbing chain

Now you'll add a navigational aid to your form—a tabbing chain that allows viewers to use the Tab key to move between form fields. To create a tabbing chain, you specify the order in which the form fields are selected by the Tab key. Adding a tabbing chain should be the last thing that you do to your form, after you are satisfied with its layout.

Note: Some Web browsers will automatically allow users to use the Tab key to move between text fields. Some browsers only allow users to use the Tab key to move between text fields and not other types of form fields. Also, be aware that the tabbing order that you create may or may not be recognized, depending on the browser and which version the visitor is using.

You can start your tabbing chain with any form field. You'll start the tabbing chain for this form with the text field for entering a name.

1 Select the text field in the document window that contains the text "Enter name here." The Inspector changes to the Form Text Field Inspector.

2   In the Form Text Field Inspector, select the Tab option. Enter **1** in the Tab text box. This specifies the text field as the first form field in the tabbing chain.

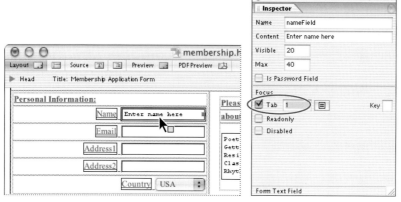

Selecting text field

Specifying text field as first in tabbing chain

3   Click the Start/Stop Indexing button (⊞). Yellow squares appear on each form field that can be part of the tabbing chain. (The yellow squares also appear on the form labels, although you can't add labels to your tabbing chain.)

The yellow square in the text field for entering a name already has a 1 in it, indicating that this field is the first in the tabbing chain.

Clicking Start/Stop Indexing button

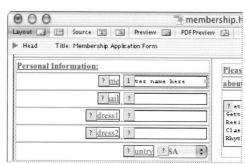

Result

4 Click the text field for entering an e-mail address. A 2 appears in its yellow square.

5 Continue to create the tabbing chain by clicking on the yellow squares for the remaining form fields. (Be sure to click on the yellow squares for the form fields, not the labels.)

Note: If you want to change the order of your tabbing chain, first deselect the Start/Stop Indexing button in the Form Text Field Inspector. Then select the form field for which you want to change the tabbing order number in the document window, and enter the correct tabbing order number in the Tab text box of the Inspector. Select the Start/Stop Indexing button to see the result.

6 When you have finished creating the tabbing chain, click the Start/Stop Indexing button in the Inspector. The tabbing chain has been created, and the yellow squares disappear.

7 Choose File > Save to save the page.

8 Click the Preview in Browser button in the toolbar. The document appears in the Web browser that you specified in the GoLive Preferences dialog box. Place your cursor in the text field for entering a name, and press Tab repeatedly to check that the tabbing chain works as it should.

9 Close your browser.

10 Choose File > Close, and close both the membership.html file and the forms site file.

In this lesson, you've learned how to lay out form fields using a table, and how to add a variety of form fields to a form. Other form fields and functions that you can add to your forms include check boxes, a file browser, a key generator, read-only and disabled form fields, bounding boxes with legends to group form fields, and hidden form fields.

For complete information about creating forms in GoLive, see "Creating Forms" in the *Adobe GoLive CS Online Help*.

Review questions

1 What are form fields?

2 Why do you need to add the Form icon to each form?

3 Why should you avoid creating forms using a layout grid?

4 How can you add a clickable image to a form?

5 How do you add an item to a list box?

6 How do you create a tabbing chain for your form?

Review answers

1 Form fields are elements that you can add to your forms, such as text fields, radio buttons, or list boxes. Viewers can interact with form fields by entering information, clicking items, or selecting items.

2 Dragging the Form icon from the Forms set of the Objects palette creates the container for a form and allows the form to display and function properly in a browser.

3 A form created using a layout grid can vary according to a visitor's browser and screen resolution.

4 To add a clickable image to a form, you can do one of the following:

• Drag a Form Input Image icon from the Forms set of the Objects palette to the form, and use the Point and Shoot button in the Form Input Image Inspector to connect the placeholder to an image file.

• Drag a Form Input Image icon from the Forms set of the Objects palette to the form, and use the Browse button in the Form Input Image Inspector to browse for an image file.

• Drag an image file directly to the Form Input Image placeholder in the form.

You should also make sure that the Is Form option is selected in the More tab of the Form Input Image Inspector.

5 In the Form List Box Inspector, click the Create New Item button to create a new item. Then enter a label and value for the item.

6 To create a tabbing chain, select any form field in your form, and click the Start/Stop Indexing button in the Inspector. Click the yellow squares for the form fields (not the labels) in the order in which you want viewers to be able to select the form fields using the Tab key. Click the Start/Stop Indexing button in the Inspector to turn off the tabbing chain.

12 | Using Cascading Style Sheets

Using style sheets, you can easily update the style of large amounts of text and maintain consistency in typography and formatting throughout a Web site. Good, consistent design makes a site more inviting to visitors and easier to explore

About this lesson

In this lesson, you'll learn how to:

- Identify styles applied to a document.

- Create styles that apply to HTML elements in a document, in blocks of text, or in selected text.

- Update styles and apply style changes globally.

- Duplicate and modify existing styles.

- Change the page color and margins using styles.

- Differentiate between internal and external style sheets.

- Link external style sheets to a document, and use them to update a document's formatting.

This lesson takes approximately 1 hour to complete.

If needed, copy the Lessons/Lesson12/ folder onto your hard drive. As you work on this lesson you'll overwrite the start files. If you need to restore the start files, copy them from the *Adobe GoLive CS Classroom in a Book* CD.

Note: Windows users need to unlock the lesson files before using them. For more information, see "Copying the Classroom in a Book files" on page 2.

Getting started

To see what you'll do in this lesson, first you'll view the final lesson file in your browser.

1 Start your Web browser.

2 From your browser, open the *index.html* file in Lessons/Lesson12/12End/poetrypond.com folder/poetrypond.com/.

3 Scroll through the page, and note its formatting.

4 Click the link "Benjamin Lucas." All the formatting, including the formatting of links, is controlled by a cascading style sheet.

Because this Web site is under construction, not all the links work and you may sometimes need to use the Back button in your browser to retrace your steps.

5 When you have finished viewing the file, close your browser.

About style sheets

HTML is a simple language intended to control the structure of information, not its presentation. Style sheets let Web designers enhance HTML's basic formatting by using styles to position text precisely, control type, and format elements on the page.

Cascading style sheets (CSS for short) are a simple way to add style to HTML documents and enhance the basic formatting of HTML elements. A style sheet is a set of stylistic rules that describe how HTML documents should appear to viewers. In HTML code, a *rule* is a statement about a stylistic aspect of one or more elements, in which a *selector* specifies what elements a *declaration*—consisting of a property and its value—will affect. For example, the style rule h1 { color : red } makes all head level 1s in a document appear red.

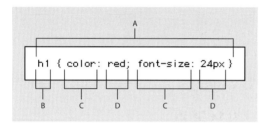

A. Rule B. Selector C. Property D. Value

In the past, designers had to understand these concepts in-depth so they could write cascading style sheet code by hand in HTML. Now GoLive writes this code for you as you apply simple formatting commands much as in familiar word-processing or page layout applications. In addition styles are applied in a cascading fashion, from the most general to the most specific.

GoLive supports Level 1 and 2 Cascading Style Sheets (CSS1, CSS2), which are part of the HTML 4.0 specification. In general, Netscape Navigator 4.0 or later and Internet Explorer 3.0 or later support many of the cascading style sheet properties that can be specified in GoLive. (Microsoft and Netscape browsers differ in which CSS features they support.) Browsers must have CSS1 or CSS2-support to be able to recognize and properly interpret style sheets.

A few considerations are key to using style sheets successfully:

• Be familiar with what style sheet properties are supported by current browsers. The CSS specification is constantly evolving. Refer to http://www.w3.org/Style/.

• Experiment with applying different properties to different HTML elements. It's important always to preview the results in the current browsers to test your style sheet's effectiveness.

Exploring style sheets

GoLive supports two different kinds of style sheets: internal and external. Internal and external style sheets differ in how they work with Web pages. Internal style sheets apply only to the document in which they were created, although their styles can be exported for use with other documents.

Far more flexible than internal style sheets, external style sheets can apply to a group of documents, or to an entire Web site. Rather than defining an internal style sheet for each and every page to which you want to apply some extra formatting, it's easier to create a stand-alone external style sheet document. You can then refer to this external style sheet from any page and make its style options available.

Exploring an internal style sheet

You'll start your work in the lesson by exploring a style sheet that was created with a document.

1 Start Adobe GoLive.

By default, an introductory screen appears prompting you to create a new page, create a new site, or open an existing file.

Note: You can set preferences for the introductory screen to not appear when you start GoLive. If the introductory screen doesn't appear, choose File > Open and go to step 3.

2 Click Open to open an existing file.

3 Open the *poetrypond.com* file in Lessons/Lesson12/12Start/poetrypond.com folder/.

4 In the site window, double-click index.html to open the home page of the poetrypond.com Web site.

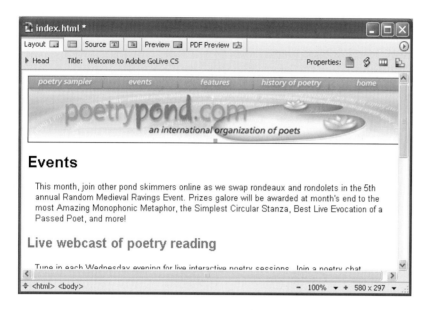

The basic structure and simple formatting of this document was achieved by applying the basic HTML elements such as h1, h2, and p to raw text. The finer styling such as the font size and color, margin widths, and even the white background of the document have been applied using a style sheet.

First you'll view the document without the style sheet formatting. You can preview your pages in one of several ways. You can choose a browser that doesn't have CSS support; you can turn off CSS support in your browser; or in the GoLive Web Settings, you can create a new browser profile that does not support CSS.

In this part of the lesson you'll create a browser profile that does not support CSS.

5 Choose Edit > Web Settings, (Windows) or GoLive> Web Setting (Mac OS) and click the Browser Profiles tab.

6 Click to select a browser profile (we used GoLive), and right-click (Windows) or Control-click (Mac OS) the browser name to display the context menu. Choose Duplicate.

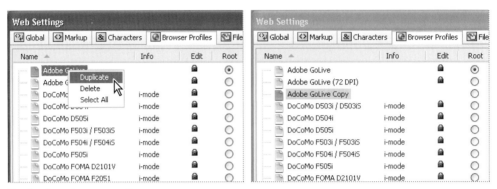

Duplicating a browser profile

Notice that the lock icon does not appear, indicating that this duplicate browser profile can be edited.

7 Choose Window > Inspector to open the Inspector palette, or click the Inspector tab if the Inspector is collapsed.

8 In the Basic tab of the Root Style Sheet Inspector, enter No CSS Support for the name of the browser profile.

9 Click the Settings tab in the Inspector, and deselect the Can Handle Style Sheets option.

10 Click the document window to make it active.

11 Choose Window > View to open the View palette, or click the View tab if the palette is collapsed.

12 In the View palette, choose No CSS Support from the Profile pop-up menu.

Choosing browser with no CSS support in View palette

Because you are now using a browser profile that does not provide CSS support, you have in effect turned off style sheets for the current document. In the document window, notice how the document display changes when the style sheet isn't used.

In this example, the headings lose their color properties and the fonts change to a larger serif face.

Style sheet active

Style sheet turned off

You can see how the document got this basic HTML structure by checking the Format menu on the toolbar.

13 In the document window, insert the text cursor in the "Live webcast of poetry reading" heading or triple-click to select the entire heading, and then notice the Format menu on the toolbar.

The Format menu displays the text's current HTML formatting. Header 2 indicates that the text is tagged as an HTML h2 element. Similarly the "Events" text is formatted as Header 1, which translates to an HTML h1 element; the body paragraphs are formatted as Paragraph, which translates to an HTML p element.

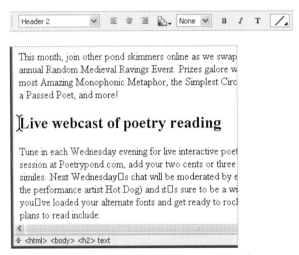

Format menu shows Header 2; corresponding text in document

14 If you're new to HTML, click the Source tab (⊤) in the document window to see how GoLive has written the HTML code and tagged the various chunks of text.

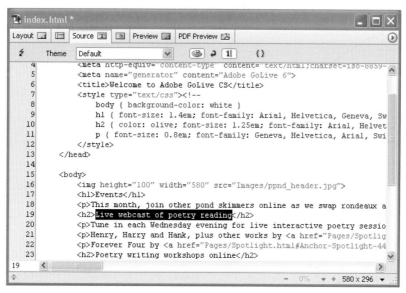

Source view

15 Click the Layout tab (▦) to return to the Layout Editor.

Now you'll take a look at the formatting that the style sheet controls.

16 Choose Explorer 5 for your platform (Windows or Mac OS) from the Profile pop-up menu in the View palette. The document window once again displays formatting with styles.

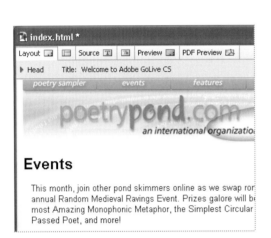

Using the Profile menu in the View palette, you can choose any of the popular browsers and see how the visual presentation changes. However, previewing with the View palette only simulates how the pages will appear in a browser; it is not a substitute for previewing pages in an actual browser.

17 To view the style sheet, click the Open CSS Editor button (🔠) in the upper right corner of the document window. This opens the index.html CSS Editor window.

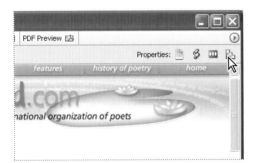
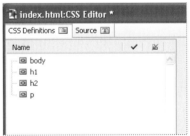

Choose the fly out menu triangle on the CSS Editor window and then select View > Folder for Sections. The Internal folder in the CSS Editor window displays the different styles defined for this document.

HTML Element styles let you reformat the visible part of an HTML document based on its structure. The designer can define a style for any HTML element, and it is applied automatically to all instances of the HTML element throughout a document. Element-based styles are fully compatible with browsers that can't read CSS1 information. So viewers with older browsers that don't support style sheets see the tag's plain HTML formatting, while viewers with newer browsers that support style sheets see the enhanced formatting. HTML Element styles are also useful for ensuring that your documents will be readable in alternative browsers or on nonstandard viewing devices, such as handheld PDAs.

Class styles apply style formatting to specific instances of a text block, rather than all instances that share a common HTML element. Unlike HTML Element styles, Class styles are independent of the document's structure; they are defined by the designer but must be manually applied. Classes are useful for creating distinctive formatting like warning notes or pull quotes that you want to stand out from the rest of your text, or for creating special effects such as varying font sizes or colors within a word. However, don't use classes to structure a document visually; the formatting won't stick if viewers have non-CSS-compatible browsers. Instead use HTML Element styles to achieve as much styling as you can, and reserve Class styles for special (but not imperative) styling, at least until browser support for cascading style sheets improves and you are sure that most of your viewers are using the latest browsers.

ID styles let you embed a specific style for a unique paragraph or range of text in your document, and create unique type treatments. Applying an ID style in GoLive requires that you edit HTML code.

18 Notice that the Internal folder in the index.html CSS Editor already lists some common HTML elements.

19 In the index.html CSS Editor window, click an HTML Element style to select it. The CSS Style Inspector becomes active.

20 Make sure that the Selector and Properties button (✐) in the CSS Style Inspector is selected.

21 In the CSS Editor window, click different elements. Notice that the styles with their associated selectors, properties, and values appear.

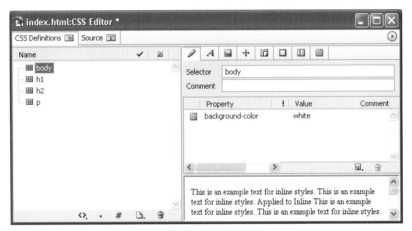

HTML Element style selected in CSS Editor window

Exporting an internal style sheet

You can easily export an internal style sheet for use with other documents or as a backup for the style sheet you're using.

1 Anywhere in the CSS Editor window, right-click (Windows) or Control-click (Mac OS), and choose Export Internal CSS from the context menu.

2 In the Save As dialog box, navigate to the styles folder in the poetrypond.com folder, name the file internal.css, and click Save.

3 Close the internal.css window.

Exploring an external style sheet

Style sheets can also be external to the current document. A link in the page to the external style sheet file will format the elements on the page. You'll be creating and linking an external style sheet to a page later in the lesson. Right now let's simply see what an external style sheet looks like.

1 Choose File > Open, and open the file alternate1.css that is located in the styles folder in the poetrypond.com folder. The style sheet opens in its own window named alternate1.css.

2 Notice that the external style sheet lists some common HTML elements.

3 In the alternate1.css window, select an element style.

The CSS Style Inspector becomes active.

4 Make sure that the Selector and Properties button (✐) in the CSS Style Inspector is selected.

5 Click different elements in the alternate1.css window.

6 In the CSS editor, notice that the styles with their associated selectors, properties, and values appear just as with the internal style sheet you examined earlier.

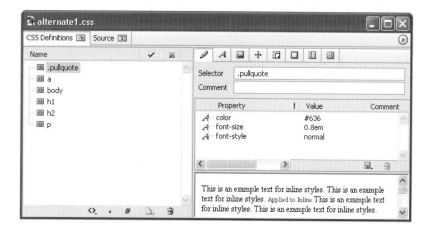

7 Close the alternate1.css CSS Editor window without saving it.

💡 *The order of the external style sheets in the CSS palette indicates their order of precedence (cascading order). Sheets that are lower in the list take precedence over sheets that are higher in the list.*

Working with styles

GoLive lets you work with style sheets and their styles in a variety of ways, including updating a style throughout a document, editing a style, and adding a style.

Updating a style throughout a document

Now you'll edit a style to see how your document is updated instantly.

1 If necessary, resize the document window so that you can see several different headings and body text.

2 In the index.html CSS Editor window, select the h2 element. Notice its attributes displayed in the Basic panel in the CSS Editor.

3 In the CSS Style Editor, click the Font button (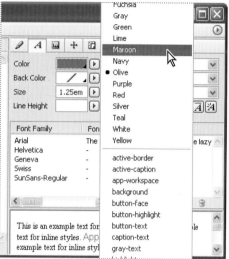). Choose a different color from the Color pop-up menu (we chose Maroon), and see how the change is immediately reflected in the document window.

Different color applied to h2 element

It's that easy to change a style that you've defined and apply it globally.

4 To make the font size a little smaller, enter **1** for Size and choose em from the pop-up menu.

> ### About absolute versus relative font sizes
>
> *Note the different units of measure in the size pop-up menu. CSS supports two types of measurements: absolute and relative. An absolute unit of measurement such as pixel is useful when you need precise control over the placement of text and graphics on a page. But type sized in pixels may not print well from some browsers, and it can limit accessibility to your site for visually impaired viewers since it forces them to view type at a fixed size. A relative unit of measurement, such as the em, sizes type in relation to the font size settings active in a visitor's browser, and is a better choice if you are concerned about accessibility issues, or if the exact placement of type and graphics on your pages is not essential.*

When you create a style using the Inspector, GoLive writes the HTML code for you. Now you'll take a look at that source code.

5 Click the Selector and Properties button (✐) in the CSS Editor, and note the properties of the h2 element.

6 Now switch to the Source Code Editor in the document window by clicking the Source tab above the document window.

7 Notice the statement in the following illustration:

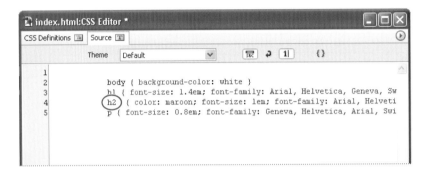

In the statement, h2 is the selector, and the information in brackets declares that the color property has a value of maroon, the font size property has a value of 1 em, and so on.

Remember that style rules are a statement consisting of a selector and a declaration on that element's property and value (that is, its specific appearance).

8 Click the Layout tab in the document window to return to the Layout Editor.

Editing a style in a style sheet

You'll continue the lesson by editing another style in the internal style sheet. This time you'll edit the style of the p element to change the margins of the body text.

1 Click the Open CSS Editor button at the top of the document window to open the CSS Editor window.

2 In the CSS Editor window, select the p element under the Internal folder. Notice its attributes displayed in the Basic panel in the CSS Editor.

3 Click the Margins and Padding Properties button (⊞) in the CSS Editor. The right and left margins are currently set to 2%.

4 Enter **5%** in the side margin text boxes, and press Enter or Return to indent the margins proportionally.

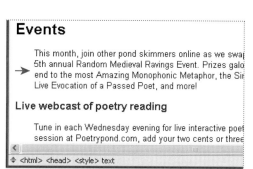

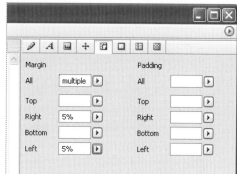

Side margins indented proportionally   *Block panel settings*

Notice how the left and right margins around all body text adjusts in the document window.

As you can see, properties can control the font, text (including the indentation, spacing, and alignment), box or document boundaries, positioning, border, background, and list elements. Values specify measurements or colors.

Note: *Browsers continue to add support for style sheet properties. For best results, test the properties that you want to use in the latest versions of the most popular browsers.*

Adding a style

Now you'll create a new element-based style to alter the way the hypertext links appear throughout this document, removing the standard HTML underline, changing the color, and applying a boldface font. The standard HTML tags for formatting hypertext links are <a></a>. Whenever you create a hypertext link using the link command, GoLive automatically writes the source code for you, tagging the element with <a></a>.

1 To add a new style to the style sheet, click the Create New Element Style button ([<>]) at the bottom of the CSS Editor window. A new item labeled "element" appears in the CSS Editor window under the Internal folder.

2 Click the Selector and Properties button in the CSS Editor, and name the style **a** to match the HTML link element. Press Enter or Return.

Whenever you create an element style, the element names must match those of the HTML code. Style definitions don't use brackets, so don't include them as part of the name. The table "Common HTML elements" on page 448 lists common HTML elements and describes the GoLive commands used to apply them.

3 Click the Font Properties button ([A]) in the CSS Editor.

4 In the Decoration options, select No Text Decoration to remove the underline beneath hypertext. Notice that the underlines are removed from the existing links in the document. You may have to scroll down the page to see the links "Benjamin Lucas" and "TW Tarwater."

Now you'll change the color of the hypertext font.

5 Choose a color from the Color menu and a weight from the Weight menu. (We chose Olive and a Bolder weight.)

GoLive features numerous ways to change the color of links. However, when you use an element-based style to change the appearance of hypertext, you can then update all links on your site globally simply by editing the style. Later in this lesson, you'll use a similar technique to update the page's background color.

Note: In Windows, to delete an element or class style from a style sheet, select the item in the CSS Editor window, and choose Edit > Delete.

6 Make the index.html document window active.

7 Choose File > Save to save the index.html document. Saving this document also saves the internal style sheet.

8 Close the document.

To create hypertext links that change color when the mouse pointer hovers over the link, use a contextual element style named after the <a> "link" tag. In the CSS Editor choose New Style > a:hover from the context or CSS Editor menu. In the Font set of the CSS Editor, choose a new color for the style.

Common HTML elements

Here are some common HTML elements that you can use when creating element-based styles in a cascading style sheet.

Element name	Abbreviation for	GoLive toolbar or menu command	Block or inline	Description
a	Link or anchor	New link	Inline	Highlighted
blockquote		Alignment commands	Block-level	Indented
body			Block-level	Inside canvas
br	Break	Shift+Return	Block-level	Breaks the line
em	Emphasis	Emphasis or Italic	Inline	Italic
h1, h2...h6	Heading levels	Header 1, Header 2, and so on	Block-level	Large fonts
i	Italic	Italic or Emphasis	Inline	Italic
img	Image		Inline	As an image
li	List item	Unnumbered list commands	Block-level	Bulleted list
ol	Ordered list	Numbered list commands	Block-level	Numbered list
p	Paragraph	Return	Inline	Regular text
strong		Strong or Boldface	Inline	Boldface

Creating a style sheet

Now that you've explored both internal and external style sheets, it's time to create your own style sheet from scratch. You'll create an external style sheet and link it to a document.

1 Double-click the spotlight.html file in the pages folder in the site window to open the file.

2 In the document window, click the Open CSS Editor button ( ) to display the spotlight.html CSS Editor window.

Notice that no styles appear in the CSS Editor window. The document has only the basic formatting from HTML elements; no styles are associated yet with any elements.

3 To create a new external style sheet, choose File > New Special > Cascading Style Sheet to open an untitled.css window (untitled2.css).

4 To add a new style to the style sheet, click the Create New Element Style button (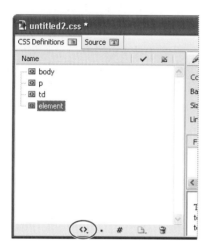) at the bottom of the palette. Select the new item named "element" that appears in the untitled2.css window.

5 Click the Selector and Properties button in the CSS Editor.

6 In the CSS Editor, name the style **h2**. Press Enter or Return to create the element.

7 Click the Font Properties button ( ) in the CSS Editor so that you can set font properties.

8 Click the Create New Font Family button (▣) at the bottom of the CSS Editor, and choose a font family from the pop-up menu. (We chose the Arial, Helvetica, etc. group for font family.)

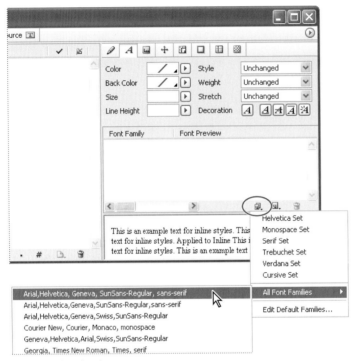

Selecting a font family

Notice that several fonts are now listed under Font Name. The font at the top of the list is the preferred font. Subsequent fonts will be used (in the order listed) if a viewer does not have the preferred font installed.

9 Use the pop-up menus to select a font color and font size. (We chose Maroon, 1 em.)

10 Leave the Line Height, Style, and Weight at their default values.

You've created the style, but notice that nothing has changed in the document. In contrast with internal style sheets that instantly update their associated document, external style sheets must first be saved and then attached to a document for the styles to be applied.

Saving and linking a style sheet

Now you'll save and link the style sheet to your HTML document. Once you link a style sheet to your document, GoLive applies its styles automatically.

1 Make sure that the untitled2.css window is active. Then choose File > Save, and name the untitled2.css document **mypoetry.css**, and save it in the styles folder in the poetrypond.com folder.

It's important to use the .css extension so that browsers recognize the document as a style sheet. Saving the style sheet in a styles folder is not mandatory, but it helps to keep your site organized and more manageable.

2 Make sure that the mypoetry.css file in your poetrypond.com site window is visible. You may have to choose Site > Refresh View to see the mypoetry.css file.

3 Drag the mypoetry.css file from the site window to the spotlight.html CSS Editor window.

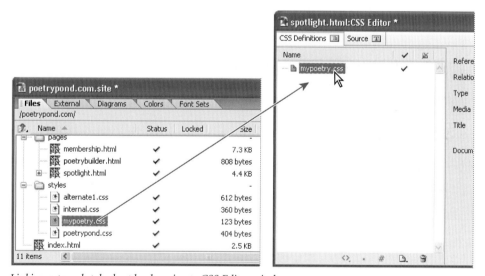

Linking external style sheet by dragging to CSS Editor window

The second heading in your document, "Started at an early age" (tagged with <h2></h2>), is reformatted automatically to reflect the style changes that you specified in the previous procedure, and the CSS Editor window is updated to reflect the linking of the mypoetry.css document to your HTML page.

It's that simple to create an external style sheet and link it to a document. Now you'll continue to refine the formatting of the spotlight.html document by linking an additional style sheet to it. This style sheet already contains several styles to give you a jump start. You'll edit those styles and add some new ones.

4 In the site window, select the poetrypond.css file in the styles folder within the poetrypond.com folder. This time, drag the style sheet to the Page icon (📄) of the spotlight.html document window.

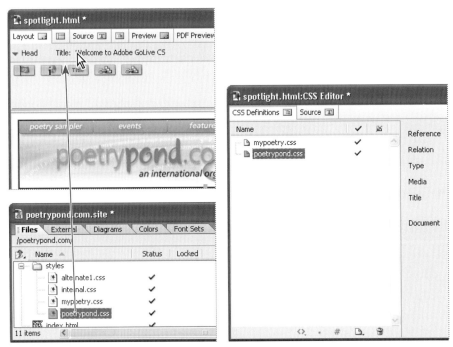

Linking to external style sheet by dragging to Page icon (left); updated CSS Editor window (right)

This is another technique for linking external style sheets to a document.

Once again the second heading (tagged with <h2></h2>) is reformatted, to reflect the properties in the style sheet that you just attached. A feature of cascading style sheets is that you can attach more than one style sheet to a document and apply styles cumulatively or separately.

When a new style sheet uses the same style names as the previous one, the newer styles will take precedence and override the styles in the old style sheet. In this case, the h2 tag overrides that in the previous one (mypoetry.css).

About cascading style sheets

A key feature of CSS is that they can cascade. That is, several different style sheets from different sources can be attached to a document, and all of them can influence the presentation of the document. For example, the default Web browser can attach a style sheet, a designer can have a style sheet to format a document, and viewers can add their own style sheets to address, for example, a larger font to compensate for poor eyesight or personal font preferences. In the case of conflicts, the CSS always chooses only one value, typically weighted first in favor of the designer, then the individual viewer, and then the default browser. (To override a designer's style rules, the viewer can turn off the designer's style sheet or mark certain style rules as "important.")

Linking and unlinking a style sheet to multiple pages

GoLive lets you easily apply an external style sheet to several pages all at once, doing away with the tedious task of linking it to each page in a site one page at a time.

1 In the mypoetry.css window, create a new element style. Name it h1, set the color to Red, and the type size to 2 em. If you need help, review the steps in "Adding a style" on page 446.

2 Save and close mypoetry.css.

3 In the pages folder in the Files tab of the site window, select poetrybuilder.html and shift-click to add spotlight.html to the selection.

4 Choose Window > CSS to open the CSS palette.

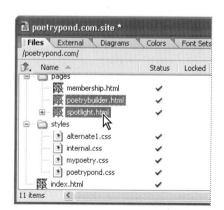 

Selecting the pages to which the style sheet should be added

5 In the CSS palette, click the Browse button, locate the mypoetry.css style sheet in the styles folder of the poetrypond.com folder, and click Open.

That's all there is to it! You can just as easily unlink the style sheet from multiple pages.

6 In the Files tab of the site window, select poetrybuilder.html and spotlight.html again if necessary.

7 In the CSS palette, select the mypoetry.css style sheet.

8 Click the Remove button.

Creating a class style

Class styles apply style formatting to specific instances of a text block, rather than all instances that share a common HTML tag. Unlike HTML Element styles, which are applied automatically to the corresponding HTML element, Class styles must be explicitly applied to a selection.

Now you'll create a new class style and apply its style to text in the Poetry page's spotlight.html file. The first class that you'll create will format a *pullquote*—some text or a quotation that is set off from the rest of the text for emphasis and for graphic impact.

1 If necessary, open spotlight.html by double-clicking it in the site window.

2 Click the Open CSS Editor button ( ) in the upper right corner of the document window to display the spotlight.html CSS Editor window.

3 In the CSS Editor window, double-click poetrypond.css to open it.

4 At the bottom of the window, click the Create New Class Style button ( ) to create a new class.

5 Click the Selector and Properties button (🖉) in the CSS Editor, name the class **.pullquote**, and press Enter or Return.

6 Click the Font Properties button (🄰) in the CSS Editor, and use the menus and text boxes to set the pullquote's font properties. (We chose Olive, a font size of 0.75 em, and Italic style.)

7 Click the Margin and Padding button (🄳) in the CSS Style Inspector, and set the left and right margins. (We used 15%.)

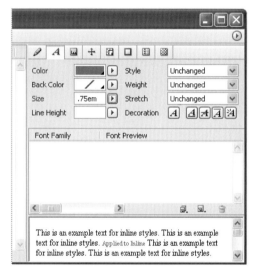

Font panel settings

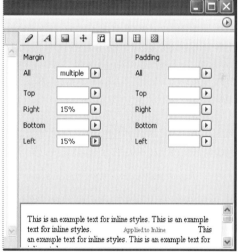

Block panel settings

Although you've created the class style, it doesn't take effect until you apply it to a selection on the page.

8 Save the poetrypond.css style sheet.

9 Save the document spotlight.html.

10 In the document window, insert the text cursor in Lucas's sample poem. The poem begins with, "Henry, Harry, and Hank." You may have to scroll down the page.

11 In the CSS palette, click the <P> next to .pullquote to apply that style to your selected text.

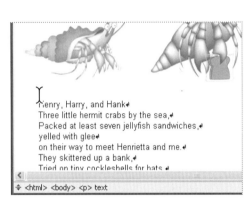

Text selection

Style applied to Par (paragraph) element

The <P> option applies a style to an entire paragraph (or HTML block element). In contrast, formatting an inline element applies the style only to the selection. See the table, "Common HTML elements" on page 448, for a list of block and inline HTML elements.

Importing an external style sheet

You can import the poetrypond.css external style sheet, changing it to an internal style sheet.

1 Right-click (Windows) or Control-click (Mac OS) anywhere in the CSS Editor window, and choose Import External CSS from the context menu.

2 Select poetrypond.css, and click Open.

All the styles defined in the external style sheet now appear under the Internal folder in the CSS Editor window as part of the document's internal style sheet.

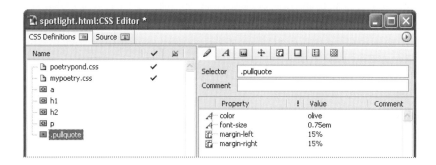

Duplicating a style

Now you'll create a new class for the author's attribution by copying the style that you just created.

1 In the spotlight.html CSS Editor window, select the .pullquote class that you created earlier. It's now part of the document's internal style sheet. You'll duplicate this class and then modify its font to create a new class.

2 With the .pullquote class selected, right-click (Windows) or Control-click (Mac OS) to display the context menu, and choose Duplicate. (You can also choose Edit > Duplicate from the GoLive command bar.) A new item called .pullquote1 appears in both the CSS Editor window under the Internal folder and in the Selector and Properties panel (🖉) of the CSS Editor.

Now you'll edit the properties of this duplicate class.

3 In the Selector and Properties panel of the CSS Editor, rename the class **.author,** and press Enter or Return. (Don't forget the leading period in the class name.)

4 Click the Font Properties button (🄰) in the CSS Editor. Notice that the attributes for the .pullquote class already appear. Change the font color to Black and the font style to Normal.

5 Click the Block Properties button of the CSS Editor, and enter a top margin of −1% to close up the space between it and the pullquote. Then press Enter or Return.

Now you'll apply this new class style to your page.

6 In your document window, select the text "Benjamin Lucas" immediately below the pullquote (poem).

7 In the CSS palette, next to author, click the Par column. This updates your text with this new format.

8 Make the spotlight.html document window active, and choose File > Save to save your changes.

Changing the background color

Now you'll change the page's background color by using a style sheet. GoLive features numerous ways to change a page's background color. Doing it by using a style sheet is convenient because you can change the backgrounds of all pages that use the style sheet with a single procedure.

To apply a background color to your document using a style, you use an element style for the HTML body element. The body element contains all the displayed content of your HTML page.

1 View the body element by clicking the Source tab (⊤) in your document window. Look at what is contained between <body> and </body>.

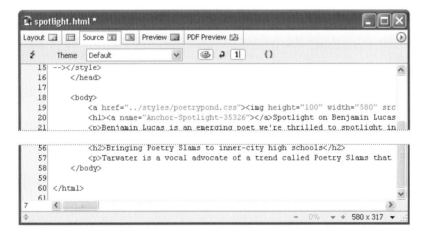

2 Click the Layout tab to return to the Layout Editor.

3 Click the Open CSS Editor button ( ) in the upper right corner of the document window. Then click the Create New Element Style button (<>) at the bottom of the window.

4 In the Basic panel of the CSS Editor, name the new element **body**, and press Enter or Return.

5 Click the Background Properties button (■) of the CSS Editor, and choose a color from the Color menu. (We chose Aqua.) The background of your document changes to the new color.

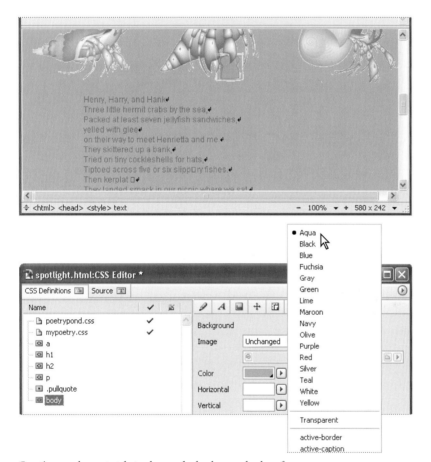

Creating an element style to change the background color of a page

6 Choose White as the background color again.

You can also use the body element to change the color of the body text by selecting the body style in the CSS Editor window, clicking the Font Properties button in the CSS Editor, and then choosing a color, and other properties.

Try experimenting with other background colors. You can also try different color combinations for the background and text font.

7 Choose File > Save to save your changes.

As you saw with the h2 element style applied to the heading level 2, cascading style sheets first apply formatting generally and then more specifically. The body element controls the color of all text in the document, until another more specific style (for example, h1 or h2) specifies a different color for a more specific text selection.

Previewing the results in current browsers

It's a good idea to have the latest versions of both Netscape and Microsoft browsers installed on your computer system, so that you can preview how effectively and accurately your style sheets work in these different environments.

Web browsers must support CSS1 and CSS2 elements to recognize and properly interpret style sheets. Version 4.0 browsers and later display some style properties. Some properties work with a single browser only, some don't work at all but cause no harm, and others cause the browser to crash. For a list of browser-safe features, visit the Web Review's Style Sheets Reference Guide at http://www.webreview.com/.

1 Click the Preview in Browser button on the toolbar in the document window to display the spotlight.html document in your browser.

Notice how the different HTML Element styles (a, body, h2, and so on) and Class styles (pullquote and author) applied to the document appear in each browser.

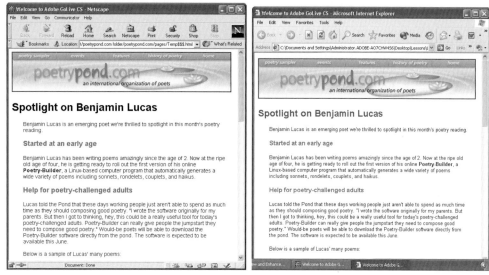

Netscape Communicator 4.0 style sheet preview   *Internet Explorer 5 style sheet preview*

2 For greater accuracy, launch your browser and then open the spotlight.html document in your browser to preview the formatting. (You can also choose File > Preview In > Live Rendering to preview the formatting).

GoLive simulates how a browser will apply the style sheet, but may not replicate the latest implementations of the style sheet standards.

3 Close your browser(s).

4 Return to GoLive, and close the spotlight.html document and its style sheets.

5 Close the poetrypond.com site window.

This concludes the lesson.

Review questions

1 How do styles differ from basic HTML formatting?

2 What does "cascading" mean when used to describe style sheets?

3 Why would a browser not display styles applied to a document?

4 How can you ensure that your style sheets work on the widest range of browsers?

5 What tools do you use in GoLive to create a style sheet?

6 What is the difference between an internal and external style sheet?

7 What is the difference between a class and element style?

8 What's the advantage of using an external style sheet to set the color of hypertext or the page background?

Review answers

1 HTML controls the structure of information (for example, different relative headings), but not its presentation. Style sheets let Web designers enhance HTML's formatting with precise positioning of text, control over type, and formatting of other elements on the page. For example, style sheets can be used to apply font size and color, margin widths, and even the background color to a document.

2 One or more cascading style sheets (CSS) can be attached to a document to influence the document's presentation. For example, a browser, then a designer, and then the individual viewer can all attach style sheets to a document. The influence of several style sheets "cascades" so that only one value is applied, typically that from the designer's style sheet. Styles within a style sheet also cascade and apply progressively to a document. In addition, if a document uses multiple style sheets, the latest style sheet can override previously applied style sheets if they share the same tags; or it can enhance previously applied style sheets.

3 A Web browser must have CSS1 and CSS2 support to recognize and properly interpret style sheets. Version 4.0 browsers display only a few style properties, and the browsers vary in which properties they support.

4 To use style sheets successfully, it's important to stay current with what style sheet properties are supported by current browsers, to experiment with applying different properties to different HTML elements, and always to preview the results in the current browsers to test your style sheet's effectiveness.

5 Several GoLive tools let you create and edit style sheets and link to external style sheets, including the CSS Editor window and its buttons.

6 Internal style sheets are part of a document and are saved with it. They must be defined individually for each page to which their formatting will apply. External style sheets can apply to a group of documents or to an entire site. You can then refer to this external style sheet from any page to make its style options available.

7 HTML Element styles are applied automatically by GoLive to their corresponding HTML elements and are fully compatible with browsers that can't read CSS1 information. HTML Element styles let you reformat the visible part of an HTML document based on its structure.

Class styles apply style formatting to specific instances of a text block, rather than all instances that share a common HTML element. Unlike HTML Element styles, Class styles are independent of the document's structure; they are defined by the designer but must be manually applied.

8 When you set the color or attributes of hypertext or the page background using an external style sheet, you can change the hypertext or backgrounds of all pages that use that style sheet with a single procedure.

13 | Managing Web Sites

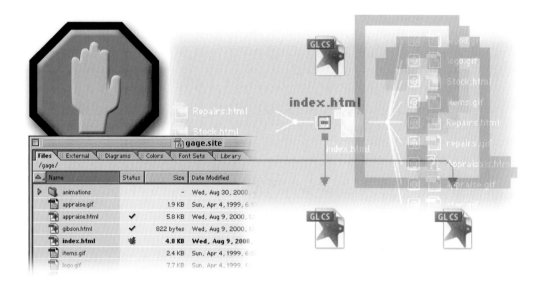

You can use the powerful Web site management tools in Adobe GoLive to create and manage your site. These tools include the site window, which shows all the objects in your site, and the Navigation view, which is a hierarchical viewer and designer. Other management tools allow you to manage folders, files, and links; import sites into Adobe GoLive; and upload your site to a Web server.

About this lesson

In this lesson, you'll do the following:

• Import an existing site created in an application other than Adobe GoLive into GoLive.

• Explore the site window.

• Correct errors in a site.

• Manage folders in a site.

• Add new pages to a site.

• Manage and modify your site using the Navigation view.

• Change links and file references.

• Import resources and remove unused resources.

This lesson takes approximately 1 hour to complete.

If needed, copy the Lessons/Lesson13/ folder onto your hard drive. As you work on this lesson, you'll overwrite the start files. If you need to restore the start files, copy them from the *Adobe GoLive CS Classroom in a Book* CD.

Note: Windows users need to unlock the lesson files before using them. For more information, see "Copying the Classroom in a Book files" on page 2.

About Adobe GoLive Web site management

To take full advantage of all the site building and management tools in GoLive, you must use GoLive to create or import a site. GoLive helps you set up all of your pages, media files, and resources in a logical folder structure and creates a special document for working with them. This document—your site project file—opens up the site window and displays an exact replica of the files and folder structure on your desktop. It is from the site window—not the desktop—that you build and restructure your site, link pages and images, store reusable site assets (such as page templates), and transfer and synchronize the site files with your server. It is important that you do all your work, especially adding, removing, or renaming files, within the GoLive site window and not on the desktop. If you do add a file from the desktop, you will need to update or refresh your site window when you next open GoLive.

Another reason to work exclusively in GoLive is that GoLive creates additional files and folders to contain the tools it uses to manage a site. For example, GoLive creates a web-data folder to hold all of the reusable site designs and site asset files, templates, components, stationeries, and site trash.

Getting started

If you have worked through the previous lessons in this book, you have already learned a lot of the principles of site management in GoLive. In this lesson, you'll review these principles and learn how to use some additional tools to resolve common problems such as broken links and orphan files. You'll also add and link files in the Navigation view of a site.

1 Start Adobe GoLive.

2 Choose File > Open, and open the *gage.site* file in Lessons/Lesson13/13End/.

This site contains a number of HTML pages and two folders, animations and images, that contain image files. When you have completed this lesson, your site will look like this.

Gage site window, showing files and folder structure and the pane containing Extras, Errors, Publish Server, and Collections tabs

The right pane of the site window usually contains four tabs: Extras, Errors, Publish Server, and Collections. The finished site contains no errors so the Errors tabs is empty.

3 Close the gage site window. This closes the Web site.

Importing an existing site into GoLive

You will now work with the files in the Start folder, which contains a site called gage, which was created in another application. Your first task is to import the site into GoLive. You will import the site as a single user.

1 Choose File > New Site.

2 In the GoLive Site Wizard, select Single User, and click Next.

3 Select Import from Folder, and click Next.

4 Click the top Browse button and navigate to the Lessons/Lesson13/13Start folder. Select the gage folder. This is the Web site that you will import into GoLive.

5 Click OK (Windows) or Choose (Mac OS). The path to the folder is entered into the top text box of the dialog box.

Importing a site using the Import from Folder option in the Site Wizard

Because the site already has an index.html page, GoLive recognizes this as the home page and automatically enters it into the bottom text box. If the index.html page were missing, you would need to browse for the site's home page.

6 Click Next, and click Browse to select a location for the imported folder.

7 In the Save dialog box, name the file **gage.site** and save it in the 13Start folder. (Be careful not to save it in the 13End folder.)

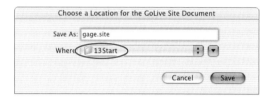

8 Click Finish to finish the import process.

The Web site is imported into GoLive, showing all its folders, files, and other site objects.

For information on creating a Web site from scratch in GoLive, see Lesson 3, "Designing Web Pages."

Exploring the site in the site window

In the site window, the Files tab shows all the objects in your site. You can use it to create, rename, move, and delete folders, files, and other site objects. The site has an animations folder, some image files, and several HTML pages. Some files have check marks in the Status column, indicating that their links are OK. Other files have red bugs () beside them, indicating that they have broken links. These broken links show up in the Errors tab of the site window, which you will look at later in this lesson.

Displaying site in Files tab of site window

1 In the site window, select (but do not open) the index.html file.

2 If necessary, open the Inspector by choosing Window > Inspector, or by clicking the tab if the Inspector is collapsed.

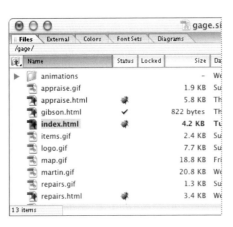

The Inspector changes to the File Inspector. The File Inspector lets you rename files, manage their properties, see their contents, and change your home page. You can use it to manage a number of different file types, such as page, image, and media files.

3 Click the Page tab of the File Inspector. The Home Page option is selected, making this your home page; however, the option is inactive. The only way to designate another file as the home page is to open it and select its Home Page option.

You can try selecting another page, making it the home page in the Page tab of the File Inspector, and then looking at how the information on the index.html file changes in the Page tab of the File Inspector. When you're finished be sure to make the index.html file the home page again.

4 In the site window, select logo.gif. The File Inspector now reflects image properties.

5 Click the Content tab of the File Inspector to see the image. Select a second image file and then a third.

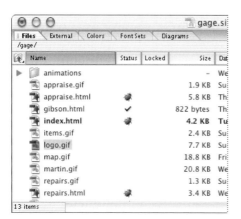 

Previewing image files in the File Inspector

The Content tab of the File Inspector is a convenient way to scroll through your images and search for the one that you want.

6 With the file logo.gif selected, choose Window > In & Out Links. This opens the In & Out Links palette.

The In & Out Links palette shows links to the image from the HTML pages in which it appears. (Select several other images to see how the In & Out Links palette changes.) The In & Out Links palette is a very useful tool that enables you to see, manage, and correct links. Its Pick Whip button (⬚) lets you easily create and change links, or correct broken links.

7 Click the index.html page icon in the In & Out Links palette. The palette changes to show all links to and from that page. (If necessary, resize the palette so that you can see all the links.)

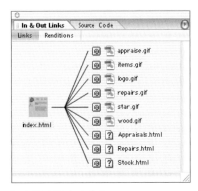

In & Out Links palette

If you click one of the files or pages linked from index.html, the focus of the In & Out Links palette changes again. In this way you can use the palette to check all the links in your site. In addition you can use the various Inspector windows to update and edit information about your site objects and their links.

8 Close the In & Out Links palette.

Reviewing the expanded site window

Now you'll review the features of the expanded site window.

1 Expand the site window by clicking the double-arrow icon ( ) in the bottom right corner of the site window.

You can drag the vertical bar between the two panes to resize them, if you wish. You may also want to move the site window to the bottom of your screen. This will help you keep it in view when you open files in the site.

Note: To collapse the expanded pane, click the double-arrow icon at the bottom of the scroll bar for the left pane.

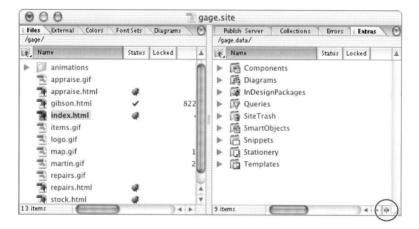

2 Click the Extras tab, if it is not already selected.

This tab contains the Components, Diagrams, Library, Site Trash, Smart Objects, Stationery, and Templates folders. These folders were created automatically by GoLive and put into the gage.data folder when you imported the site.

• The Components folder stores HTML pages (components) that you can embed inside others. You can make a single component, and use it again and again. Components are useful for buttons, logos, headers, mastheads, or other common navigation elements that you want to use throughout your site. Changes you make to elements in a component's source file are updated dynamically in the pages that use the component.

When you add a component to a page, the component remains linked to its source file until you detach it.

For more information on using components, see "Creating a component to be used as a navigation bar" on page 154.

• The Diagrams folder stores prototype designs that you have created for your current site.

For more information on creating design diagrams, see Lesson 01, "Creating Design Diagrams."

• The Library folder stores site assets that you plan on using frequently in your site. Site assets can be text, images, objects, or code snippets. You can drag or copy items to the Library palette or Library folder of the Extras tab in the site window for later insertion into a document.

• The Site Trash folder stores objects that you have removed from your site, but not your hard drive. From here you can either drag them into the desktop Recycle Bin (Windows) or Trash (Mac OS), or drag them back to your site.

About the Site Trash folder

Moving a file in the site window to the GoLive Site Trash folder is not the same as moving a file to the Recycle Bin (Windows) or Trash (Mac OS). A file or site object in the Site Trash folder remains on your hard drive, but is no longer included in your site. You can drag the file to the system trash and discard it permanently, or you can drag it back into your site structure.

You can change what GoLive does when you move items to the Site Trash folder by changing the GoLive Preferences. By default, items are not permanently thrown away, and you are warned before they are moved.

To permanently discard site items that you transfer to the Site Trash folder:

1. Choose Edit > Preferences (Win) or GoLive > Preferences (Mac) to open the Preferences dialog box.

2. Select Site, and then choose Move Them To The System Trash (Windows) or Move Them To The Finder Trash (Mac OS).

This option sends all selected items straight to the system Recycle Bin or Trash, and not the Site Trash folder in GoLive.

3. Click OK.

• The Smart Objects folder stores smart objects that you use to add images and animations to your page. GoLive optimizes these objects on your page while keeping a link to the source files in their original format. For example, when you use smart objects on your pages, resizing a Web image won't affect the source image's file size or resolution—so you can have multiple images of various sizes on your page all referring to the same source image. You can also use variables with the source image so you can change a single aspect of the image (such as type color) for each Web image on the page without changing the source image.

For more information on using Smart Objects, see Lesson 7, "Using Smart Objects."

• The Stationery folder stores page templates that may contain framesets, images, style sheets, and so on, for repeated use. Pages stored in the Stationery folder can be used as templates for creating new pages. Like page templates, you can mark areas in a stationery document's layout as editable and lock the rest of the content. Unlike page templates, stationery has no dynamic link with the pages created from it. Changes you make to a stationery file do not affect pages already created from that file.

• The Templates folder stores page templates. You can save any page as a page template and use it to control the layout and appearance of other pages in your site. Any part of the page template that is not marked as an editable region is automatically locked so that when you create new pages from the template, only the editable regions can be changed. New pages based on a template are automatically updated whenever you make changes to the template (content in the editable regions is not affected).

At this point all the folders are empty.

3 Click the Publish Server tab to select it.

This tab is also empty. When connected to your FTP server, it lists all files and folders that you have uploaded to the server, along with the date they were last revised.

4 Click the Errors tab to open it.

This tab lists any errors in your site. Notice that several types of errors appear in it: an orphan file, an unspecified link (or empty reference), and some missing hypertext links.

5 Click the plus sign or triangle to the left of the Orphan Files folder to expand it, if it is not already expanded. The one orphan file, star.gif is displayed.

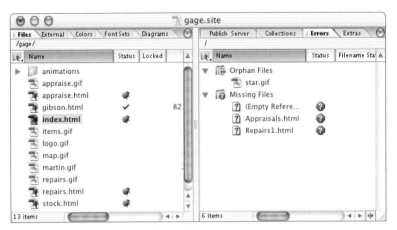

Displaying errors in Errors tab of site window

Correcting errors

You will now correct the errors displayed in the Errors tab. First you'll solve the problem of the orphan file.

Resolving orphan files

An orphan file is one that is referenced in your site, but either can't be found in the site project file, or is in the Site Trash folder. Copying the file to the Files tab of the site window will fix the problem.

1 In the Errors tab, select the star.gif file. Notice that the Inspector changes to the File Inspector. Click the Content tab to display the star.gif image—an animation that flashes on and off. This confirms that you are working with the correct file.

2 Drag the file from the Errors tab to the animations folder in the Files tab of the site window.

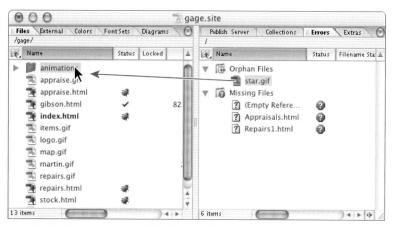

Dragging file from the Errors tab back into Files tab of site window

3 In the Copy Files dialog box, click OK to confirm that you want to copy the file into your site and update its links.

If you are too slow dropping the file on the animations folder, you may end up inside the animations folder. You can return to the root folder by clicking the Navigation button (![icon]) near the Files tab. (The icon for the Navigation button varies with your operating system.)

Why was star.gif an orphaned file? Remember that when you first created this site, you imported the gage folder. The star.gif image was not in that folder, but in the Other Files folder, and was therefore never imported into the gage.site file. Since it was referenced by index.html, GoLive marked it as orphaned.

Note: *When you drag or import HTML and image files from other locations on your hard disk into the site window, GoLive creates a copy for the site and leaves the original files in their original locations.*

Correcting missing file and hypertext link errors

Now you'll fix the missing file errors that appear in the Errors tab of the site window. You'll use the In & Out Links palette to find out which files contain the broken references or links. You can resolve missing file errors in at least three ways:

- By removing all references to the missing file.
- By changing all references to point to a new file.
- By browsing for the missing file from the Error Inspector and copying it to your site.

1 In the Errors tab of the site window, select the missing file that says (Empty Reference!). The Inspector changes to the Error Inspector, and (Empty Reference!) appears in the URL text box.

2 Choose Window > In & Out Links. The In & Out Links palette shows the empty reference, and the file containing it, Stock.html.

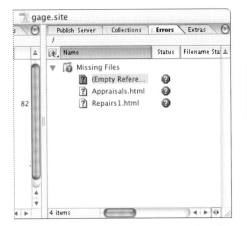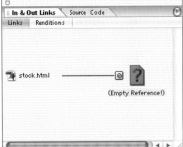

Viewing empty reference in In & Out Links palette

3 Double-click the Stock.html file in the Files tab of the site window to open the file. An image is missing from the top-left corner of the page. In its place is an empty image place-holder. If possible, resize or move the Stock.html file so that you can clearly see the Files tab of the site window.

4 Select the image placeholder in the Stock.html document window.

5 Hold down Alt (Windows) or Command (Mac OS), and drag from the image place-holder to the logo.gif file in the Files tab of the site window. The black Gage logo appears on the page.

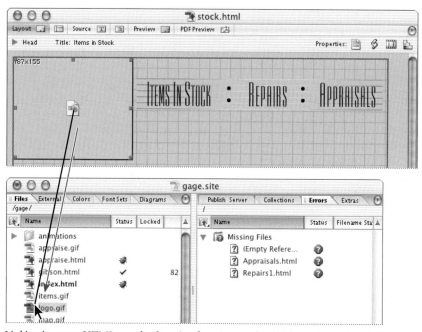

Linking image to HTML page by dragging from image placeholder to file in site window

Notice that GoLive has removed the Empty Reference error warning from the site window.

Note: *If the Files tab is partially hidden, just hold the pointer over the part of it that you can see, until the tab comes to the front.*

There is also a broken hypertext link on this page, but this error is more difficult to find.

6 If necessary, resize or move the Stock.html file so that you can see all its contents.

7 Click the Link Warnings button ( ) on the toolbar. The broken link is highlighted in red. (You may have to scroll down the page a little to see it.)

8 Double-click the highlighted text (the word "Repairs") to select the link. The Inspector changes to the Text Inspector, and the broken URL is highlighted in pink in the URL field.

9 In the Text Inspector, drag from the Pick Whip button to the Repairs.html file in the Files tab. If the Files tab is partially hidden, hold your pointer over it until the tab comes to the front. If you can't see the Repairs.html file in the tab, you can scroll down the list of files if you hold your pointer down over the lowest visible file in the pane.

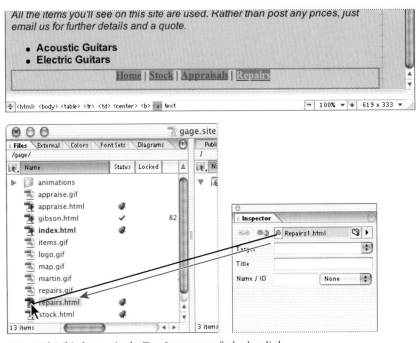

Using Pick Whip button in the Text Inspector to fix broken link

You can always use the Browse button in the Text Inspector to locate files if you have difficulty with the Pick Whip button.

The pink highlight disappears from the URL field of the Text Inspector and from the word "Repairs." Notice that the Repairs1.html hypertext link warning has been removed.

10 Choose File > Save to save your work. Close the Stock.html file, saving any changes.

Only one missing file error remains to be fixed. You will next use the In & Out Links palette to repair the connection to Appraisals.html.

11 Select Appraisals.html in the Errors tab of the site window. The In & Out Links palette shows that index.html is the only page that contains a link to the missing file.

The link from index.html refers to a file called Appraisals.html, but the Files tab contains a file called appraise.html. At some point, the file was renamed without updating all the links to it.

You will use the Pick Whip button in the In & Out Links palette to fix this error. Be sure that you can see both the site window and the appraisals.html file in the In & Out Links palette.

12 Drag from the Pick Whip button next to the appraisals.html file to the appraise.html file in the Files tab of the site window.

Fixing file references with In & Out Links palette

Note: *The Pick Whip buttons in the In & Out Links palette, Error Inspector, Text Inspector, the file itself, and the Errors Tab operate in the same way.*

13 Click OK in the Change Reference dialog box to confirm that you want to update the file.

14 Close the In & Out Links palette.

All the errors and bugs should now be gone and checkmarks should appear next to all your .html files in the Files tab, indicating that all their links are OK.

💡 *In the Files tab, click the Kind column header (scroll to the right, if necessary, to see it; or close the second half of the site window) to sort all your files by type. This groups all your HTML files making it easier to verify that all links are good.*

15 In the Files tab, click the Name column header to return to viewing files alphabetically by name.

16 Choose File > Save to save your work.

Managing folders

You will now improve the organization of the Web site by rearranging its folders and files. Because GoLive dynamically updates all your links as you go, you don't have to worry about redoing them each time that you change the files or folders.

Creating a folder and adding files to it

As your site grows, you will need to create folders to hold and organize all the files. You'll begin by creating a new folder for images and move files into it.

1 Click anywhere in the Files tab of the site window to make it active.

2 Click the Create New Folder button on the toolbar (▣).

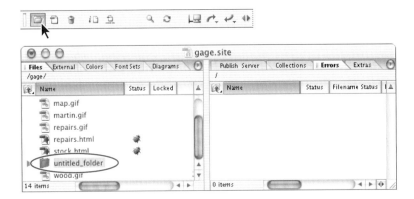

3 In Mac OS, click the Inspector, so that it changes to the Folder Inspector. The Inspector becomes the Folder Inspector automatically in Windows.

4 In the Name text box in the Folder Inspector, enter **pix**. Then press Enter or Return. The name of the folder changes.

You can change the name of any folder or file either by selecting it in the Files tab, and typing a new name directly over the old one, or by entering the new name in the Inspector.

5 In the Files tab, deselect the pix folder. Ctrl-click (Windows) or Shift-click (Mac OS) to select all the image files (any files with a .gif extension) and the animations folder.

In Windows, once you have selected all the items, release the Ctrl key or you will copy rather than move them.

6 Drag the selected items to the pix folder.

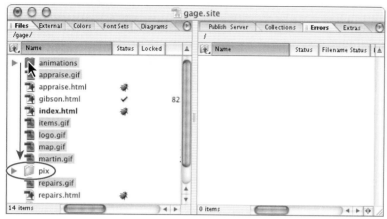

Dragging items to pix folder

7 Click OK in the Move Files dialog box. GoLive moves the files and dynamically updates all the links.

8 Choose File > Save to save the changes to your site.

Moving a folder

Next you'll move the animations folder from the pix folder back into the gage folder, and update all its links.

1 Click the plus sign (Windows) or the triangle (Mac OS) to the left of the pix folder in the site window, to expand it if necessary.

2 Select the animations folder, and move it to the root of the Gage site by dragging it to the Name title bar.

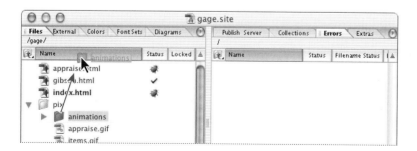

3 Click OK in the Move Files dialog box. The animations folder appears in the root of the site, and all the links are updated.

Renaming a folder

Now you'll rename the pix folder, and see how changes made inside GoLive automatically update your desktop.

1 In Windows, resize the GoLive application window to half of your screen size. Keep the site window in view.

2 In both Windows and Mac OS, open the pix folder through your operating system, and reposition the window so you can see its contents. You can do this from the GoLive site window as follows:

• In Windows, select the pix folder and click the Reveal in Explorer button (🖳) on the toolbar. (You can also right-click the pix folder and choose Open > Reveal in Explorer.) Resize the Explorer window and drag it next to the GoLive application window.

• In Mac OS, select the pix folder and click the Reveal in Finder button (🖳) on the toolbar. (You can also Command-click the pix folder in the Files tab and choose Reveal in Finder.) If necessary, resize the window and drag it next to the site window.

You should have both the GoLive and Explorer (Windows) or Finder (Mac OS) windows visible side-by-side.

3 In the Files tab of the GoLive site window, change the name of the pix folder to **images**. Press Enter or Return.

4 Click OK in the Rename Folder dialog box to confirm that you want to update the files.

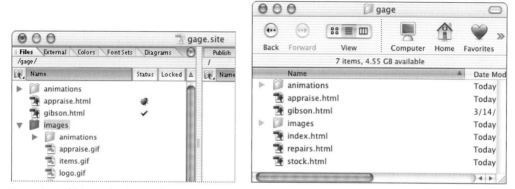

Renaming a folder in the site window automatically renames it on the desktop

Notice how the folder name has also changed on your desktop. GoLive works with your operating system to ensure reliability of the links within your site.

5 Close the Explorer (Windows) or other windows on your desktop.

6 Maximize the GoLive window, and choose File > Save to save your work.

Adding new pages to your site

You are now going to add two new pages to your site using two different techniques that automatically copy the file and place it in your site folder, without moving the original file.

You'll first use the Add Files command.

1 In GoLive, make sure that the site window is active and that nothing is selected.

2 Choose Files > Import > Files to Site, and navigate to the Other Files folder inside your 14Start folder. Open the Other Files folder, and select the hottest.html file.

3 Click Add (Win) or Choose (Mac), and then click Done. You should see hottest.html in the Files tab of the site window.

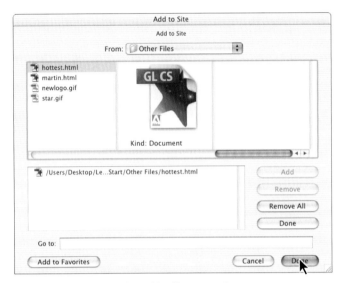

Using Add Files command to add a file to your site

The second method of adding a file is to drag it from the Explorer (Windows) or the desktop (Mac OS) to your site.

4 In the Explorer (Windows) or on the desktop (Mac OS), open the Other Files folder located inside the 13Start/gage/ folder. If necessary, resize the windows.

5 Drag the martin.html file from the Other Files folder to the Files tab in the site window.

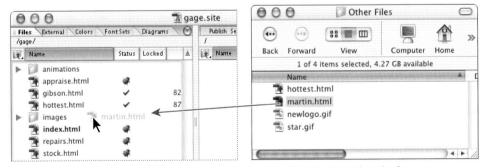

Dragging file from Explorer (Windows) or desktop (Mac OS or Windows) to Files tab of site window

If you open the gage folder in the Explorer or Finder, you'll notice how the two newly added files appear there.

6 Close the Explorer (Windows) or any desktop windows (Mac OS). Maximize the GoLive window.

Note: If you remove or add files from within folders in the Explorer (Windows only) or on the desktop without copying them into GoLive, you must use the Refresh View button (![Refresh View button]) on the toolbar to include or remove the files in your site.

Solving the site hierarchy

When you import a site, GoLive automatically analyzes the links in pages and examines the structure of folders to create a hierarchical structure for the site. This process is called solving the site hierarchy. The initial structure is based on both the pattern of links present on site pages and the hierarchy of the root folder's subfolders.

You should solve a site's hierarchy if you have made changes in your site outside GoLive or if you want to base the site's navigational structure on different principles. For example, if the hierarchy of the root folder's subfolders has nothing to do with the site's navigational logic (as with this site), you might want to base the structure entirely on links.

You solve a site's hierarchy in the Navigation view, which lets you see the overall structure of your site.

1 Choose Open Navigation View button on the toolbar to open the Navigation view.

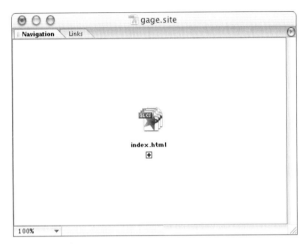

Navigation view

2 In the Navigation view, click the plus sign (⊞) below index.html to see more of the site.

The Navigation view shows the index.html page at the top of the site hierarchy and several pages on the level below.

3 Choose Diagram > Solve Hierarchy.

4 In the Solve Hierarchy dialog box, deselect the Folder Hierarchy option.

The Folder Hierarchy option bases the hierarchy shown in the Navigation view on the hierarchy of the root folder's subfolders. This option is useful if the actual folder hierarchy in your site window reflects the hierarchy of the site's pages. Because this is not true for the folder hierarchy of this imported site, you need to deselect this option. The Links option extrapolates the hierarchy in the Navigation view from the pattern of links in the site's pages. You'll leave this option checked.

5 Click OK.

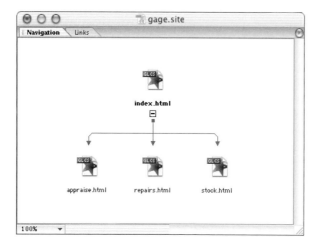

Notice how the site hierarchy is updated to reflect actual linked pages and files.

You can also collapse and expand parts of your site hierarchy. This is especially useful if you have a large site.

6 Click the minus sign (⊟) below the index.html page icon. The site collapses into the index.html page icon.

7 Expand the site again by clicking the plus sign (⊞) below the index.html page icon. The site expands to show all the other pages directly linked to index.html.

Changing the Navigation view

You can also change the way the Navigation view displays your site.

1 Click anywhere in the Navigation view window to deselect the index.html page, if it's still selected.

2 Choose Window > View to display the View palette.

3 In the Display tab of the View palette, notice that the Graphical option is currently selected. You would normally use this view to arrange and navigate across the objects in your site.

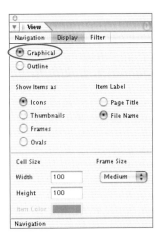

The View palette has tabs that let you set the Navigation, Display, and Filter properties of the Navigation and Links views. Take a look at the tabs and their options before continuing.

4 In the Navigation view (not the View palette), click the Links tab next to the Navigation tab to switch from the Navigation to the Links view (the two views are grouped together in a palette). Then click the right plus sign next to index.html.

5 Click the Filter tab of the View palette, and click the Toggle Media button.

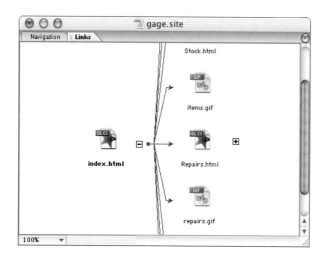 

The Filter tab lets you choose which site objects you see in the Links view. Notice how the content of the Links view has changed (you may have to scroll to see the changes). All the media files in your site are shown (or not shown) alongside the HTML pages when you click the Toggle Media button (depending on whether you have toggled the button on or off).

6 Drag the horizontal scrollbar of the Links view to the right to see all the added media files, if necessary.

7 Switch back to the Navigation view by clicking its tab.

8 Choose Scratch Pane from the Navigation view's pop-up menu. The Scratch pane lets you see pages that have been added to your site, but which remain unlinked.

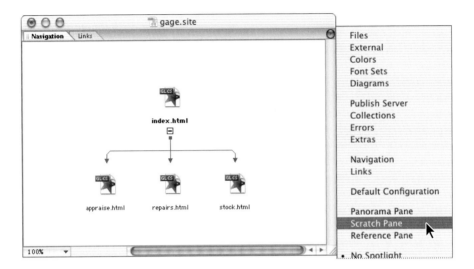

The pages that you recently added to your site, martin.html and hottest.html, as well as an unreachable image file, martin.gif, and an unused HTML page, gibson.html, are displayed. If necessary, scroll to see the files.

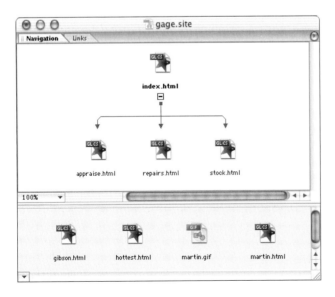

You can check that these are unused, unlinked files using the In & Out Links palette. With the In & Out Links palette open, click each unused, unlinked file in the scratch pane in turn. No links show in the In & Out Links palette. Close the In & Out Links palette when you are finished.

GoLive also provides an Outline view of the site hierarchy.

9 Click the Display tab of the View palette. At the top of the Display tab, select Outline.

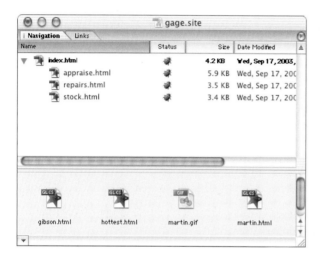

The Outline view displays a tabular view of your site. It also provides information about each object's status, type, and URL.

10 In the Outline view, click the symbol next to the index.html page to expand the tree view, if necessary. In this view, you can expand and collapse the view, as well as move site objects. Outline view provides a more compact view that resembles the site window's Files tab.

11 In the Display tab of the View palette, select Graphical to return to a graphical view of your site.

12 In the Display tab, try some of the other view options. When you have finished, select Icons and File Name, and set the Cell Size Width value to **55** and the Height value to **140**, and press Enter or Return.

For more information about how you can use the navigation view to add pages to the structure, see "Creating new pages in the Navigation view" on page 499.

Using the Site Navigator

Your monitor may not be large enough to display your entire site, so GoLive provides a Site Navigator to help you move throughout the entire hierarchical view. The Site Navigator is a separate window that displays your whole site and has a marquee that highlights the part of your site currently visible in the Navigation view.

1 Choose Window > Site Navigator.

2 Place the pointer within the marquee in the Site Navigator, and use the hand to drag the marquee back and forth across the site. Notice how the Navigation view changes as you move the marquee.

3 Close the Site Navigator window when you have finished viewing your site.

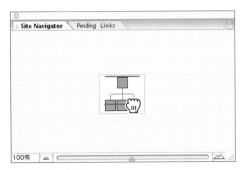

Moving Site Navigator marquee

Inserting pages into your site hierarchy

As you have seen, the two new pages that you added to your site, hottest.html and martin.html, aren't part of the main hierarchy yet—they are in the Scratch Pane. This is because you haven't created links to them, so they are unreachable from the rest of your site. One of these pages is ready for public viewing, so you'll link it to the rest of your site.

1 Drag the hottest.html page from the Scratch Pane below the index.html page in the Navigation view, and drop it when a solid horizontal line appears below index.html.

The hottest.html page moves under the index.html page, to the right of the other pages.

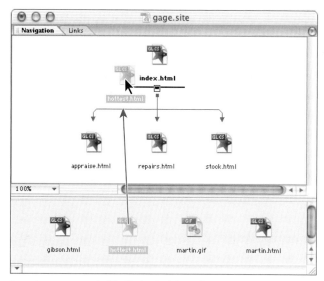

Inserting an unreachable file in site hierarchy

When you drag pages over other pages in the hierarchy, solid lines can appear above, below, or on the same hierarchical level as an existing file, allowing you to drop pages wherever you want in the tree.

2 Leave the martin.html file where it is. It's still under construction.

Creating links between pages using the Navigation view

Now you'll create the link from the index.html page to the hottest.html page.

1 In the Navigation view, double-click the index.html page to open it.

2 If necessary, resize or move the index.html page so that you can see both the Navigation view and the "Check Out This Week's Hottest Buy" text.

3 Select the text "Check Out This Week's Hottest Buy". Be sure to select the text and not the text box.

4 Hold down Alt (Windows) or Command (Mac OS), and drag from the selected text to the hottest.html page in the Navigation view. (If this page is partially hidden by the index.html page, hold the pointer over the window until the Navigation view is brought to the front.)

The Text Inspector shows the new link to the hottest.html page in the URL field.

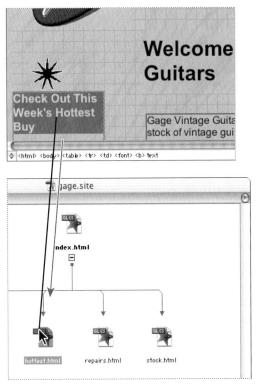

Dragging Point and Shoot line to create link

5 Save and close the index.html page.

Creating new pages in the Navigation view

Your site needs two new pages featuring your latest items. You can do this directly from the Navigation view.

1 In the Navigation view, select the Stock.html page icon.

2 Click the New Child Page button (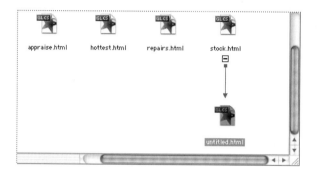) in the toolbar. A new, untitled page appears below the Stock.html page. If necessary, use the Site Navigator marquee or the vertical scrollbar to see this new page.

3 Select Stock.html again and repeat Step 2 to create another untitled page. Notice that both new pages appear on the same level of the hierarchy.

Note: *If you add a page where you don't want it, select the page and click the Delete Selected Item button (🗑) on the toolbar. Then confirm that you want to move the page to the Site Trash folder.*

4 Select the new pages in the NewFiles folder in the site window, and change their names to acoustic.html and electric.html in the Inspector.

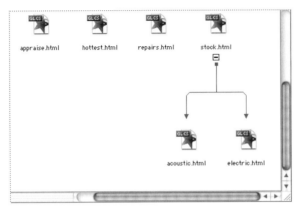

New pages in Navigation view

You'll link these unfinished pages to the rest of the site in the next section.

Creating links to new pages using the Navigation view

Now you'll link these two new pages to the rest of your site using the Navigation view. First you'll link acoustic.html to Stock.html.

1 In the Navigation view, double-click the Stock.html page icon to open the page.

2 Select the text "Acoustic Guitars" at the bottom of the page.

3 Hold down Alt (Windows) or Command (Mac OS), and drag from the selected text to the acoustic.html page icon in the Navigation view. This links the text to the page.

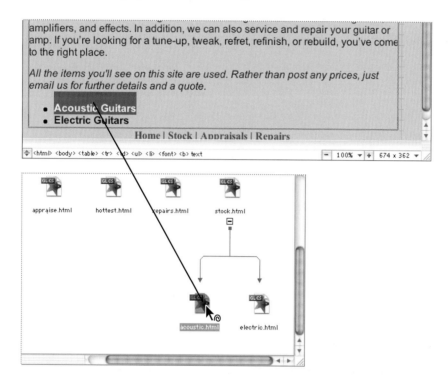

4 Select the text "Electric Guitars" at the bottom of the page.

5 Repeat Step 3, this time linking the text to the electric.html page icon in the Navigation view.

6 Save and close the Stock.html page.

You have just created two new pages, remapped your site hierarchy, and linked them to other pages.

Moving newly created files into the root folder

Whenever you create new pages in the Navigation view, GoLive creates a NewFiles folder in the Files tab of the site window to hold them. This is a useful place to keep files that are under construction, but now you'll move the files into another folder.

1 Click the Files tab in the site window to view it. If necessary, open the NewFiles folder to display the new acoustic.html and electric.html pages.

There are two construction icons (🛠) next to these pages, which indicate that they are under construction. The icons will disappear once you start adding content.

2 Click to select one of the new pages, and Shift-click to add the second to the selection. Move the two pages to the root level of the gage site by dragging them to the Name title bar, and update the links.

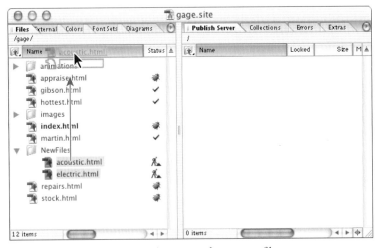

Under Construction icons appearing next to the two new files

Changing all links and file references

When you remove a page and replace it with another, you can dynamically transfer all the links to the page at the same time. This also applies to changing an image that occurs throughout your site. The Change References option is a simple way to do this.

You'll try this feature by changing the logo image that appears on most pages of the Gage site from logo.gif to newlogo.gif.

1 Double-click the index.html file in the Files tab of the site window to open the file. The Gage Vintage Guitars logo is in the top-left corner of the page. This is the image that you are going to change.

2 If necessary, resize index.html so that you can clearly see both the site window and the logo.

3 Select the logo.gif file in the images folder in the Files tab of the site window.

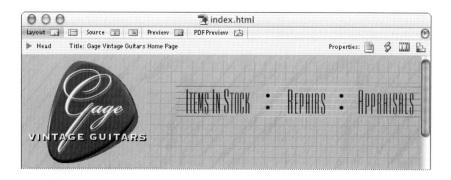

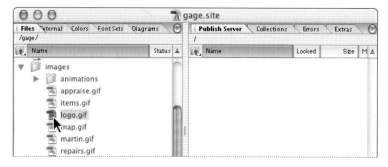

4 Choose Site > Change References. In the Change References dialog box, click the Browse button () and navigate to the 13Start/Other Files/ folder, and open newlogo.gif. The new file path appears in the Change References dialog box.

Change References
Change all references to:
file:///Users/Desktop/Lesson13/13Start/gage/images/logo.gif
Into references to:
@ ../Other%20Files/newlogo.gif
Cancel   OK

Browsing for newlogo.gif file

5 Click OK, and then click OK to confirm that you want to change all references to the image.

All references to the old file are changed, and the new red logo appears in the index.html page.

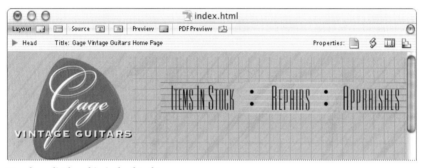

New logo displayed in index.html page

6 Save and close the index.html page.

If you want to check that the logos on other pages have been updated, open those pages.

Cleaning up a site

Your site now has a file that you don't want (logo.gif), and a file referenced by your site that is not in the site folder (newlogo.gif). The latter is an orphan file; it appears in the Errors tab in the site window. You'll import the newlogo.gif file into your site using the Clear Site dialog box. At the same time, you'll remove logo.gif and any other unused files and non-file objects, such as URLs and e-mail addresses.

1 Choose Site > Clean Up Site.

2 In the Clear Site dialog box, click OK to copy the newlogo.gif file to the NewFiles folder.

A list of all the files that need to be updated then appears in the Copy Files dialog box.

3 In the Copy Files dialog box, click OK to update the listed files.

Using GoLive to clean up the site

Note: *Cleaning up the site rescans the whole site and updates it; it also updates the files on your desktop.*

In the Errors tab of the site window, notice that the orphan file error has been resolved. GoLive has moved the orphan file (newlogo.gif) into the NewFiles folder in the Files tab of the site window.

4 Select newlogo.gif and move it from the NewFiles folder into the images folder, and update the links to it.

5 Remove the empty NewFiles folder by selecting it and clicking the Delete Selected Item button (🗑).

6 Click Yes to confirm that you want to delete the folder.

7 Save your site.

The last step is to upload your site to a Web server, so the world can enjoy your work. Because this requires certain hardware and software not included with the GoLive CS package, you can try this on your own.

Exploring on your own

Before visitors can view your Web site, you must copy it to an FTP site on a Web server. Your Internet service provider can help you with the details of uploading and maintaining your site.

You connect to a publish server in order to upload or download a site and perform any file transfer operation. Before you can connect to a publish server for the first time, you must set up access to it. See Setting up access in the online help for more information on this procedure.

Review questions

1 What is an orphan file and how do you fix it?

2 How do you create a new folder and move files into it? What happens once you move the files?

3 How do you change between a graphical and an outline layout in the Navigation view?

4 What are the two ways to add a file to your Web site from a folder outside your site?

5 How do you create a new page icon in the Navigation view below an existing page icon?

6 How do you create a link from text in a parent page to a child page using the Navigation view?

Review answers

1 An orphan file is one that is referenced in your Web site, but either is in a location not included in the site project file or has been placed in the Site Trash folder. You fix the problem either by moving the file into the site project file, by changing references to it, or by dragging the file from the Site Trash folder back to your site.

2 You use the New Folder button to create a new folder. You can add files to it either by dragging them to the folder (if they are already in your site) or by using the File > Import > Files to Site command (if they are not in your site). Once you move files that are already in your site into the new folder, GoLive dynamically updates the links to these files.

3 Choose Window > View, and select either Graphical or Outline in the Display tab of the View palette.

4 You can add a file to your site from an outside folder either by using the File > Import > Files to Site command or by dragging from the outside folder to the Files tab in the site window.

5 You select the existing page icon and click the New Child Page button on the toolbar.

6 Open the parent page, select the text, hold down Alt (Windows) or Command (Mac OS), and then drag from the selected text to the child page icon in the Navigation view.

Index

A

Action Group action 376

actions 364

    adding to floating boxes 352, 369

    adding to frames 327

    adding to images 374, 376

    adding to links 266, 382

    browser switch 191, 364

    Call Action 378, 387

    Call Function 386

    copying 380

    ForceFrame 327

    head actions 364, 374

    OnCall 364, 374

    Open Window 266

    resizing of browser window 368

    ShowHide 377

Address icon 262

aligning objects 37, 79, 92, 93, 163, 192

Alt Text box 160, 250

Anchor Inspector 253

anchors 251, 254

annotations, design diagram 11, 13, 39

ASP element, design diagram 28

B

background color 204

    changing with css 458

background image 166, 204

border size, in frame sets 317

Bring Region to Front button 273

broken links 278, 481

Browser preferences 82

browser

    profiles 138, 438

    switch 191, 364

    window resizing 368

browser, previewing with 64, 140

browsers, and frames 323

C

Call Action action 378, 387

Call Function action 386

Canvas As Single Page option 17

Cascading Style Sheets. *See* CSS

Change References option 503

Check Staging command 50

class styles 439, 454

Clean Up Site 504

code, editing HTML 238

Collision Avoidance option 17, 44

color

    background 75, 204, 458

    design diagram 20, 21

    in table cells 223

    links 264

    text 214

color palette

    custom 174

    updating 183

Colors tab 108, 174

comments, head section, body 179

comments, design diagram 11

Common Gateway Interface (CGI) 393

component 59, 154, 167, 182, 191

Component Inspector 168

Components folder 154, 475

context menus 136

Create Circle tool 272

Create Polygon tool 271

CSS 431, 439, 453

    .css extension 451

    absolute vs. relative font sizes 443

    adding a style 446

background color 458

class style 454

common HTML elements 448

creating 448

duplicating a style 457

editing 442, 444

external style sheets 432, 441

HTML Element styles 440

ID styles 439

importing 456

internal style sheets 432

linking 451

previewing 460

saving 451

CSS palette 454

CSS support 433

D

database, design diagram 33

date and time stamp 180

default configuration

    tabs 116

Delete Selected Item button 499

Design Diagram.site window 13

design diagrams 8, 14

    adding color 21

    adding pages 15, 23

    adding pages (Section Inspector) 25

    adding sections 18

    adding security 30

    adding text 47

    aligning and distributing objects 37

    anchoring 10, 48

    creating 14

    custom objects 37

    database 33

    display 16

exporting 47
grouping objects 31
labeling 45
master page 41
objects 28
opening 9, 13
PDFs 33
pending links 36
Secure object 30
staging 50
submitting 50
SWF object 35
view options 16
Design tab 13
Designs folder 475
Detect Rollover Images feature 343
Diagrams folder 476
Diagrams tab 9, 13
document window 117, 118
Down state 343, 344
drop-down menu 348
showing and hiding 352

E
e-mail link 262
EPS files, as Smart Objects 288
Errors tab 477
Export Design Diagram command 48
Export Internal CSS command 440
exporting design diagrams 47
external style sheets 432, 441, 451, 456
External tab 258
Extras tab 110, 248, 475

F
File Inspector 166, 473, 478
file references, changing 503
file structure 96
files
adding to site 151
missing 480
orphan 478

renaming 97
Files tab 97, 107
find and replace 232
Find Files in Site button 124
Find window 124
Flip Move action 372
floating box marker 341
floating boxes 60, 184
adding 186, 340
adding actions to 352, 369
adding images to 187, 347
and rollovers 340
browser support 343
hiding on loading 355
selecting 341
showing and hiding 352
folder
project 96
root 97
settings 97
folders
adding to site 67, 484
creating 68, 152
moving 485
renaming 486
font sets 227
Font Size menu 222, 399
fonts, in tables 229
in tables 229
default 227
font-size, absolute vs. relative 443
ForceFrame action 327
Form element 394, 395
form fields, aligning 404
Form icon 395
form text fields
linking to labels 405
formatting tables 219
formatting text 209
forms 394
adding fields 399–404
adding images 413, 419

address fields 402
border and cell 409, 421
creating 396, 397
custom elements 410
designing 393
form field labels 399
inserting tables 397
list box 417
name fields 399
pop-up menus 407
radio buttons 414
Reset button 421
resizing columns 413
Submit button 421
tab order 422
Frame Editor 314
Frame Regions button 273
frame sets 310
changing border properties 317
creating 314
editing 316
forcing to load 327
linking to 326
linking to home page 326
modifying 316
parent option 324
structure 311
targeted links within 324
Vertical Orientation option 317
frames
adding content 321
adding single 315
and browsers 323
linking content 319
previewing 322
scalable 320
scrolling 321
setting size 320
targeted links 324
FTP tab 477

G

General preferences 137
Generic Page icon 58
Get Colors Used command 183
GoLive CS. *See* Adobe GoLive CS
graphics
    adding 158
    as links 247
    editing 288

H

Head Action Inspector 328
head actions 364
    browser switch 364
    resizing browser window 368
head section pane 122
headings, adding column 219
Hide Palettes command 108
home page 67
Horizontal Snap option 44
hotspots 269, 273
HTML Element styles 439
HTML elements 431, 448
HTML Styles palette 214
HTML table 60
hyperlinks 255
    changing 503
    repairing 481

I

ID styles 439
Illustrator images, as Smart
    Objects 289
Image Inspector 77, 248, 269
image maps 62, 269
    linking 274
    testing 276
Image Size tab
    Save for Web 295
image, adding background 204
images
    adding 76, 158, 161
    as Smart Objects 288, 289

clickable 419
    editing 288
    linking 77
    sliced 162
Import button 217
Import Files to Site command 58, 67, 151
Import from Folder command 470
In & Out Links palette 473, 480
Include GoLive Code option
    ImageReady 345
Increase List Level button 213
Inspector 135
internal style sheets 432
    exporting 440

J

JavaScript *See also* Actions
    assigning to page elements 384
JavaServer Pages (JSP) 28

K

keywords 177

L

labels
    design diagram 45
    linking to form text fields 405
Layout Editor 118
layout grids 59, 156, 173, 205
    converting to HTML table 202, 236
    creating from table 236
    optimizing 165
Layout Preview 81, 138
Layout tab 118
layout text boxes 72, 169, 207
levels, design diagram 45
Library folder 476
library objects 59, 410
Library set 410
line breaks 213
link warnings 277

Link Warnings button 278, 481
links 245
    absolute and relative pathnames
        in 256
    active and visited 265
    adding actions to 266
    adding actions to text links 382
    adding to rollovers 351
    adding to text 255
    appearance 264
    broken 278, 481
    color 264
    creating by browsing 255
    creating with Point and Shoot 249
    e-mail 262
    empty 371
    external 258
    hypertext 255
    image maps 269
    parent option 324
    pending 36
    targeted in frames 324
    to a frame set 326
    to URLs 258
    troubleshooting 278
    updating 244
    using graphics 247
    warning preferences 277
    within pages 251
Links tab 115
list boxes, forms 417
lists, formatting 212
LiveMotion
    configuring 301
    image as Smart Objects 289

M

Make Annotations Live option 48
Make Diagram Objects Into Links
    option 48
Map Area Inspector 274
Master tab 13
menus, context 136

Microsoft Active Server Pages
(ASP) 28
missing file errors 480
Modified Date Inspector 181
Modules preferences 80

N
name field 399
names, changing file names 97
Navigation view 492, 495
adding pages 496, 499
linking pages 497, 500
moving files 502
Navigation View button 111
navigational links 63
adding 94
Netscape CSS Fix action 366, 367
in frames 311
New Action button 354, 371
New Child Page buttons 499
New Colors folder 174
New Design Diagram command 14
New Element Style button 446
New Folder buttons 484
New Folder command 68
New Item button 178, 371
New Link button 249, 371
New Page command 58, 65, 203
New Pages dialog box 23
New Site command 65
NewFiles folder 500
Normal state 343, 344

O
objects
aligning and distributing 37, 79, 163
design diagram 28
Objects palette 129, 132
OnCall actions 374, 376
Open command 65
Open CSS Editor button 438
Open Window action 266
orphan files 478

Outline Editor 239
Over state 343, 344

P
page title, changing 70, 203
pages
adding background color 75, 204
adding background images 166, 204
adding floating boxes 184
adding images 158
adding layout grids 156
adding to design diagram 15
adding to site 83, 203
anchoring 10
changing background color 458
creating from stationery 92
linking between 247
linking within 251
previewing 63, 193
pages, master
in design diagrams 41
palettes 126, 127
hiding 108
separating 115
working with 108
Paragraph Format menu 210
PDF files, as Smart Objects 288
PDF objects, design diagrams 33
pending links 36
Photoshop Smart Objects 289
Photoshop-based designs 162
PHP Hypertext Preprocessor
(PHP) 28
Point and Shoot button 135
pop-up menus, forms 407
preferences 137, 300
Browser 82
link warnings 277
Modules 80
Preview Mode 80
Preview Frame button
frames 322

Preview In Default Browser
command 82
Preview Mode
Modules preferences 80
previewing
in GoLive 237
with Web browsers 140
previewing pages 63
printing a design diagram 47
project folder 96

Q
QuickTime movies 62
adding 91

R
radio buttons, forms 414
Reference Inspector 259, 262
referencing images 77
Refresh View button 98
Refresh View command 108, 413
Remove Link button 255
Reset button 421
renaming 421
Resize Window action 368
resource links 63
reusing content *See* component
Reveal in Explorer button 486
Reveal in Finder button 486
rollovers 62, 86, 334, 340, 344
adding links to 351
and floating boxes 340
Floating Box Inspector 341
naming 343
root folder 97

S
Save for Web dialog box 292
Save Workspace command 130
Scratch pane 113, 492
Scroll Left action 382
Scroll Right action 378

sections, in design diagrams 18

security function

    adding to design diagram 30

Select Color button 273

Select Region tool 271, 273

Select Window button 124

selecting tables 397

Send Region to Back button 273

settings folder 97

Settings option

    Save for Web dialog box 292

Show in Browser button 82, 140

Show Information in Explorer
    button 126

Show Information in Finder
    button 126

Show Link Warnings command 278

ShowHide action 377, 382

Single User site 470

Site Color List 174

site hierarchy, solving 489

site management 63, 468

Site Navigator 496

Site preferences 138

site project file 58, 96

site publishing 63

Site Trash folder 475, 476

site window 58, 106, 475

    adding files and folders 151–153

    collapsing 110

    Components folder 475

    Designs folder 475

    Errors tab 477

    expanding 109

    External tab 258

    Extras tab 248, 475

    FTP tab 477

    Name title bar 485

    Site Trash 475

    Stationeries folder 477

    updating 98

Site Wizard 58, 65

sites

adding files and folders 151

adding folders 484

adding new pages 487

Clean Up Site command 504

creating 148

error handling 478

home page 470

importing 470

managing folders 484

missing file error 480

opening 107

orphan files 478

site link indicators 490

Slice Select tool 292

sliced images 162

Smart Illustrator objects 299

Smart LiveMotion objects 300

Smart Objects 288, 289

    restoring 294

    variables 302

Smart Objects folder 477

Smart Photoshop objects 289

    editing 295

    resizing 293

Smart rollovers 344

sorting table entries 225

Source Code Editor 119, 237, 437, 444

    frames 315

spell checker 234

staging

    design diagrams 50

Staging tab 13, 50

Start/Stop Indexing button 423

stationery 15, 59, 87

Stationery folder 477

Structure command 399

Structure menu 211

style sheet support 433

style sheets

    creating 448

    external 432, 441

    internal 432

linking to multiple pages 453

    removing 454

styles

    adding 446

    duplicating 457

    editing 442, 444

Submit button 419, 421

submitting a design diagram 50

Sun JavaServer Pages (JSP) 28

SVG files 293

SWF files 293, 300

SWF object, design diagram 35

T

tabbing chain 422

table

    converting to layout grid 236

table cells

    aligning 404

    color 223

Table palette 219, 220

table style 220, 231

tables 60, 216

    adding captions 221

    adding column headings 219

    adding rows 219

    changing cell color 223

    columns, spanning 413

    copying and pasting text into 217

    formatting 88, 219, 223, 229

    importing text into 172, 217

    selecting 218, 397

    setting properties 409, 421

    sorting entries 225

target file 289

templates 59

Templates folder 477

text

    adding 61, 71, 206

    adding line breaks 213

    changing color 174, 214

    copying and pasting 208

copying and pasting into tables 217

creating a style 214

design diagram 47

editing 232

formatting 61, 209, 212

importing to tables 217

in tables 172

links 255

with layout text boxes 169

text field, form 401

Text Inspector 253

text links, adding actions to 382

Ticks option 373

time

date and time stamp 180

Toggle Media button 493

toolbars 111, 124

U

Unnumbered List button 212

URLs, linking to 258

V

variables

in Smart Objects 297, 302

Version Cue projects

creating in Adobe GoLive CS 517

Vertical Snap option 44

View palette 112

design diagram 16

W

Web Settings dialog box 433

Web sites. *See* sites

Web-safe images 288, 289, 293

Window Size menu 203

windows, tiling 122

work area, setting up 131

workflow, in site building 57

workspace, custom 126

custom 126

default 126

Working with Version Cue

Getting started with Version Cue

If you own Adobe® Creative Suite Standard or Premium you can take advantage of Adobe Version Cue™, an integrated workflow feature designed to help you be more productive by saving you, and others you work with, valuable time.

With Version Cue, you can easily create, manage, and find different versions of your project files. If you collaborate with others, you and your team members can share project files in a multi-user environment that protects content from being accidentally overwritten. You can also maintain descriptive comments with each file version, search embedded file information to quickly locate files, and work with robust file-management features while working directly within each application.

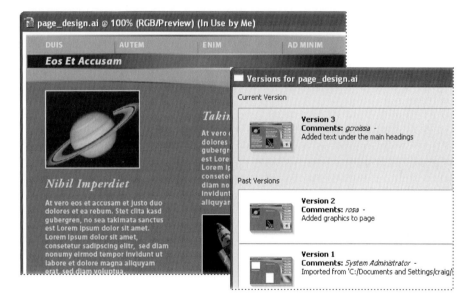

Note: The Version Cue workspace is a feature of Adobe Creative Suite. If you purchased Adobe GoLive CS, Adobe Illustrator CS, Adobe InCopy CS, Adobe InDesign CS, or Adobe Photoshop CS separately, and don't own Adobe Creative Suite, you can use the Version Cue feature in your Adobe CS application only if an owner of Adobe Creative Suite gives you network access to their Version Cue workspace.

Following are the steps you need to take before you begin working with Version Cue, and for how to use Version Cue.

1. Set up the Version Cue workspace.

You and others in your workgroup need access to a Version Cue *workspace* in order to work with the Version Cue feature. When you fully install Adobe Creative Suite, a Version Cue workspace automatically installs on your computer. Depending upon each project's needs, you may choose to work with other Version Cue workspaces located on your colleagues' computers or on a server.

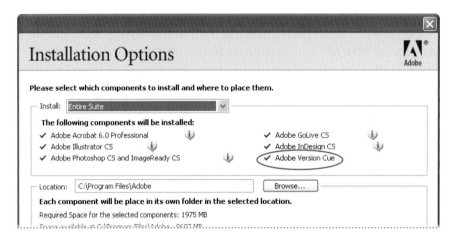

For projects and file versions that you don't need to share with others, or if you work on a laptop that isn't always connected to a network, it's easiest to use the Version Cue workspace located on your own computer. When you change your mind, Version Cue lets you immediately share any Version Cue project with other users. If you mostly intend to collaborate with others, make sure that a Version Cue workspace is located on a computer that everyone can access on a network and that the collaborative projects are kept in that workspace. For installation instructions, see "How To Install" on the Adobe Creative Suite CD.

2. Turn on the Version Cue workspace.

Before you can begin working with the Version Cue feature, you need to turn on the Version Cue workspace. Open the Adobe Version Cue preferences from Control Panel (Windows) or System Preferences (Mac OS) on the computer where the Version Cue workspace is located, and choose On from the Version Cue pop-up menu. To allow others to see and access the workspace over the network, choose This Workspace is Visible to Others from the Workspace Access menu, or, to keep it private, choose This Workspace is Private, and then click OK.

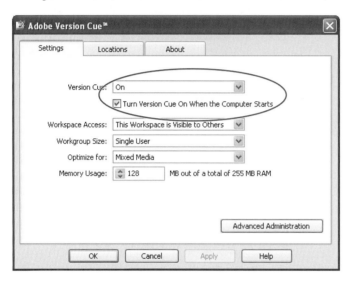

4. Create a Version Cue project for each set of related files.

Now you're ready to create a Version Cue project site, which is used to organize related files and works just like a regular GoLive site, but with additional Version Cue functionality. In addition to all the features you expect from a GoLive site window, the Version Cue project site window includes a User Activity tab and the Files tab contains a new Content Status column. You can create a blank Version Cue project, work with an existing Version Cue project, or create a new Version Cue project based on a folder or based on a GoLive site located on your computer.

In GoLive, choose File > New Site, select Version Cue Project, and then use the instructions in the GoLive Site Wizard to create a Version Cue project site. When you get to the login screen, enter the username you use on your current computer and don't enter anything into the Password text box. (After you've created or connected to a Version Cue project in GoLive, you just need to open the site project file (*.site) to work with it in the future.)

5. Add files to the Version Cue project.

You can use any method of adding files to a regular GoLive site to add files to a Version Cue project site. When you add files to a Version Cue project site, the files are added to the site folder (Web-Content folder) of working files and automatically copied (checked in) to the Version Cue workspace with an optional version comment. You can use the version comment to provide information about the file or project, such as the client, job number, or the state of the file, which can be searched using the Version Cue search feature.

6. Create file versions.

After you've saved a file to a Version Cue project, you can begin creating versions of the file and adding comments to it. File versioning with Version Cue ensures that no one overwrites the work of anyone else in a Version Cue project, but also prevents users from locking out others who need to work on the same file. You can use versioning to seamlessly retain multiple states of a single file as you work on it, in case you need to restore the file to a previous version. You can also use versioning to quickly compare file versions with team members or with a client before selecting a final version.

You can use the Version Cue toolbar to manually check out and assign files to yourself to edit in GoLive CS, or you can open and begin editing a file and check out the file when prompted by Version Cue. While you edit a file and choose File > Save, your changes only affect the working copy in the Web-Content folder on your computer. To update the master file on the Version Cue workspace and create a new file version, you need to check your file back into the workspace by click the Check In button in the Version Cue toolbar.

7. Review all versions of a file.

After you've created several versions of a file, you can click Show Version List in the Version Cue toolbar to view thumbnails of all versions of the file, alongside comments and dates for each, and then open, manage, or compare versions.

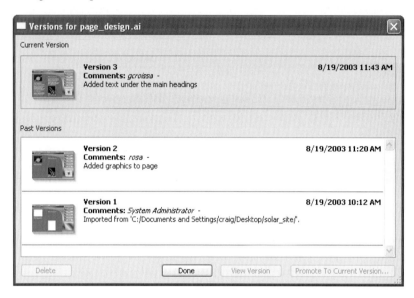

8. Collaborate on a Version Cue project.

To access your Version Cue project, other users need to be on the same subnetwork as the computer where the Version Cue workspace is installed, and then choose File > Connect To Version Cue. If a user is outside your subnetwork, they can still access the project by setting up a new Version Cue project using the GoLive site wizard with the Connect To Version Cue option. Then, instead of opening a workspace on their subnetwork, they just select Custom Server, and then enter the Version Cue Client URL (IP address) of the Version Cue workspace that is hosting your project.

9. Locate files by searching embedded metadata.

Adobe Creative Suite lets users enter a wide variety of information in the File Info dialog box. This information gets embedded into a document as XMP metadata. For example, the metadata might contain a document's title, copyright, keywords, description, properties, author, and origin. Also, any comments you add to each file version are included in the file's metadata. With Version Cue you can quickly locate a file by searching the embedded metadata of all files in a Version Cue project, including Version Cue comments. You can also view a subset of metadata to quickly check the status of a file, its last comment, version date, and who is editing it.

Choose Edit > Run Query, define a new search query, and choose Version Cue from the Find What menu. Select your search options and enter any text that may be embedded in the metadata of the file you want to locate or search by filename, and then run the query.

10. Perform advanced tasks with the Advanced Version Cue Workspace Administration utility.

You can choose to set up a simple collaboration where you share a Version Cue project with anyone using a Creative Suite application, or you can set up a more controlled environment in which users have to log in before accessing your project. Using the Version Cue Workgroup Administration utility, you can set up user IDs and define their project privileges, remove file locks, edit Version Cue Workspace preferences, and perform other project and workspace maintenance.

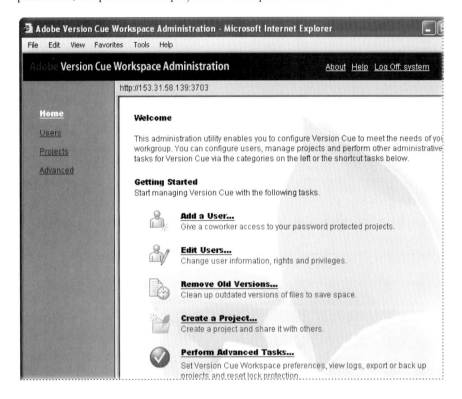

To display the Version Cue Workspace Administration utility log-in page, with the Version Cue project site window open, choose Site > Version Cue > Open Version Cue Administration.

Adobe Certification Programs

What is an ACE?

An Adobe Certified Expert (ACE) is an individual who has passed an Adobe Product Proficiency Exam for a specified Adobe software product. Adobe Certified Experts are eligible to promote themselves to clients or employers as highly skilled, expert level users of Adobe Software. ACE certification is a recognized standard for excellence in Adobe software knowledge.

ACE Benefits

When you become an ACE, you enjoy these special benefits:

- Professional recognition
- An ACE program certificate
- Use of the Adobe Certified Expert program logo

What is an ACTP?

An Adobe Certified Training Provider (ACTP) is a Training professional or organization that has met the ACTP program requirements. Adobe promotes ACTPs to customers who need training on Adobe software.

ACTP Benefits

- Professional recognition
- An ACTP program certificate
- Use of the Adobe Certified Training Provider program logo
- Listing in the Partner Finder on Adobe.com
- Access to beta software releases when available
- Classroom in a Book in Adobe Acrobat PDF
- Marketing materials
- Co-marketing opportunities

For more information on the ACE and ACTP programs, go to partners.adobe.com, and look for these programs under the Join section.